Performing (for) Survival

Performing (for) Survival
Theatre, Crisis, Extremity

Edited by

Patrick Duggan

and

Lisa Peschel

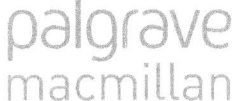

Introduction, selection and editorial matter © Patrick Duggan
and Lisa Peschel 2016
Individual chapters © Respective authors 2016

All rights reserved. No reproduction, copy or transmission of this
publication may be made without written permission.

No portion of this publication may be reproduced, copied or transmitted
save with written permission or in accordance with the provisions of the
Copyright, Designs and Patents Act 1988, or under the terms of any licence
permitting limited copying issued by the Copyright Licensing Agency,
Saffron House, 6–10 Kirby Street, London EC1N 8TS.

Any person who does any unauthorized act in relation to this publication
may be liable to criminal prosecution and civil claims for damages.

The authors have asserted their rights to be identified as the authors of this
work in accordance with the Copyright, Designs and Patents Act 1988.

First published 2016 by
PALGRAVE MACMILLAN

Palgrave Macmillan in the UK is an imprint of Macmillan Publishers Limited,
registered in England, company number 785998, of Houndmills, Basingstoke,
Hampshire RG21 6XS.

Palgrave Macmillan in the US is a division of St Martin's Press LLC,
175 Fifth Avenue, New York, NY 10010.

Palgrave Macmillan is the global academic imprint of the above companies
and has companies and representatives throughout the world.

Palgrave® and Macmillan® are registered trademarks in the United States,
the United Kingdom, Europe and other countries.

ISBN 978–1–137–45426–3

This book is printed on paper suitable for recycling and made from fully
managed and sustained forest sources. Logging, pulping and manufacturing
processes are expected to conform to the environmental regulations of the
country of origin.

A catalogue record for this book is available from the British Library.

Library of Congress Cataloging-in-Publication Data
Performing (for) survival : theatre, crisis, extremity / Patrick Duggan
   and Lisa Peschel [editors].
     pages   cm
   Includes bibliographical references and index.
   ISBN 978–1–137–45426–3 (hardback)
   1. War and theater. 2. Theater—Political aspects. 3. Theater and
society. I. Duggan, Patrick 1981–, editor. II. Peschel, Lisa,
1965– editor.
   PN2049.P535 2015
   792—dc23   2015026444

Contents

Notes on Contributors   vii

Introduction – Performing (for) Survival: Frameworks and Mapping   1
Patrick Duggan and Lisa Peschel

Part I Surviving War and Exile: National and Ethnic Identity in Performance

1. Surviving (with) Theatre: A History of the ELF and EPLF Cultural Troupes in the Eritrean War of Independence   17
   Christine Matzke

2. Theatre for Survival: Art of Creation and Protection (*Kubunda*)   37
   Ananda Breed and Alice Mukaka

Part II A Space Where Something Might Survive: Theatre in Concentration Camps

3. The Cultural Life of the Terezín Ghetto in 1960s Survivor Testimony: Theatre, Trauma and Resilience   59
   Lisa Peschel

4. Imagining Theatre in Auschwitz: Performance, Solidarity and Survival in the Works of Charlotte Delbo   78
   Amanda Stuart Fisher

Part III Tactics and Strategies: Dissent under Oppressive Regimes

5. Swazzles of Subversion: Puppets Under Dictatorship   103
   Cariad Astles

6. Against Order(s): Dictatorship, Absurdism and the Plays of Sony Labou Tansi   121
   Macelle Mahala

7 Surviving Censorship: El-Hakawati's *Mahjoob Mahjoob* and
the Struggle for the Permission to Perform 141
Samer Al-Saber

Part IV Coming in from the Outside: Theatre, Community, Crisis

8 The Council Estate as Hood: SPID Theatre Company and
Grass-roots Arts Practice as Cultural Politics 163
Katie Beswick

9 The Art of Survival: Social Circus, Youth Regeneration and
Projected Community in the North East of Scotland 185
Graham Jeffery, Neill Patton, Kerrie Schaefer and Tom Wakeford

Part V Crisis and Extremity as Performance

10 The Paradox of Dis/appearance: Hunger Strike in Athens
as a Performance of Survival 203
Aylwyn Walsh

11 'Dis-ease' and the Performance of Radical Resistance in the
Maze Prison 222
Patrick Duggan

Coda: Picturing *Charlie Hebdo* 241
Sophie Nield

Index 248

Contributors

Editors

Patrick Duggan is senior lecturer in theatre and performance at the University of Surrey. Patrick's research interests lie in critical approaches to contemporary performance and the relationship between performance and the wider socio-cultural and political contexts in which it is made. His research is interdisciplinary in nature and particularly focused on questions of spectatorship, witnessing, trauma and ethics. As well as publishing numerous journal articles and book chapters, Patrick is author of *Trauma-Tragedy: Symptoms of Contemporary Performance* (2012) and co-editor (with Prof. Mick Wallis) of a special issue of the international journal *Performance Research* entitled *On Trauma* (2011). He is series editor of Intellect's *playtexts* and co-editor of *Reverberations Across Small-Scale British Theatre: Politics, Aesthetics and Forms* (2013).

Lisa Peschel is a lecturer in the department of theatre, film and television at the University of York. She has been researching theatrical performance in the Terezín/Theresienstadt ghetto since 1998. Her articles on survivor testimony and scripts written in the ghetto have appeared in forums such as *Theatre Survey*, *Theatre Topics* and *Holocaust and Genocide Studies*, and in Czech, German and Israeli journals. She has been invited to lecture and conduct performance workshops on Terezín/Theresienstadt theatre at institutions in the US and Europe including Oxford University, University College London and Dartmouth College. Her anthology *Performing Captivity, Performing Escape: Cabarets and Plays from the Terezín/Theresienstadt Ghetto* was published in 2014. She is a co-investigator on the £1.8 million project 'Performing the Jewish Archive' funded by the UK Arts and Humanities Research Council.

Contributors

Christine Matzke teaches English and African literature at the University of Bayreuth. Recent publications include chapters on *Hamlet* in Africa (2014) and a South Sudanese *Cymbeline* (2013). Together with

Yvette Hutchison and Jane Plastow she is co-editing the next *African Theatre 14: Contemporary Women*. She is a member of the editorial board of *Matatu: Journal for African Literature and Culture* (Brill) and an associate editor of *African Theatre* (James Currey). She specializes in theatre and performance in Eritrea.

Ananda Breed is reader in the School of Arts and Digital Industries at the University of East London (UEL). An applied performance practitioner and scholar, Breed is the author of *Performing the Nation: Genocide, Justice, Reconciliation* (Seagull Books, 2014), which analyses performances and performatives related to the gacaca courts in Rwanda, in addition to several publications that address transitional systems of governance and the arts. She has worked as a consultant for IREX and UNICEF in Kyrgyzstan on issues concerning conflict negotiation and conducted workshops in the Democratic Republic of Congo (DRC), Indonesia, Japan, Kyrgyzstan, Nepal, Palestine, Rwanda and Turkey. Breed is co-director of the Centre for Performing Arts Development (CPAD) at the University of East London and former research fellow of the International Research Centre 'Interweaving Performance Cultures' (2013–14) at Freie Universität Berlin, Germany.

Alice Mukaka is a PhD candidate in the School of Law and Social Sciences at the University of East London (UEL), currently researching feminist activism for migrant rights. Her research interests developed through years of experience as an arts practitioner include the intersection between performance and politics, rights in exile, and feminist activism. Past performance credits include Koulsy Lamko's production *Corps et Voix, Paroles Rhizomes* and *Le Petit Lion Couché*, which toured Rwanda, France, Germany and Belgium; Kalisa Rugano's play *Rugali Rwa Gasabo*; Jean Marie Rurangwa's feminist production *Pour Vous Femmes*; and a choreographic collaboration in the CUA's *Iryo Nabonye* and *Des Espoirs*.

Amanda Stuart Fisher is a reader in contemporary theatre and performance at Royal Central School of Speech and Drama, London. Her research area broadly covers verbatim and testimonial theatre, witnessing and performance, and the dramaturgy of trauma. She has published articles in *TDR*, *Studies in Theatre and Performance*, and *Performance Research*. Most recently she co-edited (with Dr Alison Forsyth, Aberystwyth) a special issue for *Performing Ethos* entitled 'Acting Out Trauma and the Ethics of Remembrance' (2013). She is also engaged in

Notes on Contributors ix

practice-as-research and has directed her own adaptation of Charlotte Delbo's *Who Will Carry the Word?* (2012) and also written a verbatim theatre play, *From the Mouths of Mothers* (Aurora Metro Books, 2013).

Cariad Astles is a lecturer at the Royal Central School of Speech and Drama, where she convenes the BA (Hons) puppetry course within the theatre practice programme and is director of the Centre for Research into Objects and Puppets in Performance. She has practical and research interests in international puppetry traditions, national identity, popular performance and applied theatre. She is also lecturer at the University of Exeter where she lectures in Latin American theatre, theatre and health, puppetry and applied performance, and has published widely in the areas above. She works regularly as a performing puppeteer with the Catalan group Irènia, which won the United Nations Innovation Award for Intercultural Practice in 2012.

Macelle Mahala is associate professor in theatre arts at the University of the Pacific. She writes about the intersection of theatre, race and social justice. She is the author of *Penumbra: The Premier Stage for African American Drama* (2013). Her writing has also been published in *Theatre Journal*, *Theatre Topics*, *Women & Performance* and *XCP: Cross Cultural Poetics*. As a theatre artist she has worked with Artists in Storefronts, the Illusion Theatre, Marin Theatre Company, New World Theatre, the New York Mills Cultural Arts Center, Penumbra Theatre Company, Pillsbury House Theatre, the San Francisco Mime Troupe, the Soap Factory and Works/Plays. She received her PhD and MA from the University of Minnesota and her BA from Macalester College.

Samer Al-Saber completed his contribution to this volume during his time as a Mellon Postdoctoral Fellow (2013–15) at Davidson College in North Carolina, USA. His teaching and scholarship focus on the intersection of cultural production and political conflict. He taught courses on the cultural representations of the Israel/Palestine conflict and 'performing Arabs' in a postcolonial context. His areas of scholarly interest include Middle Eastern culture, theatre and performance, the modern history of East Jerusalem, Palestinian theatre, Arab theatre, and the performance culture in the Roman Middle East.

Katie Beswick is a lecturer in drama, theatre and performance studies at Queen Mary, University of London. Her research is concerned with theatre and performance practices in and about sites of inequality; predominately with the intersections between theatre and British social housing. Her latest project explores subway dancing in New York City. She completed her PhD, which examined representations of the 'council estate' in performance, at the University of Leeds. She is co-editor of the special issue of *Interventions: International Journal of Postcolonial Studies* 'Re-evaluating the Postcolonial City: Production, Reconstruction, Representation'. Beyond academia she has worked as a writer, performer and housing officer.

Graham Jeffery is an arts practitioner and researcher with interests in arts education, creativity and radical cultural practice. He is currently reader in music and performance at the University of the West of Scotland. Graham was Co-I on *Remaking Society*.

Neill Patton lives in Glasgow and is a cultural producer and community development worker. He was seconded from Cadispa Trust to work as a research assistant on *Remaking Society*.

Kerrie Schaefer is a researcher whose current preoccupation is completing a monograph which seeks to better define what is meant by 'community' in community performance practice. She is currently senior lecturer in drama at the University of Exeter. Kerrie was Co-I on *Remaking Society*.

Tom Wakeford is a participatory action researcher whose work is concerned with public knowledge and ways of knowing. He is currently reader in public science in the Centre for Agroecology, Water and Resilience at Coventry University. Tom was PI on *Remaking Society*.

Aylwyn Walsh is a lecturer at the University of Lincoln School of Fine and Performing Arts whose interests span political and activist performance, radical pedagogies and intercultural performance. Recent publications have included work on arts in healthcare for *Research in Drama Education* and the *Journal for Applied Arts and Health* as well as on street art in *Journal of Arts and Communities* and about women, prison and performance in *Contemporary Theatre Review*. Her artistic work has been hosted across Europe, including Germany, Greece and Finland, and in the USA and Brazil, as well as Zambia and South Africa. She co-edited *Remapping Crisis: A Guide to Athens*. Aylwyn is the co-director of Ministry of Untold Stories.

Sophie Nield teaches theatre and film at Royal Holloway College, University of London. She writes on questions of space, representation and theatricality in political life and the law, and on the performance of borders of various kinds: the international border, the former site of the Berlin Wall, and the problem of the corpse in representation.

Introduction – Performing (for) Survival: Frameworks and Mapping

Patrick Duggan and Lisa Peschel

Frameworks

In *Nation and Narration* (1990), Homi Bhabha argues that a nation shapes and narrates understandings of itself through the stories it tells about itself to itself. Such stories naturally take multifarious forms: political institutions, monuments, architecture, pageants, celebrations, commemorations and, of course, art practices such as performance. Bhabha's proposition is a useful one for the concerns of this volume in so far as it looks to the potential for theatre to help peoples cohere, to create communitas, to function as a means of embodied thinking through contexts and problems. The diverse performance practices explored here could be considered what Thompson and Schechner (2004) call 'social theatre' in so far as the 'ruling objective' is not necessarily aesthetics and the 'quality' of the performances. The objective might be political agency, group cohesion, protest, amelioration of pain, or any of the dozens of other social functions that can be served by the stories that societies in crisis tell themselves about themselves.

The volume gathers contributions from a range of international scholars and geopolitical contexts to explore why people organize themselves into performance communities in sites of crisis and how performance – social and aesthetic, sanctioned and underground – is employed as a mechanism for survival. The chapters examine a wide range of examples of what can be considered 'survival', ranging from sheer physical survival, to the survival of a social group with its own unique culture and values, to the survival of the very possibility of agency and dissent. Performance as a form of political resistance and protest plays a large part in many of the essays, but performance does more than that: it enables societies in crisis to continue to define themselves. By maintaining identities that are based on their own chosen affiliations and not defined solely in opposition to their oppressors, individuals and groups prepare themselves for a post-crisis future by keeping alive their own notions of who they are and who they hope to be.

Much of the scholarship in this volume explores work that might fit Jan Cohen-Cruz's definition of 'engaged performance'; that is, performance work that at once responds to and engages with the particular social and political conditions or contexts of its making and that draws on a wide range of peoples in order to do so (cf. Cohen-Cruz 2010: 1–16). Nevertheless, what marks this performance work out from discourses of applied, social or community theatre is that (with the exception of two examples) it is not work made by external practitioners with a particular community in order to attend to a particular 'issue', but is work that arises out of those communities as a direct result of extremity or crisis. Crucial too is the fact that 'performance' is defined broadly in this volume as authors address aesthetic performance practices, read political action as performance practice, and examine the experience of people undergoing various forms of crisis through performance (theory). In each chapter, the performance(s) analysed happen in an actual moment of crisis, rather than being retrospective interpretations or analyses of that crisis. As such, the book explores performances that are intrinsically alive to the socio-political contexts of their making and which are engaged in plural modes of challenging and changing those contexts. While we outline a more complete map of the book below, it is useful here to note that the argumentative trajectory of the volume is that by examining performance in crisis we might also be able to see crisis as performance.

In light of such plurality of approach, it seems useful at this point to outline some of the things that cohere the volume and the uses of 'performance' within it before turning to a broader gloss of the theoretical underpinnings of the volume. In line with much recent scholarship in performance studies, the cultural objects of analysis in this volume range from what Richard Schechner might delineate as 'make-believe' performances (those we associate with the fictional worlds of the well-made play) to 'real world', social dramas (cf. Schechner 2002: 35). In tandem with this we recall Joseph Roach's proposition that 'performance attend[s] not only to "the body", as Foucault suggests, but also to bodies – to the reciprocal reflections they make on one another's surfaces as they foreground their capacities for interaction' (Roach 1996: 25). For us, then, performance, wherever it might be located on the social-aesthetic continuum, is politically and socially engaged, materially participating in what theorists as diverse as Raymond Williams (1966), Jill Dolan (2001; 2005), Claire MacDonald (1996) and Peggy Phelan (1993; 1997) might think of as world-making. For Peter Dickinson (2010), defining performance broadly alongside understanding its world-making potential allows one to explore different ways in which performance can 'provide a model for, how one attends to the world socially' (4). Performance thus asks us to consider our interrelations in a given geopolitical context, but can also reflexively point beyond that context because it can involve

> the transformation of the specific forms and contours of intimacy and identification that come from being part of a local theatrical public sphere into a potentially radical re-imagining of global citizenship as an activation of still more spectacular forms of counter-publicity [...] [Furthermore] the performance event [is] emblematic of those radically contingent situations, as described by Badiou [in *Being and Event*, 2006], that have the potential to interpellate being, rupturing the established order of things and ideally producing a new 'militant' (politically, aesthetically, erotically, etc.) consciousness. (Dickinson 2010: 5–6)

The performances analysed throughout this book are not simply representing something, nor are they just about the context of their making; they are fundamentally doing something – politically, ideologically, aesthetically, culturally. For us, then, and the contributors to the book, performance is performative in Jill Dolan's sense, after J. L. Austin (Dolan 2005: 5–6).

This radical, transformative potential of performance is at the core of each of the investigations in this book and, while each of the contributions attends to different contexts and aesthetic forms, from 'well-made' plays to parades to hunger strikes, it seems to us that one useful, common thread that might be productively theorized here is the way in which each performance can be seen to make a radical intervention in 'space'. For Henri Lefebvre, and in cultural or geopolitical terms, these performances might be seen to constitute interventions into (political, social, geographic, institutional) space which can reinscribe the meaning of space or materialize new space – a space within which something can survive that might otherwise be destroyed. This is because, according to Jones et al. (2004), after Lefebvre, spaces are 'constituted through [...] social, economic and political processes' (99), they are 'the intersection of a unique mixture of social, economic and cultural relations, some of which are local in character, some of which have global reach [...]. The ways in which different actors engage with the particular combination of relations in a particular place, have real political effects' (101). As such, spaces are never neutral entities with constant and definable objective meanings; rather they are constructs in which actions and bodily relations determine social, political and symbolic meaning at different levels (social, individual, historical, governmental, etc.) (cf. Lefebvre 1991; 2009). Spaces are always in the process of being written and rewritten, made manifest in different ways through the contestation of space by bodies, physical or virtual. As cultural geographer Kirsten Simonsen argues, ' "being-in-the-world" is the everyday skilful coping or engagement with an environment including things as well as other human beings. That means that our "environment" does not arrange itself as something given in advance but as a totality of equipment dealt with in practice' (2010: 222). For Lefebvre, human action changes and manifests space, but also the history of a space will reveal 'conflictual coexistence of works and products from different periods [...] [that] generate tensions that animate space [and] make it difficult to decipher' (2009: 229). Thus performance within situations of extremity can be seen to be part of the constitution of the meaning of the space even in the face of violence, confinement, migration, dictatorship or domination. In such contexts, performance can be seen as a form of agency, as the ability to take some form of action.

Given that all performance happens in and produces space, both representational and material, it seems vital to examine the political implications of performances in the context of extremity. Only some of the contributions focus on what might be thought of as overtly political protest performance. However, each performance, in its own way, represents a protest in time and space as each is a reaction to conditions and contexts in which some form of amelioration of pain or suffering, escapism or political intervention became urgent and necessary.

We choose to focus on performance as a meaningful response to crisis because, as Franz Fanon has powerfully proposed, in situations of extremity, there is often a sudden and urgent desire, even a fundamental need, to speak creatively to, from or about the socio-political context of the 'exceptional circumstances' being enacted upon the body (individual or collective) of those affected. As Fanon puts it, in such circumstances people often 'feel the need to speak to their nation, to compose a sentence which expresses the heart of the people and to become the mouthpiece of a new reality in action' (1990: 179). The notion of a 'new reality' is particularly important to the concerns of this volume, suggesting that creative processes can provide modes of engagement that might facilitate, or at least point towards, different ways to experience the present and future beyond the contemporary crisis.

Each of the chapters takes as its central case study an example of performance that emerged from within the space and time of the socio-political context under discussion, even if, as Chapters 8 and 9 demonstrate, outsiders might have initiated a creative process that culminated in the community's taking ownership of the work. Thus, the performances analysed here are not performances which seek retroactively to comment upon, understand, discuss, 'act out' or 'work through' a past moment in history, but are from/of that moment. The chapters seek to discover what functions the performances served for performers and their audiences in that moment, and what each case study might tell us about the functions of performance within situations of extremity more broadly. These social functions might correspond with what de Certeau would call a tactic: a means of fighting back against different forms of oppression in responsive and flexible ways. In a striking echo of Brecht's call for theatre to make audiences look afresh at and question the social realities being represented in a play (principally through *Verfremdungseffekt*), for de Certeau 'a tactic boldly juxtaposes diverse elements in order suddenly to produce a flash shedding a different light on the language of a place and to strike the hearer' (1984: 37–8). The inclination to consider these performances as tactics becomes more striking when we consider that tactics are 'an art of the weak' (1984: 38) and in the majority of the cases discussed throughout the book those performing are those discernibly without state or institutional power. As such, these performances might be seen to operate within the 'space of the tactic', which is 'the space of the other', where the deployed tactic 'must play on and with a terrain imposed on it and organized by the law of a foreign power [...] it is a manoeuvre "within the enemy's field of vision" [...] and within enemy territory' (de Certeau 1984: 37). The tactic is deployed by the 'powerless' to inflict blow-by-blow damage to those in power as opportunities present themselves, rather than with any 'strategy' guiding that deployment (cf. 1984: 37). Thus 'strategy' is formulated as the preserve of the powerful (cf. 36–8).

De Certeau goes further to argue that power brings with it a particular visibility that prevents 'deception' and 'feints' because 'it is dangerous to deploy large forces for the sake of appearances [...] Power is bound by its very visibility. In contrast, trickery is possible for the weak, and often it is his [*sic*] only possibility, as a "last resort"' (1984: 37) and so 'a tactic is determined by the absence of power just as a strategy is organized by the postulation of power' (38). While such distinctions might be true in a military context, in which a more powerful force faces a lesser one, the situation might be more complex for our concerns. Although the idea of the tactic is productive, it also seems to negate, or perhaps ignore, the possibility of tactics being deployed strategically. At the same time it relegates those without institutional power to being reactionary, concerned only with grasping unexpected opportunities to strike out at their oppressors rather than taking advantage of the tactic as a way to engage with and define their own communities.

Many of the chapters throughout this volume worry at this distinction in exploring the space and function of performance within a range of international, transhistorical situations of 'extremity'. The contributions suggest that, far from being opportunistic one-offs, many of the performance practices deployed might be thought of as what Duggan terms a 'strategy of tactics' in which performative or theatrical events are used as tactics – with great flexibility of form, place or timing, for example – but in determinedly strategic ways, where, for example, visibility and changing of aesthetic form are used in a deliberate and sustained, campaign-like way to ideologically and materially alter the space that the performers inhabit or are subject to. Our authors attend to the specificity of the historical events under discussion, to the possibility of performance as a means to political agency through spatial and bodily practices and representations, and to the possibility that those practices provide a means of surviving the situation (literally, politically, historically, for example).

Thus, the work aims to expand upon and, crucially, move beyond existing scholarship regarding performance in 'camp' environments (concentration, labour, prison, refugee, etc.) by investigating the possibility that both aesthetic performance events and social performance strategies might be employed as a means of 'survival' in multiple environments of/in crisis, which might, for different reasons, be conceptualized as 'extreme' contexts.

Mapping: organization of the volume

Each of the contributions in this volume has been (informally) guided by a steer to attend to three interrelated research questions:

1. How do people living in oppressive conditions or conditions of danger and deprivation use performance to survive and to express dissent or a desire for change?

2. What role is (the) performance fulfilling within the context being explored?
3. What might the example/s being analysed tell us about performance, extremity and survival within their historical context and at a broader socio-political (and/or theoretical/philosophical) level?

In supplying this steer our editorial intention has been to gather together scholarship that explores multiple and differing geopolitical and social contexts and types of performance while ensuring a shared research imperative. This shared territory or focus has, we believe, allowed the contributors to develop chapters that absolutely and concretely stand on their own, but that draw further strength and impact through a dialogic engagement with and inflection on their section partners and more broadly across the volume as a whole.

We have also intentionally included chapters that demonstrate varying levels of historiographic versus critical engagement. That is, just as performance spans a continuum from the aesthetic to the social, scholarship on performance ranges from the largely descriptive to the critically reflective. We have found value in accounts of virtually unknown theatrical interventions for their ability to ensure the historiographic survival of rare performance practices, as well as in chapters that engage with and build upon contemporary critical thought.

In Part I, titled 'Surviving War and Exile: National and Ethnic Identity in Performance', the authors examine the role of performance during political upheavals in two African countries. Matzke describes theatrical and musical performances by Eritrea's guerrilla cultural troupes during the war with Ethiopia and the Eritrean civil war, and Breed and Mukaka examine the exile theatre of the Tutsis of Rwanda as they waited in neighbouring countries for the longed-for return to their homeland. In both cases, as Bhabha argues, a nation shaped its understanding of itself through the stories it tells to itself about itself, but for these societies in crisis, their stories were complicated by ethnic and linguistic diversity. In Eritrea, although 'cultural combatants' were first and foremost engaged in rallying against the Ethiopian enemy, a secondary goal was the struggle to create a pluralist Eritrean national identity. Tutsi playwrights, during their time in exile, wrote works that strengthened their own sense of ethnic identity. After their return to a country in which the terms 'Hutu', 'Tutsi' and 'Twa' have been forbidden, they have created plays that attempt to enforce 'Rwandanicity' as an integrated national identity. The juxtaposition of these two chapters also highlights the unexpected risks that emerge when tactics become strategies:

in both cases, when formerly disempowered groups (re)gained power, strategies of representation that were developed in extremity became potentially oppressive and/or destabilizing forces once the crisis had passed.

In Christine Matzke's chapter, musical and dramatic performances developed by the cultural troupes of the Eritrean Liberation Front (ELF) and Eritrean People's Liberation Front (EPLF) in wartime exemplify the notion of a 'strategy of tactics' designed to serve overtly political goals. Touring the countryside to persuade the Eritrean people to fight the Ethiopean emperor's annexation of their country and, after 1974, the corrupt Marxist military junta that had ousted him, members of the ELF and EPLF used improvised materials and sets to perform songs and plays that portrayed Ethiopian atrocities and the heroic deeds of Eritrean fighters and civilians. Ironically, while attempting to preserve their own political, religious and cultural identities and construct an integrated yet pluralist Eritrean national identity, actors ran the risk that they might not survive their own performance practices; for example, those playing hated political figures were sometimes attacked by their own audiences. After independence was won, however, survival presented dangers of its own: the EPLF has become an oppressive force in a one-party state where all cultural work is subject to strict censorship.

Performances by Tutsi artists enduring the crisis of exile, as analysed by Ananda Breed and Alice Mukaka, drew on a mythical past representing specifically Tutsi culture, both to preserve that culture while in exile and to motivate their audiences to return to a homeland that those born abroad had never experienced. Playwrights, for example, embedded traditional war poems in their works to illustrate that Rwanda was a homeland worth fighting for, and trained spectators to speak like the heroes depicted in the plays during the moments when they participated through vocal response in the performances. As in Eritrea, however, the practices adopted to deal with past crises present dangers in the present: the persistence of Tutsi cultural forms in performances that are now intended to perform an ethnically neutral 'Rwandanicity' may actually jeopardize lasting peace.

The chapters in Part II, 'A Space Where Something Might Survive: Theatre in Concentration Camps', explore performance in conditions of extreme oppression. Paradoxically, in sites where power exerted a radical degree of control over the prisoners' physical existence, policing of their cultural activities was comparatively lax. Both chapters in this section speak to Lefebvre's concept of space as constituted through processes: prisoners took advantage of this relative freedom to create a space, through the process of performance, where elements of their prewar lives and identities could be preserved. That is, although they were cut off from engagement in normal social, economic and cultural relations, they were symbolically able to perform these normal relationships within the theatrical space and thus exercise choice and agency in sites where those possibilities were radically curtailed.

Lisa Peschel examines testimony from the 1960s by Czech-Jewish survivors of the World War II Jewish ghetto at Terezín (in German, Theresienstadt) to argue that theatrical performance in the ghetto functioned as a performative, not only representing something, but doing something: it enabled the prisoners to convert potentially traumatizing experiences into manageable narratives and thus enhanced their ability to cope with the conditions of their captivity. By creating a safe space, sharing these narratives with their fellow prisoners and reconnecting with themselves, others and what they considered to be 'their world', they refused to succumb to what psychiatrist Judith Herman calls 'the essential insult of trauma': helplessness (1992: 41). Their testimony, as a rhetorical performance, also effected change in the present: by referring to cultural touchstones shared with non-Jewish Czechs, the survivors created narratives that helped them reintegrate into Czech society after a long period of state-sanctioned anti-Semitism.

In Stuart Fisher's study of Charlotte Delbo and her theatre-making in World War II concentration camps, she draws on several autobiographical works and two post-war plays to explore what survival and theatre meant for Delbo in the context of the concentrationary world. Rather than engaging with their oppressors in their performances, Delbo and her companions, all French political dissidents, drew upon classic texts that opened up a space of togetherness and what Jean-Luc Nancy calls a being-with and being-for the other. They reinscribed the meaning of the brutal camp environment by creating a space defined by a sense of communitas, solidarity and indebtedness to others. Theatre-making contributed to Delbo's capacity to redefine her relationship with her fellow prisoners and this, Stuart Fisher argues, contributed to an existential process of survival by establishing a sense of solidarity amidst the harsh and unrelenting environment of the camps.

In Part III, 'Tactics and Strategies: Dissent under Oppressive Regimes', the authors examine symbolic resistance as expressed through seemingly 'minor' or 'harmless' theatrical forms: puppetry, absurdism and comedy. Working from a position of weakness within a political terrain imposed upon them – the Nazi occupation of Czechoslovakia, authoritarian regimes in the Congo, the Israeli annexation of East

Jerusalem – artists created works that inflicted damage upon those in power by demonstrating the possibility of dissent, even if that dissent was carefully coded (successfully or not) to escape the censor's reach.

Cariad Astles' transnational and transhistorical study of puppetry as a response to dictatorship encompasses both subversion and resilience. As a seemingly trivial performance form, yet at the same time a powerful metaphor for the total control of one being by another and, simultaneously, the desire to break free, puppetry is particularly suited to speak to totalitarian rule. In Nazi-occupied Czechoslovakia, puppet shows kept Czech-language popular and folk culture alive while providing a forum to condemn the regime. Astles then engages with more subtle forms of crisis that arise in the aftermath of dictatorship and the lifting of censorship: in Catalonia immediately after Franco's death, puppetry that revelled in scatological and grotesque imagery celebrated Catalonian culture and enabled people to release years of collective rage through laughter, and in Chile after Pinochet, puppet theatre represented the absence and trauma associated with the disappeared and enabled performers and their audiences to acknowledge the scars left on the present by the past.

Macelle Mahala examines the plays, novels and political essays of Congolese playwright Sony Labou Tansi, who lived and wrote through a series of political coups and authoritarian governments. Tansi thought about performance explicitly in terms of space, writing that '[t]heatre leaves us ample space while the world around us unrelentingly seeks to take it over'. Within that space, shaped by ancient Greek drama from his colonial education, traditional Kongo theatre practices and religious traditions and Afro-francophone interpretations of absurdism, Tansi's ebullient humour and wild imagination enabled him to critique abuses of state authority yet avoid censorship until nearly the end of his career.

Samer Al-Saber explores the potentially subversive effects of a comic play about a politically indifferent Palestinian 'everyman' who simply tries to survive in East Jerusalem after it is annexed by Israel. He is thwarted, however, in a series of increasingly absurd comic scenarios; for example, he is fired from his job at an Israeli factory because he is supposedly wearing the colours of the Palestinian flag. The troupe was similarly thwarted in their attempts to produce the play. Drawing on Edward Said's concept of 'permission to narrate', Al-Saber traces their long struggle against Israeli attempts to censor the production and the obstacles they faced even while on a tour of several European countries, during which Orientalist discourse and attempts to brand the troupe a mere mouthpiece of the PLO (Palestinian Liberation Organization) limited the performers' capacity to present their message outside of Israel.

The chapters in Part IV, 'Coming in from the Outside: Theatre, Community, Crisis', constitute an exception in this volume because the performance practices described were brought into depressed communities by outsiders. Both case studies, however, posit the initially 'outsider' artists as practising a potentially radical form of global citizenship by creating performances that reconfigured the established order in the sites where they worked and enabled a change in the consciousness of the local participants as well as themselves. The artists' long-term engagement with local youth potentially enabled restructuring what Bordieu calls their 'habitus': a repertoire of behaviours conditioned by social structures that can limit or expand the opportunities available to them. Within the crisis context of the growing gap between wealth and relative poverty, performance has the potential to help young people survive what Jeffery, Patton, Schaefer and Wakefield in Chapter 9 call 'a disturbingly quotidian "situation of extremity" affecting many communities in the UK today'.

Katie Beswick's study focuses on SPID (Specially Produced Innovatively Directed) Theatre Company, a collective of professional film and theatre makers that has been based permanently on the Kensal House estate in Ladbroke Grove, West London since 2005; a number of residents have joined the company as professional and amateur members. The residents' work with SPID enables them to resist dominant narratives about council estates as dysfunctional, deprived criminal breeding grounds by creating counter-narratives that may assist in breaking open the enduring stigmas that limit the opportunity structures available to estate residents.

Jeffery, Patton, Schaefer and Wakefield examine the work of Theatre Modo in Peterhead and Fraserburgh, two economically depressed fishing towns located on the northeast coast of Aberdeenshire. *Maelstrom, The Shell Fireworks Parade* was performed in Fraserburgh in 2012 as the culmination of a four-year programme of community partnership, public engagement and creative practice. During this programme, Modo held workshops in puppet-making, lantern-making, stilt-walking, drumming, mural painting, fire juggling/breathing and circus and street performance that enabled them to engage masses of young people. Interviews with participants revealed evidence of informal learning, of subtle forms of apprenticeship, the making of new identities and the imagining of possible futures.

In Part V, 'Crisis and Extremity as Performance', the authors turn from aesthetic performance events to social performance strategies. They explore hunger striking as an act that is 'performed' for the public, even when it takes place within the framework of incarceration. Parodoxically, as the starving body slowly disappears, it creates exceptional visibility for the strikers' cause and presents a crisis for state power: wilful self-destruction positions the government as ultimately having no power over the 'survival' of the strikers.

Aylwyn Walsh examines the case of 300 men – all asylum seekers and economic migrants – who embarked on a hunger strike in order to pressure the Greek government to pay attention to their demands for legal status. This strike was exceptional in that, rather than taking place in a carceral space, it was staged in a highly symbolic space related to Greek national identity: the Law School building in Athens. Although the strike conferred upon them valuable bargaining power at the time it was conducted, the rapid decline in social and economic conditions led to the political gains made by the strikers being overruled.

Duggan describes much more 'successful' performative acts by Irish prisoners in the H-blocks of the Maze prison. Triggered by the abolishment of their political prisoner status and classification as ordinary criminals, their initial acts of protest – the learning of Gaelic and then the so-called 'dirty protests' – broke down normal penal narratives as the prisoners first defied rules against 'talking out the door' with a language the prison staff could not understand, then radically changed the nature of the carceral space by writing themselves on it with their own bodily wastes. Finally the hunger strikers themselves performed death, as a way to make visible the wider politics of the Republican cause; in the process they created a crisis for the British government as politicians struggled to find a way to deal with the hunger strikers.

The volume ends with a coda by Sophie Nield which turns the book's concerns to the contemporary moment by looking at the January 2015 murders in Paris and the *Je suis Charlie* 'movement' that followed. The coda focuses not only on a timely example, but one that explores 'the intertwining of material and symbolic gestures' as fundamental components of the meaning of those events. In so doing, Nield dialogically refracts the arguments of the foregoing chapters to suggest that theatre and performance have an important and ongoing role to play in situations of crisis and extremity.

This book, then, not only highlights theatre's performative potential – the fact of its material agency – but also demonstrates an urgent imperative for theatre and performance scholars to look at such situations of crisis and extremity from plural perspectives.

Bibliography

Bhabha, H., 1990. *Nation and Narration*. London: Routledge.
Cohen-Cruz, J., 2010. *Engaging Performance: Theatre as Call and Response*. London: Routledge.
De Certeau, M., 1984. *The Practice of Everyday Life*. Berkeley: University of California Press.
Dickinson, P., 2010. *World Stages, Local Audiences: Essays on Performance, Place, and Politics*. Manchester: Manchester University Press.
Dolan, J., 2001. *Geographies of Learning: Theory and Practice, Activism and Performance*. Middletown: Wesleyan University Press.
Dolan, J., 2005. *Utopia in Performance: Finding Hope at the Theater*. Ann Arbor: University of Michigan Press.
Fanon, F., 1990. *The Wretched of the Earth*. London: Penguin Books.
Herman, J. L., 1992. *Trauma and Recovery*. New York: BasicBooks.
Jones, M., R. Jones, and M. Woods, 2004. *An Introduction to Political Geography: Space, Place and Politics*. London: Routledge.
Lefebvre, H., 1991. *The Production of Space*, trans. Donald Nicholson-Smith. Oxford: Blackwell Publishing.
Lefebvre, H., 2009. *State, Space, World: Selected Essays*, eds Neil Brenner and Stuart Elden. Minneapolis, MN: University of Minnesota Press.
MacDonald, C., 1996. 'Joining Up the Dots'. *Performing Arts Journal*, 18: 1, pp. 89–102.
Phelan, P., 1993. *Unmarked: The Politics of Performance*. London: Routledge.
Phelan, P., 1997. *Mourning Sex: Performing Public Memories*. London: Routledge.
Roach, J., 1996. *Cities of the Dead: Circum-Atlantic Performance*. New York: Columbia University Press.
Schechner, R., 2002. *Performance Studies: An Introduction*. New York: Routledge.
Simonsen, K., 2010. 'Encountering O/other Bodies: Practice, Emotion and Ethics'. In B. Anderson and P. Harrison (eds) *Taking Place: Non-Representational Theories and Geography*. Farnham: Ashgate, pp. 221–40.
Thompson, J., and R. Schechner, 2004. 'Why "Social Theatre"?' *TDR: The Journal of Performance Studies*, T183, pp. 11–16.
Williams, R., 1966. *Modern Tragedy*. London: Chatto and Windus.

Part I

Surviving War and Exile: National and Ethnic Identity in Performance

1
Surviving (with) Theatre: A History of the ELF and EPLF Cultural Troupes in the Eritrean War of Independence

Christine Matzke[1]

Introduction

Eritrea looks back on a long history of colonialism, occupation and military conflicts which have always found expression in the performing arts. Of particular importance remains the war of independence against Ethiopia (1961–91), which broke out in response to mounting Ethiopian domination in the 1950s and 1960s. After half a century of Italian colonialism (1890–1941) followed by a British Military 'care-taker' Administration (BMA, 1941–52), Eritrea was federated with Ethiopia in 1952 as the result of a UN resolution. Her constitutionally guaranteed autonomy, however, was systematically undermined by the Ethiopian crown until the country was annexed to Ethiopia in 1962 as an ordinary province. The already-fraught political situation was complicated still further in 1974 when Ethiopian Emperor Haile Selassie was ousted, and eventually killed, by a Marxist military junta known as the Derg. Eritrean opposition became ever more radical and resulted in a ferocious 30-year liberation struggle, with the Eritrean Liberation Front (ELF) and the Eritrean People's Liberation Front (EPLF) as the two major liberation movements. Both used performance as a tool for entertainment, propaganda and nation-building, but also to boost morale and develop stamina in the protracted battle for sovereignty and survival.

In this chapter I focus on two crucial moments in the narrative of Eritrean theatre in 'the field' – the areas in which the liberation movements operated – during the 1970s and early 1980s.[2] I begin with the much-neglected history of the ELF cultural troupes to argue that the ELF

18 *Surviving (with) Theatre*

laid the foundation for a unique fighter culture to emerge – one that drew upon reinvented Eritrean traditions – but that the EPLF troupes developed that culture further and used performance to maximum effect for the project of independence and national survival. In conclusion I question briefly why these modes of performance have persisted into the post-war period and whether they may even contribute to the current state of arrested democratization.

While this essay essentially provides an introductory cultural history of an important phenomenon in the Eritrean war of independence – the emergence and problem-ridden continuity of cultural troupes – I will also enquire into the 'functions' of performance in relation to mechanisms for survival. Life was immensely hazardous in the field and did not allow for a sharp distinction between culture, creativity and combat. Often 'performing for survival' referred not only to the liberation war, but also to the continued existence of cultural troupes in the field.

Historical background: the ELF and EPLF

In 1960 the first armed liberation movement, the ELF, was founded and started to stake out its power base. While the leadership remained located in Egypt, the Eritrean Liberation Army was established in Eritrea, with a Revolutionary Command based in Sudan. In Eritrea a zonal organization was introduced whose ultimate drawback, most sources agree, was the rise of ethnic and religious parochialism, social exclusion and personal patronage.[3]

Eritrean historiography is unequivocal that the ELF as a liberation movement eventually failed and that from 1970/71 reformist splinter groups were on the ascent. Critical accounts of the fragmentation of the ELF differ considerably; in the given context it is only necessary to understand that three main factions split off from the ELF, which, after a complicated consolidation process, emerged as the EPLF in 1976. In 1977 the new liberation movement officially constituted itself at the first EPLF Congress. For the sake of simplicity all groupings which eventually merged as the EPLF will be referred to as such.[4]

In 1972 the core ELF declared war against the secessionists, which led to a prolonged civil war, the fiercest periods being between 1972–4 and 1978–81 (Iyob 1995: 122). By the early 1980s the ELF was virtually powerless inside Eritrea, the majority of fighters having fled to Sudan to seek refuge in the Arab and western diaspora. Even today, bitterness stemming from the civil war, which separated families and caused casualties totally unrelated to combating the common enemy, Ethiopia, is rife on both sides of the divide.[5] Inside Eritrea the role of the ELF in the liberation struggle continues to be relatively neglected, as is its contribution to the cultural field. I encountered few attempts at ELF/EPLF reconciliation until the onset of the so-called Eritrean-Ethiopian 'border war' in 1998–2000, one of the largest and deadliest conventional inter-state conflicts at the turn of the millennium (Jacquin-Berdal 2004), when a number of distinguished ELF artists returned to Eritrea to lend their support. In the capital of Asmara I had to wait until 2008 before I was actively encouraged to research into ELF cultural troupes. That was also the first time I heard an ELF song during the official independence celebrations. The internecine strife between the two camps has continued over more than four decades and has often impeded fruitful discussions and the collation of data (cf. Pool 2001: 71).

These factors have long contributed to the underestimation of ELF cultural work, especially in official historical narratives. Creative impulses originating in the ELF, if not earlier in civilian theatre associations, were sometimes implicitly credited to the EPLF. Yet for both fronts the institutionalization of cultural work, and the recognition of its importance, was a genuine challenge.

The first ELF cultural troupe

Research into the ELF's cultural activities has suffered not only from the tensions between the two liberation fronts, but also from lack of contemporary documentation for triangulation. It can, however, be safely assumed that no cultural group existed before 1968, when the ELF began a major structural overhaul of the organization (Iyob 1995: 113–14). Changes were also called for with regard to the role of culture. A cultural group was needed for political ends and Ramadan Gebre, a Tigre-speaker from Keren,[6] the third-largest city in Eritrea, was given the task. Ramadan was an old hand at performance, having run his own theatre group, *Abna Keren* ('Sons of Keren'), as early as the mid-1950s. Now he travelled with the new ELF troupe, mostly in the western lowlands, where they performed political agit-prop and revolutionary music in languages such as Tigre, Arabic and Tigrinya. At some point between 1969 and 1971 Ramadan Gebre mounted the first known drama in the field. The play, *Emperor* (*Imberator*), was classic propaganda material[7] and prefigured theatrical tendencies for both liberation movements in the coming two decades, including the portrayal of Ethiopian atrocities and the heroic deeds of Eritreans, fighters and civilians alike. It told the story of an Eritrean son incarcerated by the Ethiopian emperor's army for being a member of an ELF underground cell, and the heroic, if tragic, resistance of his mother. She is killed, but is eventually avenged by ELF fighters (I 20, I 21, I 22).

Emperor portrayed the bravery of the fighters, but also highlighted the sacrifices made by (and expected of) the civilian population for the nation's survival. It also acknowledged the role of mothers in the struggle for independence. At this point women were not yet frontline fighters,[8] and mothers in theatrical representations had mainly served as (passive) allegories of the suffering nation.[9] The heroic mother figure was to become a staple representation in the two liberation movements, the image appealing to both reformist and conservative elements at the fronts and to the civilian population: a woman comfortably settled into her traditional role, yet resolutely fighting the enemy with all her available resources, even if it meant sacrificing her life. The play left no doubt about its message: this war was not about personal survival; it was about the survival of Eritrea as a nation.

The ELF's cultural heyday

The outbreak of the civil war in 1972 considerably weakened the ELF cultural troupe, but further political developments led to its rejuvenation. In 1974 Ethiopian Emperor Haile Selassie, who had ruled since 1930, was ousted by the Derg, a Marxist military junta. The new Ethiopian regime under Colonel Mengistu Haile Mariam proved to be more oppressive than that of the emperor, which resulted in an increasing number of new recruits to the liberation fronts, male and female. By 1975 many highlanders, largely Tigrinya-speakers, had joined the ELF. These included a number of established artists.[10]

In 1975 Bereket Mengisteab, a well-known singer and former member of the Haile Selassie I Company in Addis Ababa (based at the emperor's 1,400-seater theatre in the Ethiopian capital), joined the ELF, as did Negusse Haile 'Mensa'ai', a songwriter, playwright and key player in the highly influential *Mahber Teyatr Asmera* ('Asmara Theatre Association'), known as Ma.Te.A. (cf. Matzke 2008a). Initially Bereket was appointed as the new director of the 'Eritrean National Theatre and Music Revival Troupe' (ELF 1977/8: 15), with Negusse as deputy. In 1976–7 they switched roles, and Negusse continued to direct the group until the early 1980s.[11] Ramadan Gebre, although he was no longer running the group, stayed with them until 1977 (I 12/08).

The cultural heyday of the ELF lasted from 1975 to 1981, when the cultural troupe disbanded. Particularly from 1975–7 they had a clear artistic advantage over the EPLF because of their many seasoned performers. Some 20–30 artists made up the troupe, with numbers fluctuating. Following a performance formula time-tested by urban theatre associations, their shows were divided into modern (i.e. 'liberation war') music, long-established performance arts (especially songs and dances), and the occasional dramatic skit. Music was most prominent, having always been an essential element of creative expression among all nationalities in Eritrea. It proved to be an effective tool for political propaganda. As performer Sediq, today with the national dance troupe *Sbrit*, recalls:

> Particularly the people and the fighters liked it very much. They used to say 'a show on one night is better than a series of seminars and lectures'. It proves that people realized the importance of our work. The shows were also helpful in recruiting new fighters to the ELF because after every performance, particularly those in Sudan [where many Eritrean refugees lived], young people joined the ELF in large numbers. (I 5/08)

As there was only one official cultural troupe, the artists lived the life of creative nomads in order to reach their potential audiences: fighters at the frontline, civilians in the liberated areas, and the exile community in Sudan. A large Fiat truck served as the means of transport and, more often than not, as a makeshift upper stage, often used for traditional dance performances. A plastic tarpaulin was spread out at the side of the lorry to mark the lower performance space and to protect the artists from dust. The band took a position in front of the vehicle, a banner with slogans serving as backdrop.[12] With the help of a generator, two 700-watt floodlights and some smaller spots, this mobile performance space metamorphosed into a theatre at night. In the highlands, a *hidmo* – the traditional house of Tigrinya people – was sometimes used as theatrical space, the anterior room serving as the changing room and backstage area, and the company performing in front of the house while the band sat on the roofed veranda.

In Eritrea, then, the military phrase 'theatre of war' has always had a rather literal meaning, for war has continued to be the prime motif in the performing arts, often embedded in historical narrative as a means of political education. Plays recounting the history of the nation were a staple in both liberation movements, even if drama was a minor, because historically alien, performance form for most fighter and civilian audiences alike. Often plays were reduced to ten-minute skits in the ELF for want of professional actors (as opposed to musicians) and lack of audience appreciation.

The Corrupt Derg (*Dergi Zergi*) by Negusse Haile was one of the few full-length plays recalled by former ELF members. Conceived as a national epic, it recounted Eritrea's troubled colonial history until the coming of the Derg regime. Mounting a play outside an urbanized context was a novel experience for Negusse, and rather a challenge. Audiences in Asmara and other towns had been familiar with theatre conventions initially brought to Eritrea by Italian and British performers, and they did not call for explanatory commentaries during the shows. In the rural countryside, however, a moderator was needed to guide the spectators through the play. In 1978, in an attempt to provide the historical background during a village show, Negusse explained the ascent of Colonel Mengistu in Ethiopia. When a Mengistu lookalike appeared on stage, a panicky outcry rippled through the audience with a group of female spectators taking to their heels. The company did not understand the commotion and continued to play, only to be informed by the local militia that the women had taken the actor for real. Audience members also tried to beat up the unfortunate impersonator after the show.

It is thus not surprising that music and long-established performance forms remained the most popular elements. Too many drastic changes in too little time had been imposed upon combatants and civilians alike. The old order had been violently disrupted in all imaginable ways – social, political, economic and cultural – and smooth reception of what many still perceived as a foreign aesthetic could not realistically be expected. Traditional performance forms, on the other hand, enabled both fighters and civilians to assert themselves against foreign intrusion and provided a point of imagined stability. This holds true for both liberation movements. For civilian audiences, traditional performance forms constituted familiar elements in which they recognized themselves or learned about other Eritrean nationalities; for combatants they played an important integrative role in the effort to create a sense of unity among the heterogeneous fighters (I 5/08, I 12/08). Ernest Gellner, with a critical view of nation-building and the emergence of nationalism, has observed that

> [n]ationalism usually conquers in the name of putative folk culture. Its symbolism is drawn from the healthy, pristine, vigorous life of the

peasants, of the *Volk*, the *národ*. There is a certain element of truth in the nationalist self-representation when the *národ* or *Volk* is ruled by officials of another, an alien high culture, whose oppression must be resisted first by a cultural revival and reaffirmation, and eventually by a war of national liberation. [...] Society no longer worships itself through religious symbols; a modern, streamlined, on-wheels high culture celebrates itself in song and dance, which it borrows (stylizing it in the process) from a folk culture which it fondly believes itself to be perpetuating, defending and reaffirming. (Gellner 2006: 56–7)

Performance elements rooted in ancestral patterns certainly supported the creation of an imagined community in both movements. While the EPLF eventually embellished customary choreographies for greater stage effect and incorporated 'genuine' peasant performers for a more 'authentic' feel, the ELF can be credited with the reinvention of Eritrean traditions in the field, bringing together artists and performance forms from almost all nationalities.[13]

For the military survival of the ELF, however, these cultural mediation measures came too late. In the early 1980s the movement disintegrated when they were attacked by EPLF forces in a second flare-up of the civil war and driven across the Sudanese border. This also put an end to their cultural work, even if individual performers continue to be active in both Eritrea and the diaspora until the present. It was the newly constituted EPLF which would come to use performance to maximum effect for the project of independence and national survival.

Theatre in the EPLF: the story of the first cultural troupe

I would like to begin this section with a contemporaneous account of theatre work in the EPLF, which provides an impression of how cultural work was initially conceived. Dan Connell describes a performance that served not only to support Eritrean nationalism and condemn the Ethiopian oppressors but also to distinguish the EPLF from the ELF:

> A group of twenty-five students, including nine women, had also formed their own theater company and begun improvising plays and dramatic readings. The night I visited them, they performed the history of the national liberation struggle in five acts.
>
> Several hundred people sat on the rocky ground in a broad semicircle around the makeshift outdoor stage, lit by two strings of bare

bulbs. The show opened with a tribal dance by a scantily clad boy carrying a long spear and wielding a wooden sword as he leapt about the stage to the beat of the hand-held drum. The audience murmured and giggled throughout, unsure how they were supposed to react.

Next, one of the players spoke to the audience on the need for a new 'people's culture'. Then he led the assemblage in a song of praise for the martyrs who had given their lives for the liberation of their nation, before stepping off the stage and joining the audience.

Behind him a group of swaggering guerrilla fighters moved to stage left, opposite a man and a woman at stage right dressed as nomads. (This was the ELF in its starting phase.) One of the fighters sashayed across the platform to demand taxes from the nomads. As the man started to pay, his wife demanded to know why the fighter was living an easy life at their expense while they suffered and starved. Her vehemence had the audience roaring.

Women were not supposed to involve themselves in politics, he snapped, as she made the Eritrean version of an obscene gesture at him behind his back. More raucous laughter, especially from the women in the audience. Back in the fighters' camp, the leader ostentatiously smoked a cigarette and threw the butt on the ground where his fawning comrades fought over it.

And so it went with a mixture of slapstick comedy and biting satire in scene after overacted scene, until the EPLF was portrayed as emerging in the 1970s to lead the people in a social revolution. (Connell 1997: 107–8).

Though the first factions to separate from the ELF did so as early as 1969, the intricate amalgamation and constitution process of the EPLF did not allow culture to play a central role until the mid-1970s when the EPLF 'expanded its geographical and social base' (Pool 1997: 12). It can nevertheless be inferred that informal entertainment existed on all levels of the splinter groups whenever the situation allowed or required. Often, it was a pastime during *maetot* (communal work) when people sang while engaging in some other occupation. On the whole, these performances drew upon aforementioned customary forms and do not seem to be associated with a noteworthy socio-political agenda. The attempt to level ethnic affiliations and constitute a unified, if diverse, Eritrean identity through the conscious mounting of a 'putative folk culture' (often by members of other nationalities) was yet to come. In the early to mid-1970s, fighters still tended to mingle with their own ethnolinguistic group, with whom they practised ancestral performance forms for festivities and recreation.

Organized cultural work in the EPLF started in 1975, in all likelihood after the ELF's National Theatre and Music Revival Troupe had been established. The striking similarities between the creation and the management of the two groups suggest that EPLF cultural work was initiated in reaction to arts activities in the rival organization. It also seems to have contributed to the initial confusion regarding the difference between the liberation movements. New recruits who flocked to the fronts in the mid-1970s often did not – or could not – distinguish between the two.[14] Atrocities committed by the new Ethiopian regime under Mengistu had made civilian life intolerable and participation in the liberation struggle became the common goal. Among the new recruits joining the EPLF were some experienced artists, including Ma.Te.A. veterans Tebereh Tesfahunei and Asmerom Habtemariam, and the singer Idris Mohamed Ali. Idris and his band had come from Sudan. Tebereh, a well-known and very beautiful singer, joined from Sweden where she had been living as a refugee since leaving Addis Ababa in the early 1970s. On completing their military training the artists were brought together to form the first *Bahli Wdb* or Cultural Troupe (CT). The first CT, also known as the Division of Culture, was administered by *Ziena*, the Department of Information, whose objectives were mobilization and propaganda work.

Initially, the troupe was a purely musical band under the direction of Idris Mohamed Ali and Tsadu Bhata. As Asmerom Habtemariam recalled:

We trained day and night and all was about songs, not drama. We started to mount shows in our vicinity. The contents of the songs were meant to strengthen the people. Tebereh, for example, sang about the '*Kumandis*', that is Eritreans recruited to the Ethiopian army, and Idris Mohamed Ali had a song which said 'I prefer to die like my martyred brother'. Since these songs were influential, we were asked to perform in the highlands rather than remain in Sahel. We first went to *Semenawi Bahri* [the Northern Red Sea Region]. When we mounted our first show there, people began to flock to us, even from Asmara. Asmerom Geregzhier was the leader of this area. He told us that our shows were a better tool of politicization than two or three people telling the masses about the liberation struggle. He then ordered the show to be performed everywhere in the highlands. (I 38).

Tebereh Tesfahunei's account of the very first EPLF troupe is more critical than Asmerom's, referring to tensions between members of different political factions and describing Ethiopian attacks which disrupted the shows. Above all, she objected to being deployed in the cultural field rather than as a frontline fighter – a sentiment which was shared by a number of performers thereafter. It was the actual combat that held the highest prestige, and women felt a particular need to prove themselves on the frontline (Selassie 1992: 69). Tebereh had reinvented herself in compliance with the organization – both in appearance and attitude – only to find herself back where she had started: singing on stage.

> Before the military training I had cut my hair Afro-style. The training included military training, political lessons and criticism and self-criticism.[15] [...] Three months later the training was over. Some of us joined the army, some went to the health department and one of my comrades and I were sent to the Cultural Bureau to work with the cultural troupe. I was very disappointed by this assignment. I wanted to go to the front. But it was a precept in the EPLF that you must not refuse any orders. Solomon was one of the fighters who told us about our assignments. I asked him why I wasn't sent to the frontline. Solomon smiled and said: 'You must hit the enemy with your songs like you would hit them with a bullet.'[16]

The 'cultural bullet' and the 'cultural combatant' were to become set ideas at the front,[17] especially as awareness grew regarding the importance of '[c]ulture and education as vehicles for mobilization and construction of a pluralist Eritrean national identity' (Iyob 1995: 129). First and foremost, 'cultural combat' meant rallying against the Ethiopian enemy and its cultural and socio-political stranglehold; secondly, it entailed the battle against customs practised by the various cultures of Eritrea which were considered reactionary and 'harmful'. A projected 'revolutionary' society reorganized according to the tenets of the revolution needed egalitarian laws which did not discriminate based on ethnicity, religion or gender because everyone – woman and man, highlander and lowlander, Christian and Muslim – was needed to help fight the war of independence. Performance and other cultural activities were thus seen as vital tools of social and ideological propaganda work, and as instruments of instruction, exploration and learning.

Despite its auspicious beginnings, personal rapport in the first CT deteriorated by the end of 1975, largely due to political factionalism during the constituting phase of the EPLF. Among the members of the EPLF cultural troupe, tensions were of both a personal and political nature. There were accusations of certain factions boycotting communal 'criticism and self-criticism' sessions, and of receiving better provisions

(Tesfahunei 2000: n.p.); others noted more general dissent and conflict among the performers. The cultural troupe seemed to mirror, in microcosm, the problems among the guerrilla fronts and the lack of unity even within one organization. As one former liberation fighter recalled:

> We did not have experience in the struggle and were without a framework of unity. We did not really have deep thoughts about the struggle. All we had were strong national feelings. This meant we were not united enough in our daily life. For instance, those who came from Asmara used to socialize among themselves, while others did the same among their own people. I talked with 'Tebereh' but not with 'Sadiya' because I didn't know her. This was seen as a complete separation by foreign observers – they thought it was a religious divide. [...] The language too was not unified. But you should have something to unify the differences. This was the biggest problem, though we didn't understand at the time. (I 38)

It is thus not surprising that the first CT began to disintegrate. Some performers left for Sudan; others were rumoured to be spies or infiltrators. Less than a year after its foundation, it was dissolved and the remaining artists were assigned to various tasks. Mostly, they were sent to combatant forces to experience what the struggle was 'really' about. Tebereh Tesfahunei was deployed in the 3rd Battalion, joyful that she would now be engaged in frontline combat. Within the first year of her deployment, she sustained a serious head injury while stationed near Decamhare. The injury left her marked for the rest of her life, resulting in severe mental instability, and was the end of her singing career. One of Eritrea's most treasured artists would survive the liberation war, but she would not survive as a performer.[18]

EPLF cultural work after the strategic retreat

By 1978, events at the front called for a complete reconsideration of military strategies and organizational structures. The new Ethiopian regime under Mengistu attracted massive Soviet military assistance and, beginning with a setback at the strategically important port of Massawa in December 1977, Eritrea suffered five major Soviet-backed Ethiopian offensives up to mid-1979 (Iyob 1995: 174). While the ELF was hardest hit during the First Offensive, the EPLF surrendered territory in subsequent attacks. When the Second Offensive broke through critical frontlines, the EPLF decided on an orderly military withdrawal into the inaccessible northern highlands of Eritrea. This so-called 'strategic retreat' – drawn from Mao Zedong's long-term tactics to win a guerrilla war – allowed the EPLF 'to defend its base area against all further assaults and thus survive the most difficult days of the war for independence' (Connell and Killion 2011: 482). As a result, the Fourth and Fifth Offensives failed.[19]

Together with the retreating fighters, tens of thousands of civilians fled their homes. Some followed the EPLF into Sahel, others tried to find their way into Sudan in the desperate attempt to save their lives. While former pastoralists found themselves nomadic refugees, the fighters, paradoxically, had to adapt to a more sedentary existence. For the cultural work of the EPLF, exodus, retreat and the prospect of a protracted war had tremendous consequences and led to a comprehensive restructuring. Culture was now encouraged on all levels and units of the liberation movement, not only in the military, but also in supporting departments, such as medical services or schools. In addition, culture in the field began to be promoted more aggressively as 'revolutionary culture'. Influenced by relatively generalized ideas about socialist realism in the communist world, 'revolutionary culture' had to be relevant to and supportive of the liberation movement; it had to be typical of the fighters' lives; and it had to be realistic in a representational sense in order to avoid allegory and potentially hidden meanings.

At first these ideas met with resentment and difficulties; they were only fully implemented from the early to mid-1980s. Initially, fighters were simply ordered to get engaged in cultural work. Grass-roots work started within smaller units – the platoons and companies – before CTs were established at battalion, brigade and finally army division levels. Initially, no one in the military units had any cultural experience and shows were rather humble events. Fighters were selected for their voices or their outgoing personalities and people who had never sung, acted or made music started to get engaged. 'Most of us didn't want to be in the cultural troupes,' recalled Ibrahim Ali 'Akla', today a senior cultural administrator. 'Most of us preferred combat to culture. [...] However, they told us that all occupations were equal in the field' (I 67). Since the EPLF defined 'fighting' more broadly than engaging in frontline battles, comrades who refused to get involved in performance activities were strongly criticized by their peers (Zerai 2001: 28). Gradually, the importance of culture became more accepted. 'There were awareness campaigns regarding recreation in the companies to refresh the minds of the members,' the actress Tsega Hagos explained (I 93). 'You accepted and adopted the idea because you had been told that it [culture] was part of the struggle' (I 67).

Wednesday had been declared the official day of rest in the EPLF, as opposed to the usual Christian Sunday and Muslim Friday, to avoid privileging one religious community over the other. Tuesday night was reserved for partying and recreation should the military situation allow. *Suwa* (a local alcoholic brew) was prepared and enjoyed while the fighters watched the impromptu shows. The actress Nechi Fesehatsion recalled her first singing performance in the military training camp when a cluster of stones served as a 'stage'. 'I sang standing on these stones, but then I wanted to dance and jumped down. Obviously, my voice no longer reached the audience and people started to shout and complain' (I 87). Her colleague Atsbehet Yohannes confirmed that the shows 'were not particularly organized. There was no training or capable leadership or any ordered programme. The performances were put on whenever they were needed. It was just for the fun and enjoyment of our unit or group' (I 7). 'It was everywhere in the trenches,' Tsega Hagos confirmed. 'You just shared things, and after you had put on a show, you went back to the trenches and continued guarding' (I 93).

While platoon and company entertainment remained an ad-hoc affair, some performers were recruited to higher level cultural troupes where they were given more resources to develop their talents. Fatuma Suleiman, for example, became a long-term member of the 31st Brigade CT. She had originally been selected for her Saho ethnic background because fighters from minorities (such as the Kunama, Nara, Afar or Saho) were scarce, and higher level cultural troupes aspired to a broad ethnic spectrum among their members. In 1981 the Central Cultural Troupe (CCT) was revived and Alemseged Tesfai – lawyer, writer and one of Eritrea's most prominent intellectuals until this day – was appointed director of drama (cf. Matzke 2008b). Fatuma was recruited to the CCT and, although she had initially pursued a career as painter, singer, songwriter, dancer and actress in the field, she ultimately distinguished herself in tailoring and wig-making, becoming the EPLF's most prominent costume designer.[20]

Even that activity, however, was not without its hazards. Given the ubiquitous 'Afro' sported by male and female fighter-performers, wigs became essential in frontline theatre, especially for the mounting of traditional performance forms. Hair and head movements were an essential part of certain dance choreographies, such as *shellil* (a Bilen dance performed only by women, which involves turning the head left and right and swinging one's braids), and a signifier of ethnic and marital status in civilian Eritrea. As Fatuma recalled:

> The first time I prepared wigs was in Brigade 31. Initially, real hair was not available, we used sacks and dyed them with used battery powder. There was nothing but these batteries, and at that time we were not aware of the health hazard they constituted. When the women danced, the battery powder came off and coloured their faces.

Another occupational hazard for performers was spectators' inability to distinguish between an offstage 'reality' and onstage 'performance'. The actress Weyni Tewolde recalled how a number of actors were beaten up after a play about feudal exploitation in front of traditional village authorities who did not seem to have taken too kindly to such 'revolutionary' ideas. Sadyia Omer, in her first role as the Eritrean wife of an Ethiopian, had to cope with people throwing stones at her and insulting her as a 'prostitute'. Even artists could fall prey to such attitudes, as did a member of a smaller CT who unexpectedly refused to be seized during a scene, afraid that he might be nicknamed 'captive' later.[21]

With the reconstitution of the CCT in 1981 and the creation of a section of literature and drama, concerted efforts were made to promote dramatic literature in the field in order to deepen understanding among audiences and performers (Matzke 2008b). While performers still had to cope with the haphazardness of war, cultural work became more professionalized, thematically focused and aesthetically refined. Occasionally, performers would break out of the 'revolutionary' mould to mount plays by Shakespeare and other classics of 'world theatre' (Matzke 2004). On the whole, however, the tenets of 'revolutionary culture' still applied: theatre had to be relevant to and supportive of the aims and objectives of the EPLF; it had to be realistic in a representational sense; and it had to be typical of people's lives.

Conclusion

The war against Ethiopia ended in 1991 and a UN-supervised referendum in Eritrea led to independence and international recognition in 1993. Most cultural work in the late 2000s, however, still seemed to follow the artistic principles of the liberation war. Why have such modes of performance survived and continued to be central to contemporary cultural practice in Eritrea? While such theatre certainly keeps alive the memories of the war of independence, it also seems to calcify the government's claims to power and sustain the current state of arrested democratization. The country is now a single-party state run by the People's Front for Democracy and Justice (PFDJ), the EPLF turned civilian post-independence.[22] Other political groups are not allowed to organize; national elections have never been held.

There is very little experimentation today with new topics and forms in the cultural realm; all cultural work is now state-controlled and goes through various forms of screening. Performance thus seems to reflect Eritrea's current position in the global community of nations: a pariah state with no freedom of the press, in which human rights abuses abound and which is accused of supporting Al-Shabab and other terrorist organizations.[23] Scholarly discourses on the Eritrean liberation struggle changed long ago from hagiography to disillusioned criticism (cf. Müller 2012: 451). Such polarized views, however, do not do justice to theatrical innovation during the war of independence. Further research, it is hoped, will provide ever more nuanced insights into Eritrean performance practice in order to defy any form of one-dimensional reading and enhance our understanding of the sociocultural history of Eritrea – and of performance for and survival in the Horn of Africa.

Notes

1. I wish to thank former cultural workers in the field, both ELF and EPLF, for reading and commenting on earlier drafts in the early 2000s and again in 2008, Richard Boon and Bettina Conrad for their constructive comments on drafts in 2013, and the editors of the present volume for their patient and careful guidance. Thanks also to Bruce Parkhurst for providing me with picture material. All errors, inaccuracies and interpretations are obviously mine.
2. While the scope of this chapter does not allow me to go into more detailed methodological considerations, it is important to understand that this essay is essentially a chronologically ordered collage of stories, which I constructed out of the memories of participants and survivors of the Eritrean liberation war. These recollections are embedded in, and read against, a historical narrative based on published and unpublished sources. Memory always 'finds itself under the yoke of the current political situation' (Mwembu 2005: 447), which affects how recollections are related at a particular time (cf. Matzke 2010: 7) and how the narrative is constructed by the researcher at the time of writing. For this chapter there are three main timelines: the period with which this chapter deals (1970s–1980s); the periods of collating data (1995 and 1997, 1998–2003, and 2008); and, finally, the time of writing in summer 2013 (with earlier drafts dating back to 2003 and 2008).
3. Pool (2001: 49–54), Iyob (1995: 109–14), Markakis (1987: 109–20).
4. For older sources on the different factions see ELF (1979: 44–50), Markakis (1987: 126–41), Iyob (1995: 114–16). For more recent accounts see Pool (2001: 63–70, 140–42) and Connell and Killion (2011: 210–18).

5. This was exacerbated by one ELF faction siding with Ethiopia in the latest Eritrean-Ethiopian war in 1998–2000 (Ghirmai 2005: 199–202).
6. Today Eritrea acknowledges nine ethno-linguistic groups, which are generally referred to as 'nationalities'. They are divided into two dominant communities, the Tigrinya- and Tigre-speakers, and seven minorities: the Bilen (or Blin), Kunama, Nara, Rasheida, Saho, Hedareb (Beja) and the Afar. Languages correspond eponymously to these groups except for the Rasheida who speak Arabic. Tigrinya-speakers are often considered to be the dominant group in Eritrea, also in terms of relative political power.
7. In this chapter propaganda is generally defined as '*expression of opinion or action by individuals or groups deliberately designed to influence opinions or actions of other individuals or groups with reference to predetermined ends*' (Institute for Propaganda Analysis 2010: 496).
8. Eventually, all members of the fronts were called 'fighters', whether they were engaged in frontline combat or not.
9. Plastow (1997: 152), Matzke (2008a: 73).
10. Most of this section is based on ECBTP 95/24, ECBTP 95/25, ECBTP 95/30, I 20, I 21, I 22, I 133, I 2/08, I 5/08, I 6/08, I 7/08, I 9/08, I 12/08.
11. By then Bereket Mengisteab had already left Eritrea for Sudan; later he moved to Saudi Arabia before returning permanently to Eritrea during the 1998–2000 Eritrean-Ethiopian war.
12. For a filmic documentation of their work see *The Land by the Sea* (1982).
13. All nationalities were represented except for the Rashaida who had no contingent in the ELF; one former group member also mentioned a 'traditional' troupe with just Nara and Tigre performers (I 5/08). For EPLF examples see the video *Music and Drama of the EPLF* (mid-1980s).
14. Cf. Pool (2001: 142, fn 10). I too heard a number of such stories. In the mid-1970s, many new recruits did not bother too much about which liberation movement they joined. Others were said to have been 'rejected' by one organization – asked, for example, to finish their education or form a civilian cell – only to become frontline combatants with the other.
15. Criticism and self-criticism sessions were a measure taken by the EPLF to tighten discipline. They were practised at all levels of the organization.
16. Tesfahunei (2000: n.p.). Tebereh published two autobiographies in rapid succession, in 1999 and 2000, which differ somewhat from each other. Part of the 1999 version can now be found on the web at http://www.crcstudio.org/eritrean/Pages/viewfulltext.php?tid=108.
17. Visual artist Terhas Iyasu, for example, mentioned that 'during the struggle, we also struggled with paintings' (I 106); while Berhane Adonai, one of the most prominent arts teachers in Eritrea, recapitulated that: 'We were fighting the enemy not only with bullets, we were also fighting them with cultural bullets' (I 75). Personally, I have borrowed these terms from the South African arts and culture activist Bongani Linda (1966–2013).
18. Tebereh Tesfahunei died in March 2007 in Asmara.
19. Pateman (1998: 135–7). In my narrative of EPLF cultural work, I have omitted the story of the 2nd Cultural Troupe (1976–8/9), largely for reasons of space, and because it was less impactful than its predecessor.
20. For more details on her life see Christmann (1996: 118–22) and Gerezgiher (1995).

21. I 51, I 93, I 97. The inability to distinguish between stage action and reality was of course not an exclusively Eritrean phenomenon. For examples in Ethiopia see Pankhurst (1986: 187–8).
22. For more details see Connell and Killion (2011: 418–19).
23. Plaut (2013: 323–6), Amnesty International (2013), Human Rights Watch (2013).

Bibliography

Eritrean and Ethiopian authors are listed with their father's name ('surname') first to comply with international citation systems. Texts originally published in Tigrinya are quoted in the English translation available to the author.

Amnesty International, 2013. 'Annual Report 2013: Eritrea', available online at http://www.amnesty.org/en/region/eritrea/report-2013, accessed 12 September 2013.
Christmann, S., 1996. *Die Freiheit haben wir nicht von den Männern: Frauen in Eritrea*. Unkel: Horlemann.
Connell, D., 1997. *Against All Odds: A Chronicle of the Eritrean Revolution* (1993). Asmara: Red Sea Press.
Connell, D., and T. Killion, 2011. *Historical Dictionary of Eritrea*, 2nd edition, African Historical Dictionaries, 114. Lanham, MD: The Scarecrow Press.
ELF, 1977/8. *Eritrean Revolution*, 2: 4 (Dec. 1977/Jan. 1978).
ELF, 1979. *Eritrea: The National Democratic Revolution versus Ethiopian Expansionism*. Beirut: The ELF Foreign Information Centre.
Gellner, E., 2006. *Nations and Nationalism*, 2nd edition (1983). Malden, MA: Blackwell.
Gerezgiher, W., 1995. 'A Woman Moving Forward: Fatuma Suleiman', transl. (from the Tigrinya) by Mussie Tesfagiorgis. In *Mosana*, October 1995, n.p.
Ghirmai, A., 2005. *Eritrea zwischen Einparteienstaat und Demokratie: Die Bedeutung der Opposition im Demokratisierungsprozess*. Marburg: Tectum.
Human Rights Watch, 2013. 'Eritrea', available online at http://www.hrw.org/world-report/2013/country-chapters/eritrea, accessed 12 September 2013.
Institute for Propaganda Analysis, 2010. 'How to Detect Propaganda'. In Gary Goshgarian (ed.) *Exploring Language*, 12th edition. New York: Longman, pp. 496–500.
Iyob, R., 1995. *The Eritrean Struggle for Independence: Domination, Resistance, Nationalism, 1941–1993*. Cambridge: Cambridge University Press.
Jacquin-Berdal, D., 2004. 'Introduction: The Eritreo-Ethiopian War'. In Dominique Jacquin-Berdal and Martin Plaut (eds) *Unfinished Business: Ethiopia and Eritrea at War*. Trenton, NJ: Red Sea Press, pp. ix–xxi.
Markakis, J., 1987. *National and Class Conflict in the Horn of Africa*. Cambridge: Cambridge University Press.
Matzke, C., 2004. 'Shakespeare and Surgery in the Eritrean Liberation Struggle: Performance Culture in Orota'. In *Journal of Eritrean Studies: Research Journal of the Colleges of Arts and Social Sciences* (Asmara), 3: 1 (May 2004), pp. 26–40.
Matzke, C., 2008a. 'The Asmara Theatre Association, 1961–1974: *Mahber Teyatr Asmera*'. In James Gibbs (ed.) *African Theatre 7: Companies*. Woodbridge: James Currey, pp. 62–81.

Matzke, C., 2008b. ' "Life in the Camp of the Enemy": Alemseged Tesfai's Theatre of War'. In Ernest N. Emenyonu (ed.) *African Literature Today 26: War in African Literature Today*. Woodbridge: James Currey, pp. 15–32.

Matzke, C., 2010. 'Looking for "Eritrea's Past Property" (1947): Archives and Memories in Eritrean Theatre Historiography'. In Yvette Hutchinson (ed.) *African Theatre 9: Histories 1850–1950*. Woodbridge: James Currey, pp. 1–22.

Müller, T. R., 2012. 'Beyond the Siege State: Tracing Hybridity During a Recent Visit to Eritrea'. In *Review of African Political Economy*, 39: 133, pp. 451–64.

Mwembu, D. D., 2005. 'History and Memory'. In John Edward Philips (ed.) *Writing African History*. Rochester, NY: University of Rochester Press, pp. 439–64.

Pankhurst, R., 1986. 'Shakespeare in Ethiopia'. In *Research in African Literatures*, 17: 2, pp. 169–96.

Pateman, R., 1998. *Eritrea: Even the Stones are Burning*. Trenton, NJ: Red Sea Press.

Plastow, J., 1997. 'Theatre of Conflict in the Eritrean Independence Struggle'. In *New Theatre Quarterly*, 13: 50, pp. 144–54.

Plaut, M., 2013. 'Briefing: How Unstable is the Horn of Africa?'. In *Review of African Political Economy*, 40: 136, pp. 321–30.

Pool, D., 1997. *Eritrea: Towards Unity in Diversity* (Minority Rights Group International Report). London: Minority Rights Group.

Pool, D., 2001. *From Guerrillas to Government: The Eritrean People's Liberation Front*. Oxford: James Currey.

Selassie, W. W., 1992. 'The Changing Position of Eritrean Women: An Overview of Women's Participation in the EPFL'. In Martin Dornboos et al. (eds) *Beyond Conflict in the Horn: The Prospects for Peace, Recovery and Development in Ethiopia, Somalia, Eritrea and Sudan*. The Hague and London: The Institute of Social Studies, The Hague, in association with James Currey, pp. 67–71.

Tesfahunei, T., 1999. *The Two Lives: Based on a True Story: Autobiography of Tebereh Tesfahunei*. Trans. Mohamed Salih Ismail ([Asmara]: n.p.). For a different translation see http://www.crcstudio.org/eritrean/Pages/viewfulltext.php?tid=108, accessed 10 September 2013.

Tesfahunei, T., 2000. *Short Autobiography of Tebereh Tesfahunei* (Doris Day), translated from the Tigrinya by Mohamed Salih Ismail ([Asmara]: n.p.).

Zerai, Mesgun [also: Misgun Zerai Asghedom], 2001. 'The Theatre Experience in Eritrea'. Unpublished MA dissertation, Workshop Theatre, University of Leeds.

Films

The Land by the Sea: A Film about Eritrea. Christina Björk, Bengt Danneborn and Göran Aslun. Viking Film, 1982.

Music and Drama of the EPLF. Video. EPLF Cine-Section (mid-1980s).

Interviews

Memberships of liberation movements, bands and theatre associations are provided. Professions, if stated, were those at the time of the interview.

Eritrea Community-Based Theatre Project (ECBTP) 1995

Numbers after the stroke refer to the catalogue number of the ECBTP.

ECBTP 95/24	Isaak Abraham, ELF and EPLF, member of Venus Band before joining ELF in 1975.
ECBTP 95/25	Isaak Abraham, 2nd interview.
ECBTP 95/30	Zemheret Yohannes, ELF and EPLF, today head of PFDJ Research.

Interviews 1999–2001

Abbreviations: interviewer (int), notes (nts), recorded (rec), translator (ttr), transcript (tpt), unrecorded (unrec), Christine Matzke (CM), Mohamed Salih Ismael (MSI), Mussie Tesfagiorgis (MT), Samson Gebregzhier (SG), Tedros Hagos (TH), Tesfazghi Ukubazghi (TU), Yakem Tesfai (YT). Thanks to my Eritrean colleagues for their invaluable help.

I 7	**Atsbehet Yohannes**, actress, PFDJ Cultural Affairs. Rec. interview in English/Tigrinya, 23 September 1999, Asmara, Eritrea. Int: CM, ttr: Beneam (X), tpt: SG.
I 20	**Negusse Haile 'Mensa'ai'**, Ma.Te.A., Merhaba, ELF. 3rd unrec. interview in German, 7 November 1999, Kassel, Germany. Int/nts: CM.
I 21	**Negusse Haile 'Mensa'ai'**, Ma.Te.A., Merhaba, ELF. 4th unrec. interview in German, 4 December 1999, Kassel, Germany. Int/nts: CM.
I 22	**Negusse Haile 'Mensa'ai'**, Ma.Te.A., Merhaba, ELF. 5th unrec. interview in German, 12 December 1999, Kassel, Germany. Int/nts: CM.
I 38	**Asmerom Habtemariam**. 2nd rec. interview in English/Tigrinya, 14 February 2000, Asmara, Eritrea. Int: CM, ttr/tpt: MT.
I 49	**Fatuma Suleiman**, singer, artisan, owner of Roble Traditional Gift Article Shop, demobilized fighter. Rec. interview in English/Tigrinya, 24 February 2000, Asmara, Eritrea. Int: CM, ttr/tpt: MT.
I 51	**Weyni Tewolde**, actress, PFDJ Cultural Affairs. Rec. interview in English/Tigrinya, 29 February 2000, Asmara, Eritrea. Int: CM, ttr: TU, tpt: MT.
I 67	**Ibrahim Ali 'Akla'**. 2nd rec. interview in English/Tigrinya, 29 March 2000, Asmara, Eritrea. Int: CM, ttr: TU, tpt: MT.
I 75	**Brehane Adonai**, painter, former head of the Asmara Arts School. Rec. interview in English, 6 April 2000, Asmara, Eritrea. Int: CM, tpt: MT.
I 87	**Nechi Fesehatsion**, actress, demobilized fighter. Rec. interview in English/Tigrinya, 1 May 2000, Asmara, Eritrea. Int: CM, ttr/tpt: MT.
I 93	**Tsege Hagos**, actress, PFDJ Cultural Affairs. Rec. interview in English/Tigrinya, 11 May 2000, Asmara, Eritrea. Int: CM, ttr/tpt: MT.
I 97	**Sadyia Omer**, actress, *Abbot*, PFDJ Cultural Affairs. Rec. interview in English/Tigrinya, 22 July 2000, Asmara, Eritrea. Int: CM, tpt: MT.
I 100	**Tebereh Tesfahunei**, singer, Ma.Te.A. Rec. interview in English/Tigrinya, 31 July 2000, Asmara, Eritrea. Int: CM, ttr/tpt: MT.

I 106 Terhas Iyasu, painter, Curriculum Department, Ministry of Education. Rec. interview in English, 14 August 2000, Asmara, Eritrea. Int: CM, tpt: MSI.

I 133 Negusse Haile 'Mensa'ai'. 6th unrec. interview in German, 11 December 2001, Frankfurt/M., Germany. Int/nts: CM.

Interviews 2008

I 02/08 Ibrahim Idris Totil, ELF. Unrec. conversation in English/Tigrinya, 30 August 2008, Asmara, Eritrea. Int: CM, ttr: TH.

I 05/08 Sediq, ELF. Rec. Interview in Tigrinya, 2 September 2008, Asmara, Eritrea. Int: CM, ttr/tpt YT.

I 06/08 Baba John, ELF, Tsebah School. Rec. Interview in Tigrinya, 3 September 2008, Asmara, Eritrea. Int: CM, ttr/tpt: YT.

I 07/08 Bereket Mengisteab, ELF. Rec. Interview in Tigrinya, 4 September 2008, Asmara, Eritrea. Int: CM, ttr/tpt: YT.

I 09/08 Ibrahim Idris Totil, ELF. Unrec. conversation in English/Tigrinya, 7 September 2008, Asmara, Eritrea. Int: CM.

I 12/08 Wad Gebru, ELF. Rec. Interview in Tigrinya, 10 September 2008, Asmara, Eritrea. Int: CM, ttr/tpt: YT.

2
Theatre for Survival: Art of Creation and Protection (*Kubunda*)

Ananda Breed and Alice Mukaka[1]

Kubunda

Tutsi artists-in-exile sought to use performance as a mode of cultural survival, both to preserve Tutsi culture in the countries of refuge and to fuel a militaristic return to Rwanda, 'the land of milk and honey'. Performance was used to survive displacement and to create a utopian vision of Rwanda, the ancestral land that many young Tutsi refugees had never lived in nor experienced. In Ananda Breed's interview with Rwandan playwright-essayist Jean-Marie Rurangwa on 25 April 2006 in Kigali he stated: 'I wrote poems and plays to sensitise the diaspora to go back to their homeland. I have played a big role in Rwandans coming home'. Many of these artists took refuge in neighbouring countries including Tanzania, Kenya, Burundi and the Democratic Republic of Congo (DRC) at various historical points when Tutsi were hunted down to be killed, including 1959, 1973 and the genocide against Tutsi in 1994.[2]

In this chapter, we examine the function of culture during the Tutsi diaspora between 1959 and 1994 and, subsequently, in post-1994 Rwanda to argue that survival mechanisms that were effective in certain conditions may be dangerous when transferred to a new setting. That is, while the performances constructed by Tutsi artists-in-exile functioned as a mode of ethnic survival, the persistence of Tutsi cultural forms in performances that are now intended to perform an ethnically neutral 'Rwandanicity' may actually jeopardize lasting peace. There is an agonistic tension between the use of the arts for creation and protection (and in the case of our essay for a militaristic return to Rwanda). Malcolm Miles quotes Herbert Marcuse in this regard: 'Marcuse says that aesthetic sublimation both has an affirmative character (making suffering acceptable) *and* is simultaneously "a vehicle for the critical, negating function of art. Art stands as reconciling other *and* rebellious subjectivity, at the same time"' (Miles 2012).

As we argue in our essay, art served to protect the consciousness of the Tutsi refugees while in exile. The use of the arts made suffering acceptable to reify Tutsi identity, while at the same time instigating rebellious subjectivity towards the reclaiming of Rwanda as a reimagined homeland. The mass exodus of Tutsi to neighbouring countries exposed them to the plight of exilic conditions in their host countries. In order to combat psychological and material loss, exiled Rwandans in Burundi settlements sought to rediscover cultural identity through an artistic journey from a narrative of loss to a narrative of recovery. This transformative process will be referred to using the Kinyarwanda term *kubunda*: the tradition of sending dynastic heirs far from their home in order to protect them from potential assassination attempts. The years spent in exile could be compared to the same *kubunda* process: they were the result of forced migration following imminent threat to one's life, but also featured the transformative power of the arts to protect oneself against injustices suffered while in exile.

Theatre for social recovery

In tracing the historic and artistic narratives constructed by contemporary Rwandan playwrights, it is important to note that many of the playwrights were both part of the exodus from Rwanda in 1959 and the return of the exiles in 1994. Although theatre by artists in the diaspora was used to militarize a return to Rwanda via the Rwandan Patriotic Front (RPF) led by President Paul Kagame, post-1994 theatre continues to be led by some of the same playwrights and artists.[3] Social performance events propagated Tutsi culture as will be evidenced by the plays *Rugari Rwa Gasabo* (1991) by Kalisa Rugano and *Ruganzu* (1988) by Jean-Marie Vianney Kayishema.

In order to explore the intra-cultural links between performances conducted on the main stages of Rwanda today and performances from the Tutsi exiles in neighbouring countries, Alice Mukaka argues that drama in Rwanda is a ritual stemming from theatrical enactments of history and legend that date back centuries (Mukaka 2005). Mukaka claims that Rwandan drama contains a complex system of symbols, metaphors and proverbs that ultimately create and maintain social order and hierarchy. Her analysis of the Tutsi exile plays *Rugari Rwa Gasabo* (1991) by Kalisa Rugano and *Ruganzu* (1988) by Jean-Marie Vianney Kayishema suggests that the imagery and ideology in the plays are an invocation of the traditional past. Mukaka states:

> In both plays, the authors use elements of oral history, myth and legend through their plays in a subversive manner by exploiting the considerable power which tradition exerts in an effort to positively influence contemporary Rwandan life. In these plays, they radically revise and reshape familiar history, myth, and legend in the light of contemporary realities in order to stress their dialectical dynamism, and to seek out fresher meanings from them. Furthermore, they expose the ills of the society and provide the audience with their vision of a new social order. History is for this widely used to establish the will for change and the return to customs of traditional Rwanda as long as it does not stop from progressing and emancipating. (Mukaka 2005: 59)

Although Mukaka claims that the exiled poets developed a sense of identity through myth and legend, there is a distinct difference between national identity and ethnic identity.[4] In terms of identity formation, the quest of Tutsi exiles to enrich culture, heritage and history through the arts reinforced their ethnic identity. The plays Mukaka explores in her thesis, *Rugari Rwa Gasabo* (1991) by Kalisa Rugano and *Ruganzu* (1988) by Jean-Marie Vianney Kayishema, illustrate dynastic order through the journey of heroes fighting for the king under the divinity of *Imana* (God). Similarly, Marcuse argues for the revolutionary and protective potential of art to create an alternative reality:

> Aesthetic form, autonomy, and truth are inter-related. Each is a socio-historical phenomenon, and each *transcends* the socio-historical arena...The truth of art lies in its power to break the monopoly of established reality...to *define* what is *real*. In this rupture...the fictitious world of art appears as true reality. (Marcuse 1978: 9)

The forced migration of the authors from Rwanda to Burundi influenced their desire to transmit the culture of their country of origin and to artistically manifest the embodied memory of their homeland. Both authors drew from their respective personal journeys and exilic conditions to project a desirable outcome to reclaim their lost land and heritage. The plays *Rugari Rwa Gasabo* (1991) and *Ruganzu* (1988) were strategically written, staged and directed to explore the social and cultural memory of Rwandan – and specifically Tutsi – identity. The use of legendary characters in their plays reveals the original intention of the authors to encourage the recruitment of exiles to join the RPF for a militarized return to Rwanda. The playwrights' knowledge of their country of origin, language and culture is expressed through the ideas of abundance versus the conditions of poverty, freedom versus captivity, sense of belonging versus exile, heroism and patriotism versus cowardice as evidenced with *Rugari Rwa Gasabo* (1991) and *Ruganzu* (1988).

Ruganzu: heroic appeal of King Ruganzu II Ndoli

The play *Ruganzu* was written in 1988 by Jean-Marie Vianney Kayishema. Heir to the crown King Ruganzu II Ndoli was forced into exile at an early age following his father Ndahiro II Cyamatare's battle with the foreigners, *Abanyoro*, who eventually kill him. In order to protect the future king from life-threatening situations, Ndoli is sent to a hiding place, *kubunda*, in *Karagwe k'Abahindi* (Tanzania), to his aunt, Nyabunyana, who is married to King Karemera of *Karagwe*. King Ndoli is burning with the desire to liberate his homeland from foreign invasion, to repatriate the exiled and to restore peace to his father's kingdom. The foreigners' reign over Rwanda has damaged the country. Not only have they killed Ndahiro II Cyamatare and captured the dynastic drum, *Rwoga*; they have also killed Ndoli's mother, the queen mother, Nyirangabo ya Nyantaba, and the king's other wives at *Ku Muko w'Abakobwa* (across Nyabarongo River in the current Kibirira region in Rwanda's Northern Province). A quote from the play reveals a scene of desolation:

> They looted and destroyed the land, they ate sorghum and their stalks; they ate banana trees up to their roots, they ate fresh grass and trees; they burned the dried one, they left nothing on the land (Rwanda).[5]

Historians state that Ruganzu returned to Rwanda after 11 years in exile. Young and inexperienced, Ruganzu obeys his calling as the keeper of his father's dynasty and legacy, returning to Rwanda to fight the invasion of foreigners and consequently bringing the longed-for salvation to the people of Rwanda who have been in captivity. The play propagates preparation for battle by overcoming challenges and shortcomings with the reward of the promised land, abundant with milk and honey. Jan Vansina argues that both King Ndoli's exilic and returning journeys were in fact 'a long struggle' towards his assumption of power (Vansina

2004). King Ndoli was treated as a foreigner by his aunt's husband, King Karemera, who plotted to kill Ndoli on several occasions. *Ruganzu I Ndoli* liberated his country from foreign invasion and brought back the rain to the dry land after a long period of drought. After his return from exile, the cattle multiplied, the households prospered, barren women gave birth, and the sound of drums that hadn't been heard for a long time were heard again. The drum *Kalinga*, symbol of the dynasty, was reinstated. Life was restored with hope and a new social order.

Rugari Rwa Gasabo: heroic appeal of Ruganzu I Bwimba

The play *Rugari Rwa Gasabo* was written in 1991 by Kalisa Rugano. Ruganzu I Bwimba established the nation-state Rwanda in the region of Bwanacambwe in the sixteenth century, through expansion of small kingdoms around central Rwanda. During the fifteenth and sixteenth centuries, clans and kingdoms fought battles in order to enlarge their kingdoms or to challenge the rival clans ruling over them. King Ruganzu's enormous conquests set an example for the generation of warrior kings that followed, thus representing the pride of Tutsi dynastic conquests and the expansion of Rwanda from a small kingdom to almost the size it is today.

The play recalls the 'founding father of Rwanda', Gihanga Ngomijana, who migrates from the Mpororo na Mubari region to settle in a small territory, Gasabo, in the now Eastern Province of Rwanda. Gihanga was the mythical founder of the Banyiginya dynasty in the eleventh or twelfth century, according to oral tradition as documented by poet and historian Alexis Kagame (1959: 799–800). Gasabo was the location for the first settlement of Gihanga and the starting point for the progressive hegemony of Banyiginya that would eventually create the vast Rwanda of Gasabo, Rwanda Rugali rwa Gasabo. *Rugari Rwa Gasabo* (1991) propagates the extreme patriotism that promotes fighting for one's country (*kurutabarira*) even though it may lead to shedding one's own blood as a sacrifice for the country (*kwitangira igihugu*).

The characters of King Ruganzu I Bwimba and his sister Princess Robwa were fourth-generation descendants of Gihanga Ngomijana. Both die in heroic circumstances. The myth propagated by the play is based on the sacrifice of one's own life in order to purify the land and simultaneously poison the enemy (*amaraso azabere abanzi indurwe*). The play narrates King Bwimba's decision to arrange a political marriage for his sister to the rival king, Kimenyi Musaya of Gisaka, the vast neighbouring kingdom at the time. The strategic alliance was intended to facilitate the conquest of Gisaka, consequently annexing it to Gasabo kingdom. Princess Robwa, however, did not consent to her brother's arrangement with the king of Gisaka, afraid of giving birth to an heir to/of/for the enemy. The rivalry led to a battle between the two kingdoms Rugari Rwa Gasabo and Gisaka. King Bwimba was killed during the battle to protect his country at a time when, ironically, his sister Princess Robwa was heavily pregnant with the son of her brother's killer. In order to console his wife after the loss of her brother, King Kimenyi presented her with the drum. However, the latter saw it as an overwhelming proof of Gasabo's loss of sovereignty and a symbol of Kimenyi's dynasty presiding over her own. As an act of sacrifice for her country, Princess Robwa decided to take her own life in order to terminate her pregnancy by dramatically piercing her stomach with the edge of the drum. The concept of shedding one's own blood on the battlefield is a symbol of martyrdom and patriotism in Rwanda, largely used to encourage war recruitment at different points in the history of war in Rwanda.

The play addresses issues of betrayal and cowardice through the character of Nkurukumbi. Whereas every man voluntarily joined the battle to show support for the king, Nkurukumbi refuses to join the battle against the attack from Gisaka. His character symbolizes cowardice, which is in direct opposition to Rwandan values based on heroism. Nkurukumbi is framed as a traitor and outside the realm of warriors.

The above exploration of the plays *Rugari Rwa Gasabo* (1991) and *Ruganzu* (1988) demonstrates that, in contrast to the strategies of abduction and forced recruitment that have prevailed in most African wars in recent decades, the exilic playwrights suggest participation (in war) was motivated by voluntary recruitment and pursued on the basis of collective common action (Humphreys and Weinstein 2006).[6] In the political context of the 1980s and 1990s, when the plays were written and performed, the exilic conditions determined the need for survival based on issues concerning land, social mobility, issues of citizenship, power, identity and captivity among others. Audiences identified with the plots and characters, such as King Ndoli's own exilic experience in Karagwe and his quest for identity and homeland. The emphasis in the play on Ndoli's youth and relative inexperience could be further compared to RPF strategies for recruiting young and inexperienced members who personified Ndoli's traits. Similarly, the character of King Bwimba is used to exemplify the necessity of self-sacrifice for the sake of one's country.

The use of iconic liberator and conqueror figures in the plays strategically involves the audience emotionally in the characters' journey from exodus to the promised land and in individual acts of bravery leading to eventual conquests. King Ndoli's heroic appeal represents exemplary leadership, loyalty to his dynastic succession and risk-taking. For example, Ruganzu I Ndoli in *Ruganzu* (1988) is driven by patriotism even though he is young and inexperienced.[7] Likewise, King Bwimba's heroic appeal involves the shedding of his blood for the betterment of his country. Princess Robwa's tragic death in the play is celebrated as martyrdom, thus asserting that the concept of sacrificing one's own life in order to save your own applies as equally to women as it does to men. Robwa's role as a princess of the people comes with great agency as her story challenges the discursive portrayal of stereotypical images of passive Rwandan women. Robwa's loyalty and patriotism had a heroic appeal for women who would have doubted their role and place in joining the RPF militarized front. There are high-ranking women in the military and government today who exemplify the role of women as leaders of the country.

Embedding cultural memory

The playwrights use rhetoric that conveys the ideology of reclaiming their homeland, but which also contains prose and war poems called *ibyivugo* to illustrate that Rwanda is a homeland worth fighting or dying for. Audiences learn how to speak like the heroes depicted in the plays by developing vocal intonations as they participate in the performances. For instance, there are moments in the plays when audiences respond to the folk songs and lyric poetry as they are instructed to act like heroes through *Ruganzu* qualities such as pride, confidence, boldness, fearlessness, etc. In the midst of attempts within the country of exile to diminish and ban the influence of all cultural forms related to the Tutsi dynasty, the plays *Rugari Rwa Gasabo* (1991) and *Ruganzu* (1988) not only safeguarded the Kinyarwanda language, but also safeguarded the monarchy and the Tutsi dynasty's linguistic symbolism and aristocracy.

The playwrights strategically embedded cultural memory into the plays through the exploration of migration, transmission and conservation of indigenous Rwandan culture to recreate a mythic narrative of 'saving the nation from the oppressor' that was, in this case, related to inter-regional and inter-ethnic conflict. Children born in exile from 1959–90 inherited cultural traditions that were originally developed through generations by their ancestors and transmitted to their parents through the arts. In most African oral narratives, the narrator demonstrates the ability to evoke mental pictures of the scenes described, to choose pattern images that have the proper affective appeal, and to achieve the right diction and vocal modulations (Conteh-Morgan 1994: 37). *Rugari Rwa Gasabo* (1991) and *Ruganzu* (1988) offer a simulation of the 'homeland' that keeps the imagination of nation-ness alive, where the land not only communicates identity, but also serves as a physical expression of their being. Catherine Palmer argues that land or landscape is one of the symbols of national belonging. She argues that a nation's landscape is not merely a physical expression of boundaries, but a symbolic expression of a nation's past (Palmer 1998: 191–5). Both kings' conquests and battle victories manipulated Tutsi exiles into believing in the Rwandan utopia dramatized in the plays: the land of milk and honey.

Rwandan citizenship was evoked by means of incantation through ritual and mythology. In one example from *Ruganzu* (1988), Ndoli encounters *Abanyabyinshi* people on his return to Rwanda from Karagwe. After crossing the river, Ndoli fills an *igicuba* (wooden jug) with water and repeats incantations saying:

> I overthrow the Banyabyinshi people, I overthrow Bahinza people, I overthrow the foreign countries and I re-enthrone Rwanda back to its prominence.[8]

Ndoli performed the ritual repetitively to reclaim citizenship through the mythic power of incantation. Plays and poems, among other art forms, were means by which the Rwandan Tutsi identity was shaped through the glorification of Rwandan customs, traditions and landscapes. The conscious intention of the playwrights in exile was to create a popular theatre form with which the masses could easily identify. Through this form, they were able to elicit responses from their audiences and to mobilize them to participate in the drama, thus training audiences to participate in the political return to Rwanda. The use of traditional Rwandan song, music and dance serves as a means through which the audience actually partakes of the action on stage by singing along. In both plays evidenced in this section, the authors use elements of oral history, myth and legend to radically revise and reshape familiar history, myth and legend with their vision of a new social order. However, as explored through the historic backdrop of the productions and the poets and playwrights, there are discrepancies between the claim concerning a unified cultural history and how culture has been used in the past and present and will be used in the future for identity re-formation.

Ethnic identities and the new Rwandan identity

The distinction between ethnic identities and national identities is crucial to understanding how collective memory has shaped these identities through theatre, and how these identities are either forged or eroded in Rwanda. Nationalism and ethnicity are in conflict on multiple levels in contemporary Rwanda. On the legal level, ethnic identities are being erased by law and repressed due to government efforts to enforce national identity as conceived through Rwandanicity. Although Rwanda has legally forbidden the use of the terms Hutu, Tutsi and Twa through law number 47/2001 of 18/12/2001 titled 'Instituting Punishment for Offences of Discrimination and Sectarianism', these ethnic labels are still used in neighbouring countries, including Burundi, Uganda and the Democratic Republic of the Congo.[9] Cultural forms related to these ethnic identities can therefore not be completely erased or reimagined due to their continued use elsewhere.

Literary critic Ebere Onwudiwe makes the distinction between ethnic identities and nationalism and explains how the two forms of identity can have separate and potentially disparate social functions:

> Ethnicity and nationalism are different expressions of collective public identity. Their core difference lies more in their distinctive records and social foundations, even when both exist simultaneously in the same country. The resultant diverse experiences of ethnicity and nationalism endow each with varying meanings and historical memories. In this sense, the two concepts, while closely related, are not equivalent. (Onwudiwe 2001: 213)

Ethnicity and nationalism have come into sharp conflict throughout the Great Lakes region, usually when land rights are involved as an inheritance of colonially drawn borders. Before colonization, borders were fluid within Africa and identity distinctions were primarily based on the cultural fabric of a community. To some extent, this changed when colonizers fixed definite national borders throughout the Great Lakes region. Yet even here the history is complex. At times, colonial policy sought to submerge ethnicity within a larger sense of nationalism, as when Belgian colonizers gave for a time the name Ruanda-Urundi to the topography now known as Burundi and Rwanda. In other cases, ethnic elites succeeded in harnessing the colonizer-led drive to nationalism to expand their own power. For example, the Tutsi oligarchy, operating from its stronghold in central Rwanda, had long sought to extend its power over the north, which was dominated by Hutu, but the Hutu had not succumbed. The Tutsi aristocracy succeeded where it had previously failed with the help of the Belgian colonizers who drew the modern-day boundaries of the nation-state of Rwanda in the early 1900s.

When thinking about the current cultural and political practices in Rwanda, it is easy to assume Rwanda is a sovereign nation-state, without placing current events in the context of Rwanda's historically fluid borders. However, when the Tutsi refugees migrated to neighbouring areas, there were political issues inherent in the ethnic identities of Hutu and Tutsi that were, and remain, also embedded in groups throughout the Great Lakes region. For example, the 'Banya-Mulenge' in Congo were Tutsi who '... fled Rwanda because of King Rwabugiri's administrative/military campaign and the heavy taxation system... They settled between Mulenge and the upper Sange river', giving them the title Banya-Mulenge (Pottier 2002: 16). Also, Johan Pottier notes the significance of Rwanda's regional north and south divide, stating that '[t]he Belgian colonists also amplified, one might say created, Rwanda's regional north-south divide, another strong identity marker, when they aided the central court in its campaign to subjugate those areas still outside its influence, especially the north-west and the Hutu kingdoms of Bukunzi and Busozo (15)'. These regional considerations of ethnicity inform the context of diaspora theatre creation and performance in the country of refuge.

In the next section, we move from an analysis of how performance was used to inculcate Tutsi culture in diaspora to the stages of Rwanda. Contemporary theatre in Rwanda illustrates the ideal of Rwandanicity often extolled through themes of genocide, reconciliation and culture. Rwandan dance and music is performed as symbolic of a united Rwanda with one culture and one language. Aimable Twahirwa's *Iryo Nabonye* (2004) will serve as an example of a production that toured nationally to foster reconciliation and justice following the genocide, but contains remnants of the historic use of theatre during the period from 1959–94.[10]

Iryo Nabonye ('What I Saw')

Iryo Nabonye was directed by Aimable Twahirwa and Odile Gakire Katese, the former director of the Centre for the Arts at the National University of Rwanda. The production was originally commissioned by the Survivors Fund for the tenth anniversary of the genocide in 2004, but was revamped for a national tour in 2005. According to Aimable Twahirwa in an interview with Ananda Breed on 10 January 2005 in Kigali, the original concept for *Iryo Nabonye* began with a group of 20 artists (musicians, dancers and actors) made up of both Hutu and Tutsi, who sought to use theatre as a method of dialogue. Over the course of six weeks, the participants discussed how events led to the genocide and how they should represent that history. In an interview with Twahirwa, he relayed the general content of the production:

> The play illustrates the role of religion, life in Rwanda before the white man, choreography of rape, construction of the play between a young person and his grandpa, and elements that characterize Rwanda yesterday and today. The play ends with hope, a time for all of Rwanda to return to school.[11]

The open-air stage area had a cement floor with a natural brick backdrop; to the left of the stage sat three musicians with instruments including drums, *inanga* (traditional guitar) and flute. The stage directions in the text for the play *Iryo Nabonye* state:

> The play will be divided into three parts all surrounded by the homestead of Rwanda, in such a way that it will help the performers to enter and exit. On the right, there is a big *Igiseke* (the woven basket), on the left is a small hut of Rwandan origin that is constructed the same way as *Igiseke*. In the middle towards the back there are cultural materials to be used like *Intara* (very big trays) and *Inkoko* (small tray).[12]

Traditional props and set pieces were used to evoke the imagery of traditional community practices and environments. The performance began with three women who used the *Intara* trays to mime the separation of beans from rocks. The women placed their hands on either side of the tray, making a circular motion, and then tossed the imaginary beans in the air. The stage directions for *Iryo Nabonye* continue, 'When the play begins, there is an introduction of activities that characterise the culture of Rwanda of long ago.'[13]

The characters of the grandfather and grandchild entered from out of the large *Igiseke* hut and the grandfather began the tale of Rwanda's mythical past and its descent into genocide. The grandfather is symbolic of Rwanda's traditional past, and the grandson, the future of Rwanda.

The stage description in the text of *Iryo Nabonye* states, 'The grandfather is talking about the real history of Rwanda before, during and after colonisation.' The performance of *Iryo Nabonye* began with a one-minute timeline of the history of Rwanda, as the character of the grandfather relayed historic events to his grandson:

> When the colonialist came to Rwanda
> The country Rwanda became his
> He divided its natives
> He eliminated clans, he eliminated cultural rituals
> The country of Gasabo becomes dirty
> He blackmails the country
> He divided the people into many groups
> He strengthens it and becomes history
> He writes them down and becomes history
> When people came to power, they picked it
>   [the colonizer's revised version of history]
> 1959 people died
> 1973 repeated history
> 1994 they finished the game
> One million people were killed[14]

Although the beginning speech could be interpreted as government propaganda to disseminate the RPF version of national history, the remainder of the production addressed the complexity of genocide through visual images, dance and song. The selected dialogue presented the invasion of the colonizers and the stripping away of clanship ties and cultural rituals. Subsequently, dates including 1959, 1973 and 1994 were included as major points in Rwanda's history in which the Tutsi were persecuted. The one-minute rendition of history was aligned with the RPF national portrayal of history, in which genocide is the major point of reference from which history is written or rewritten. The instructive phrases throughout the text – including 'old Rwanda' and 'real history' – were descriptors indicating a reimagining of the past. Historical references evoked what Rwanda was like prior to the genocide, prior to colonization.

Iryo Nabonye used set design to exhibit the crafts and trade of Rwanda. The stage design incorporated the traditional *Igiseke* (woven basket), made from vegetal fibres that are woven along a spiral frame. The larger *Igiseke* was traditionally used to store tobacco, food and pipes. The smaller *Igiseke* was used for small personal items like jewellery. The women used the *Intara* (tray) to winnow the beans. The 'traditional' staging devices of Rwandan culture were illustrated through fabric, basketry, music and food preparation. These practices are inherently inter-ethnic and not designated to particular ethnic groups.

Iryo Nabonye specifically addressed the events of the genocide and the post-genocide reconstruction period. The production may embed the political stance of the RPF, but also might provide an example of how the arts have been used for a period of redress. In a post-show interview that Ananda Breed conducted on 16 January 2005 with an actor from *Iryo Nabonye*, Kenneth Kamugisha, he provided a philosophical and artistic perspective on how *Iryo Nabonye* sought to discover the roots of genocide:

> People blame the genocide on colonization, but that isn't what caused the genocide. Although some of the colonizers are responsible, how does one person tell another person to kill and they do it? It is the quality of the people that killed others that caused the genocide. Just the nature of human beings that caused the genocide. Just like in the play, some leaders in the play asked people to commit genocide and they listened. Genocide is independent of ideology. All of us have evil in us. It is the purpose of the arts to prevent genocide. The main purpose is to give a message about what happened before and after the genocide. The message is to reconcile, that is the main purpose – reconciliation. The arts are used to show strong images, to represent the evil. Drama is used to show that evil people can carry out their acts. There is a character clad in a burlap sack in the play that represented the reduction of humanity and evil of the genocide.

The quote from Kamugisha provides less emphasis on the roles of Hutu as perpetrator and Tutsi as victim, but rather the consuming force of the genocide and the encompassing suffering for the whole of Rwanda. One scene in particular related the genocide to a wave into which everyone was swept. Several actors entered the stage enclosed in a white sheet. The heads were visible from holes cut in the sheet, but otherwise, the sheet illustrated one undifferentiated mass. Kamugisha elaborates:

> Another scene is with the characters with a white sheet over them, heads poking out...some were victims, some were perpetrators...an image of death, to show how victims and others suffered. A boy is looking for his mother and is swallowed up by it. This is why

I thought that the images in the play were particularly potent, that the audience could identify in different ways that weren't literal. The uplifting song that the young boy and the performers sang in the play was to soothe, to calm down the victims.[15]

In a post-show interview with the actors on 16 January 2005, Breed asked what the sheet signified, to which one actor replied, 'The white sheet was the genocide, death. Both the perpetrators and the victims were wrapped up and swallowed up by it.' Symbols and images were deployed in the play in order to encourage the audience to identify in different ways with the production, allegorically rather than literally. The use of the sheet as an allegory for the genocide demonstrated the wave of devastation that spread throughout Rwanda, allowing individuals to witness how genocide occurred rapidly en masse, without pinpointing individual acts by the perpetrators. In this way, *Iryo Nabonye* aims to promote reconciliation through an investigation of genocide by the artists who created the work, to try to understand how and why it happened. In this case, it was a mutual and joint effort to understand the genocide. However, at the end of *Iryo Nabonye* there was a turning point from the use of theatre to explore the genocide to the use of theatre for justice.

The final scene of *Iryo Nabonye* enacted a school classroom, representing the *gacaca* courts.[16] The analogy reflects reality; following the genocide, the public was mandated to incorporate policies and systems of reconciliation and justice, including their attendance at *ingando* and *gacaca*.[17] The classroom scene portrayed a teacher asking her students to conjugate the verb 'to forgive'. The students refused to recite the word because they had witnessed their families being killed and could not bring themselves to utter the word 'forgive' in any of its variations. A young person of ten years stood up to face the classroom of students and stated 'I forgive, you forgive', and then pointed to the audience to say '[y]ou tell the truth. You must ask for pardon. Tell me what happened during that period because you were there during the time of murders.' The scene moved from a metaphoric relation between an individual's moral responsibility and the genocide, into a plea for justice.

At the beginning of this section, the work of *Iryo Nabonye* is characterized as being consistent with the canon of Tutsi exile plays in that it promotes a mythical utopian past and embeds RPF ideology in its history telling, yet the production also serves as an investigative tool into the cause and effect of genocide. Even though *Iryo Nabonye* may foster an ideal for reconstruction post-genocide, epitomized through *gacaca* and 'truth-telling', the closing sequence following the classroom scene illustrated national unification through a modern dance performance. *Iryo Nabonye* contained traces of development rhetoric and addressed issues concerning reconciliation and justice, linking the production with larger political and social considerations in connection to the RPF. The play vacillates between ethnic and national references and histories, yet there are moments in which contemporary and non-ethnic signifiers, like the use of the white sheet to portray the genocide, provide the potential for a more nuanced aesthetic that allows space for the viewer to explore events during the genocide and genocide itself.

Conclusion

A vast majority of the Rwandan diaspora whose families fled after 1959 never saw their homeland and endured hardships while abroad, including discrimination and exclusion from society.[18] According to Rurangwa, theatre was utilized in neighbouring countries to build nationalism and to provide sustaining, hopeful imagery of the homeland.[19] Rurangwa stated in an interview with Ananda Breed on 25 April 2006 that, after 1994, when he brought his family back to Rwanda for the first time, his young son remarked, 'Papa, is this the Rwanda of milk and honey that you've always talked about?' He replied to his son, 'It might not look like the country you've heard about, but it is your country. No one can take it away from you. It is your motherland.' Rurangwa stated how his work as a playwright contributed to the making of the new Rwanda: 'I work for this country to be prosperous. There is nothing better than my country. The image of Rwanda was like a myth, because when you don't know your country you idolize it. For us, Rwanda was everything. Nothing could be preferred to other than living in Rwanda.'[20] However, it can be argued that the mythic imagery of Rwandanicity as illustrated through theatre has the potential to mask dangerous historical and ongoing power imbalances, both during exile and currently in Rwanda.

In *Iryo Nabonye*, there was a warning regarding what may happen if one does not adopt the ideology of Rwandanicity: 'If you don't pass the school, it will be difficult to have a place in the country of Rwanda. Rwanda wants its children and grandchildren to live in peace, tolerance, and love... living with each other in harmony to reconcile without betraying one another.'[21] The passage explicitly states that one who does not adhere to the lessons taught will not be accepted in the new

Rwanda. Following the warning of rejection, the descriptive stage directions in the text of *Iryo Nabonye* state, '*Ishimwe* (you must pardon), there is traditional dance, singing, playing instruments, and an illustration of what would unite Banyarwanda, including the use of one common dance.'[22]

In this way, Rwandan playwrights have promoted Rwandanicity by disseminating the image and ideology of the new Rwanda. There are inherent dilemmas regarding the ethics of remembering or forgetting, and the nature of how historical events are recorded and performed in the name of nationalism. Historian John R. Gillis argues, 'National identities are, like everything historical, constructed and reconstructed; and it is our responsibility to decode them in order to discover the relationships they create and sustain' (Gillis 1994: 4). Gillis continues, 'Identities and memories are not things we think *about*, but things we think *with*' (5).

This essay has aimed to deconstruct how survival and nationalism have been staged through performance, analysing the role of the formerly exiled Tutsi poets and playwrights, as well as examining how the representation of genocide through theatre can be used for particular political and social objectives. However, Victor Turner also warns against the potential rupture of reconciliatory practices:

> Redressive procedures may break down, with reversion to crisis. Traditional machinery of conciliation or coercion may prove inadequate to cope with new types of issues and problems, and new roles and statuses. And, of course, reconciliation may only seem to have been achieved in phase four, with real conflicts glossed over but not resolved. Moreover, at certain historical junctures in large-scale complex societies, redress may be through rebellion, or even revolution, if the societal value-consensus has broken down, and new unprecedented roles, relationships, and classes have emerged. (Turner 1982: 71)

The production of Rwandanicity has in large part been constructed through the negation of ethnic differences. Although the RPF currently seeks ethnic unification through Rwandanicity devoid of ethnic signifiers that were formerly embroiled in violence, the denial of continued power imbalances between ethnic groups could propagate future violence. In terms of Rwanda in its redressive phase, the denial of ethnic differences may actually jeopardize lasting peace, especially since ethnic identities are embedded in the cultural forms used to perform Rwandanicity. We would argue that while the performances constructed by Tutsi artists-in-exile employed culture as a mode of survival to maintain ethnic identity that was threatened by annihilation, these cultural forms contain inherent power imbalances that must not be overlooked. Survival mechanisms that were effective under certain conditions can be dangerous or run counter to original intentions when deployed in new contexts.

Notes

1. The authors used a mixed research approach including interviews with playwrights, observations of rehearsals and performances, and participation in workshops with the artists and productions noted in this chapter. Alice Mukaka performed as a company member of Kalisa Rugano's production *Rugari Rwa Gasabo*. Additionally, Alice Mukaka served as a company member of the original production *Iryo Nabonye* and was supervised by Jean-Marie Kayishema during her MA degree at the National University of Rwanda, Butare.
2. The years 1959, 1973 and 1994 were major points of violence against Tutsi. This violence can be traced back to colonial roots. Rwanda was colonized in the 1890s by Germany and later ceded to Belgium in 1916 through the League of Nations mandate following the First World War. The hierarchical power structure of ethnic identities – Tutsi (pastoralists), Hutu (agriculturalists) and Twa (artisans) – was exacerbated and racialized through colonial divide-and-rule tactics. Tutsi were the elite recipients of colonial favour until the revolution of 1959, in which the Hutu majority overthrew the Tutsi-dominated government and monarchy with the support of Belgium. Thousands of Tutsi were massacred by their Hutu compatriots during this time, spurring 400,000 Tutsi to flee to neighbouring countries (Prunier 1998: 119, 121 n11). Grégoire Kayibanda led the Republic of Rwanda from 1962 to 1973, when he was overthrown by a coup and replaced by General Juvénal Habyarimana who stayed in power until his assassination at the beginning of the 1994 genocide.
3. See Phil Clark and Zachary D. Kaufman who provide a detailed account of the RPF rebel invasion in October 1990: http://papers.ssrn.com/sol3/papers.cfm?abstract_id=2368824
4. The playwrights who we discuss in this study are also poets. Poetry was a powerful form of expression in Rwandan oral history. For example, war poems are embedded with the emotions of war, conquest and violence. Kayishema, Rugano and Rurangwa lyrically stylize and dramatize their sense of activism throughout their works.
5. Translated by Alice Mukaka. For contextualization of the quote from Ruganzu see http://www.kimenyi.com/ruganzu-ndori-ajya-kubungira-ikaragwe.php (accessed 16 January 2014). Also see Jan Vansina (2004) and Alexis Kagame (1951).
6. See Humphreys and Weinstein (2006).
7. Ruganzu was a name given to war kings in Rwanda. Bwimba is the first king recorded as being named Ruganzu and Ndoli was the second to have that name. However, four kings reigned in-between. The list goes: Ruganzu

54 Theatre for Survival: Art of Creation and Protection

      I Bwimba, Cyirima Rugwe, Kigeli Mukobanya, Mibambwe Sekarongoro I Mutabazi, Yuhi Gahima, Ndahiro Cyamatare, Ruganzu II Ndoli, etc. See Jan Vansina (2004) for an account on the Nyiginya Kingdom.
8. See http://www.kimenyi.com/ruganzu-ndori-ajya-kubungira-ikaragwe.php (accessed 16 January 2014). Translation by Alice Mukaka. Also see Jan Vansina (2004) and Alexis Kagame (1951).
9. Law No. 47/2001 of 18/12/2001 Instituting Punishment for Offences of Discrimination and Sectarianism, Government of Rwanda.
10. The script of *Iryo Nabonye* was translated from Kinyarwanda to English, and subsequent script analysis was undertaken with the director, Aimable Twahirwa, following the production.
11. Ibid.
12. Aimable Twahirwa, *Iryo Nabonye* (unpublished play, National University of Rwanda, 2004), p. 1. Translation of the original script. Script written by Aimable Twahirwa, translated on 4 May 2005.
13. Ibid.
14. Twahirwa, *Iryo Nabonye*.
15. Ibid.
16. Gacaca (pronounced ga-cha-cha) is Kinyarwanda for 'grass' or 'lawn'. The gacaca court is based on an indigenous, pre-colonial form of mediation in which opposed parties 'sit on the grass and resolve community conflicts' (umucaca is a type of grass eaten by livestock). Gacaca was first launched in June 2001, followed by a pilot phase and national implementation in 2005. These courts officially finished their work in June 2012.
17. Ingando is Kinyarwanda for 'military encampment' – an assembly area where troops traditionally received their final instructions while readying for a military mission abroad. According to the National Unity and Reconciliation Commission (NURC), the ingando was used in pre-colonial times to prepare for war under the guidance of the mwami (king). Similar to the pre-colonial emphasis on unification through a militarized notion of nation, following the 1994 genocide the ingando was initially revived as a vehicle to reintegrate ex-FAR (Rwandan Armed Forces) soldiers from the DRC. Over time, the ingando was redefined as a broader vehicle for civic education to encompass returned refugees, university students and various community groups.
18. It should be noted that great variation can be observed in experiences from country to country. See Johan Pottier for more information regarding the refugee crises in Uganda and Congo.
19. The authors note that the RPF used theatre to promote Tutsi culture while in exile. Additionally, Liisa Malkki (1995) writes about the use of culture to promote Hutu culture in refugee camps in Tanzania.
20. Ibid.
21. Twahirwa, *Iryo Nabonye*, p. 14.
22. Ibid., p. 1.

Bibliography

Bale, J., 2002. *Imagined Olympians: Body Culture and Colonial Representation in Rwanda*. London: University of Minnesota Press.

Borneman, J., 2002. 'Reconciliation after Ethnic Cleansing: Listening, Retribution, Affiliation'. In *Public Culture*, 14: 2.
Brah, A., 1996. *Cartographies of Diaspora: Contesting Identities*. London: Routledge.
Clark, P., and Z. D. Kaufman, 2013. 'Recent History'. In Iain Frame (ed.) *Africa South of the Sahara*. London: Routledge, pp. 980–88.
Conteh-Morgan, J., 1994. *Theatre and Drama in Francophone Africa: A Critical Introduction*. Cambridge: Cambridge University Press.
Coupez, A., and T. Kamanzi, 1962. *Récits historiques Rwanda*. Tervuren: MRAC.
Coupez, A., and T. Kamanzi, 1970. *Litérature de la Cour au Rwanda*. Oxford: Clarendon Press.
Fujii, L. A., 2009. *Killing Neighbors: Webs of Violence in Rwanda*. Ithaca: Cornell University Press.
Gillis, J. R., 1994. 'Memory and Identity: The History of a Relationship'. In John R. Gillis (ed.) *Commemorations: The Politics of National Identity*. Princeton: Princeton University Press.
Humphreys, M., and J. M. Weinstein, 2006. 'Who Rebels? The Determinants of Participation in Civil War', available online at http://www.sscnet.ucla.edu/polisci/cpworkshop/papers/weinstein.pdf, accessed 16 January 2014.
Kagame, A., 1947. 'Le code ésotérique de la dynastie du Rwanda'. In *Zaïre*, I: 4, pp. 363–86, Bruxelles, Éditions universitaires, résumé dans M. d'Hertefelt et D. de Lame (1987), pp. 783–4.
Kagame, A., 1951. 'La Poésie Dynastique au Rwanda'. In *Institut royal colonial belge*, 22: 1.
Kagame, A., 1959. 'Inganji Karinga (The Conqueror's Drum Karinga)', Kabgayi, s.n., 2 vols, 116 pp., 164 pp. (2ème éd.; 1ère éd. 1943 [vol. I], 1947 [vol. II]), résumé dans M. d'Hertefelt et D. de Lame (1987), pp. 799–800.
Kanimba Misago, C., and T. Mesas, 2000. *Regards sur le Rwanda: Collections du Musée National*. Paris: Maisonneuve et Larose.
Lemarchand, R., 1970. *Rwanda and Burundi*. London: Pall Mall Press.
Lemarchand, R., 1994. 'Managing Transition Anarchies: Rwanda, Burundi, and South Africa in Comparative Perspective'. In *Journal of Modern African Studies*, 32: 4.
Malkki, L., 1995. *Purity and Exile: Violence, Memory, and National Cosmology Among Hutu Refugees in Tanzania*. Chicago: University of Chicago Press.
Marcuse, H., 1978. *The Aesthetic Dimension: Towards a Critique of Marxist Aesthetics*. Boston, MA: Beacon Press.
Miles, M., 2012. *Herbert Marcuse: An Aesthetics of Liberation*. UK: Pluto Press.
Mukaka, A., 2005. *Revivifying Rituals as the Engine for Drama Development in Rwanda: A Socio-Critical Approach*. Unpublished undergraduate thesis, National University of Rwanda.
Muzungu, B., 1997. 'L'Heroisme au Feminin'. In *Cahiers Lumière et Société*, Histoire IV, 8. Butare, Rwanda.
Onwudiwe, E., 2001. 'A Critique of Recent Writings on Ethnicity and Nationalism'. In *Research in African Literatures*, 32: 3.
Palmer, C., 1998. 'From Theory to Practice: Experiencing the National in Everyday Life'. In *Journal of Material Culture*, 3: 2, pp. 190–95.
Pottier, J., 2002. *Re-imagining Rwanda: Conflict, Survival and Disinformation in the Late Twentieth Century*. Cambridge: Cambridge University Press.

Prunier, G., 1998. *The Rwanda Crisis: History of a Genocide*. London: Hurst and Company.

Rusagara, F. K., 2005. 'Gacaca: Rwanda's Truth and Reconciliation Authority'. In the *New Times*, 16 May, available online at: http://allafrica.com/stories/200505170174.html (accessed 11 July 2015).

Sarkin, J., 1999. 'The Necessity and Challenges of Establishing a Truth and Reconciliation Commission in Rwanda'. In *Human Rights Quarterly*, 21: 3, pp. 785–6.

Straus, S., 2006. *The Order of Genocide: Race, Power, and War in Rwanda*. Ithaca: Cornell University Press.

Straus, S., and L. Waldorf, 2011. *Remaking Rwanda: State Building and Human Rights after Mass Violence*. Wisconsin: University of Wisconsin Press.

Turner, V., 1982. *From Ritual to Theatre: The Human Seriousness of Play*. New York: PAJ Productions.

Uvin, P., 1988. *Aiding Violence: The Development Enterprise in Rwanda*. West Hartford, CT: Kumarian Press.

Vansina, J., 1961. 'De la tradition orale'. In *Essai de méthode historique*, 36. Bruxelles (Tervuren): Musée Royal de l'Afrique Centrale.

Vansina, J., 2001. *Le Rwanda ancien, le royaume nyiginya*. Paris: Karthala.

Vansina, J., 2004. *Antecedents to Modern Rwanda: The Nyiginya Kingdom*. Madison: University of Wisconsin Press.

Part II

A Space Where Something Might Survive: Theatre in Concentration Camps

3
The Cultural Life of the Terezín Ghetto in 1960s Survivor Testimony: Theatre, Trauma and Resilience

Lisa Peschel

In the World War II Jewish ghetto at Terezín (in German, Theresienstadt), a stunningly active cultural life sprang up on the initiative of the prisoners themselves. Although their activities, which ranged from lectures to concerts to theatrical performances, were officially permitted by the Nazis, today they are often described as 'spiritual resistance'. In this chapter, however, rather than focusing on what theatrical performance did *against* the Nazis, I will concentrate on what theatrical performance might have done *for* the prisoners. Drawing upon an unusual body of testimony collected in the 1960s from a group of Czech-Jewish survivors, I argue that theatrical performance enabled the prisoners to carry out the steps that psychiatrist Judith Herman claims are necessary for recovery from traumatic experiences: they were able to establish a safe space, to create coherent narratives of potentially traumatizing experiences, and to reconnect with themselves, each other, and the world outside the ghetto.

The testimony

European Jews were deported to the Terezín ghetto, located just 40 miles northwest of Prague, from several different countries during the course of the war. The largest groups arrived from Czechoslovakia, Germany and Austria.[1] Although artists from all three countries were active in the cultural life, in this chapter I engage with the testimony of a particular group: Czech-Jewish survivors who remained in Czechoslovakia after the war. Interwar Czech Jewry had been a diverse population; they spoke

Czech or German and covered a wide range of political and religious affiliations. Most German speakers and Zionists left the country after the war, and the Communist coup in 1948 led to the emigration of many of their political and class enemies. Those who remained by the early 1960s were almost exclusively Czech-speaking communists or 'fellow travellers' who had believed in the ideals of the party and had hoped to build an egalitarian Czechoslovak society after the war.[2]

A remarkable body of testimony by these survivors was collected in 1963 by a 19-year-old student of theatre history at Prague's Charles University, Eva Šormová.[3] One of her tutors, Jan Kopecký, had known many of the young Terezín theatre artists personally and he suggested that she write her seminar paper on the topic of theatre in the ghetto. At that time there was virtually no secondary source material she could draw upon, so she gathered information by conducting interviews with 23 survivors. As Šormová described her methodology to me in 2004, she had presented to her interviewees a few basic questions regarding fellow theatre artists or specific performances and then simply 'let them speak' (2004). Šormová kept the handwritten notes she took during her interviews and, upon my request in 2007, typed up her notes from conversations with ten of the 23 survivors.

Most of the texts I analyse in this chapter are Šormová's fragmented and telegraphic interview notes, reconstructed more than 40 years after the interviews were conducted. In the absence of other narratives it might be tempting to assume that their fragmentary nature stems from the effects of traumatic experience upon the survivors' narratives, as many scholars who study trauma suggest. Some of the same survivors, however, also wrote and published perfectly coherent essays about the ghetto during this period, thus revealing that the fragmentary nature of the testimony is an effect of the way it was collected, preserved and reconstructed, then subsequently translated by myself. These highly mediated texts suggest, rather than perfectly capture, the survivors' own feelings and turns of phrase, but they provide an astonishing wealth of information on the theatrical life of the ghetto from various individual points of view.

From Šormová's ten sets of testimony I chose six that were exceptionally detailed and vivid. These survivors were born between 1910 and 1921 (in 1963, aged 42 to 53), and had worked together in various Terezín performances that I will analyse below. Actors Jan Fischer and Jana Šedová, composer Karel Reiner and director Norbert Frýd participated in the Terezín performance of *Esther*.[4] František Miška, Šedová and Fischer performed together in Gogol's *The Marriage*. Reiner's wife,

Hana Reinerová, was an avid spectator and, as a caretaker in a children's home, put on performances with her young charges. I also draw from essays written in the 1960s by Šedová, Frýd and a survivor just a few years younger, Eva Kavanová, who had also performed in *Esther* (in 1963 she was 39). In their testimony they expressed opinions on performances they were all familiar with and fellow theatre artists they all knew, including two young Terezín directors who perished: Karel Švenk (1917–45) and Gustav Schorsch (1918–45).

The testimony of these survivors suggests that theatrical performance may have helped the prisoners cope with some of the potentially traumatizing aspects of life in the ghetto, for their descriptions correspond with several steps that Judith Herman, a professor of clinical psychiatry, identifies as the sequence of recovery of traumatized individuals.

Judith Herman's three steps

I draw upon Herman rather than literary scholars such as Cathy Caruth because Herman's approach corresponds more closely to the conditions the prisoners faced in Terezín. In *Unclaimed Experience*, Caruth defines the traumatic event as an event that '...is experienced too soon, too unexpectedly, to be fully known and is therefore not available to consciousness until it imposes itself again, repeatedly, in the nightmares and repetitive actions of the survivor' (1996: 4). As diaries and other works by the prisoners that describe life in the ghetto reveal, events taking place in Terezín, even when potentially traumatizing, were clearly still available to consciousness, perhaps because the environment of the ghetto was not as brutal and shocking as in other concentration camps. Terezín's main function was as a transit camp: a central location where the Nazis gathered the Jews of Central Europe before sending them on to the death camps and slave labour camps. Therefore the Nazis kept conditions relatively liveable, so that news that might escape the ghetto would not incite those to be deported to rise up against the transports to Terezín. We must never forget that over 33,000 prisoners, mostly the elderly, died in the ghetto of hunger, disease and despair, but there were no gas chambers in Terezín, and very little random violence.[5] Young and healthy prisoners like those who subsequently provided the testimony for this study could reasonably hope to survive. All, however, lived in a constant state of anxiety about the transports that left Terezín at irregular and unpredictable intervals. As survivor and chronicler of the ghetto H.G. Adler wrote, 'Fear of deportations made fear of death seem insignificant or even replaced it' (2005: 669).

Given the conditions in Terezín, the danger of traumatization stemmed not from the inability to fully perceive a threat, but from the inability to do anything about it. As Herman puts it, 'helplessness constitutes the essential insult of trauma' (1992: 41). What I propose is that theatrical performance offered a way to 'do something' that, while it did not change the fundamental conditions of the ghetto, prevented the prisoners from being paralysed by fear and despair and enabled them to go on with the daily fight for life.

But what kind of 'doing something' was theatrical performance? According to Herman there are three steps that people who have experienced traumatic events must go through to recover psychologically: create a safe environment, construct a story of the traumatic event that includes a full and vivid description of the traumatic imagery, and reconnect with themselves, others and their world (1992: 155). As my analysis of the 1960s testimony will reveal, theatrical performance in the ghetto enabled the prisoners to carry out these steps, but with an essential variation: because the Terezín prisoners were dealing with a present crisis that was unfolding right before their eyes, they did not need to capture the full traumatic imagery of the events. Instead, they rewrote traumatic events into psychologically manageable narratives that enabled them to engage with the ghetto and integrate their experiences into a larger life narrative.

A safe space

Terezín theatre, as an institution, consisted of a whole network of performance and rehearsal spaces located all over the ghetto. One of the reasons the prisoners perceived them as safe spaces was because theatrical performances were officially allowed. The first cultural activities of the ghetto – simple and improvised programmes of songs, poems and sketches – began in the prisoners' barracks shortly after the first transports arrived in late November 1941 (Weiner 1999: 209). The Jewish Council of Elders, apparently in an attempt to legalize these performances and head off the possibility that the prisoners would be punished for them, requested and received permission from the Nazi leadership. They announced in the Daily Orders of 28 December 1941 that such *Kamaradschaftsabende* (friendship evenings) could be held on the condition that the programme be submitted in advance for approval (Šormová 1973: 22).

By February 1942 cultural activities had expanded to the point where the Council of Elders established an administrative body to oversee them: the *Freizeitgestaltung* (Office for the Administration of Leisure

Time). Although permission for cultural activities had been granted, there was apparently some uncertainty regarding exactly what was allowed. As Šedová recalled, in the early months of the ghetto, they performed secretly in their barracks:

> The first signs: at the beginning of 1942 Švenk's cabaret began. They played in the attics, everything was illegal.
>
> Theatre started... in 1942, when all of Terezín was changed into a ghetto. Official permission... (1963)

Although, according to other sources, the status of Czech-language theatre was ambiguous rather than illegal, even during the period when prisoners were confined to their barracks (Weiner 1999: 213), Šedová correctly captures the transition when, in the summer of 1942, all the non-Jewish inhabitants of Terezín had finally been moved out and the prisoners were free to move about the ghetto rather than being confined to their barracks. The new openness of the cultural scene was reflected in the way performances were administered; as the head of the *Freizeitgestaltung* wrote in a 1943 report, by the autumn of 1942 their activities had become a 'totally official undertaking' (Weiner 1999: 220).

The Nazis left the cultural life of the ghetto in the hands of the prisoners. They did not become involved in its operations until late in the war, when they exploited it for their own purposes. The most notorious occasion was in June of 1944: officials from the International Red Cross were allowed to visit the ghetto and viewed a concert and a performance of the children's opera *Brundibár* (Adler 2005: 172–8). As a rule, however, they did not interfere. Frýd, in his testimony, remarked on their lack of interest: 'The commandant was actually not concerned about what people did in the camp – they were condemned to death all the same' (1963).

Another reason the prisoners perceived performance spaces as safe spaces was the fact that, because the performances were officially allowed, the SS never violated them. In all other aspects of life in the ghetto, the prisoners had to be prepared for chance encounters and unannounced inspections. However, interestingly, there is not a single report of Nazi guards entering a performance space and breaking up a show. Prisoners soon discovered that they could count on being undisturbed for those few hours. As Šedová wrote:

> In the beginning we had some innocent texts ready to put in instead of the risky passages, in case of German inspection. Later on we grew

less careful. The SS left the internal camp administration to a great extent in the hands of the so-called self-government. (1965: 221)

Of course, creating a truly safe space was beyond the prisoners' power. However, as Herman makes explicit, it is not true safety but a 'strong perception of their ability to control their destiny' that makes people resilient in the face of potentially traumatizing experiences (1992: 58). The prisoners' subjectively experienced sense of control over the space and time of a performance allowed them to forget their powerlessness for a few hours and recover, temporarily, from the 'essential insult of trauma' (Herman 1992: 41). Within those safe spaces they also worked through other steps in the process of recovering from traumatic experiences.

Reconstructing the trauma narrative

It is here, in the types of narratives the prisoners constructed and performed, that we find the greatest difference between Herman's three steps and the prisoners' choices in the ghetto. According to Herman, once a safe space has been established,

> The next step is to reconstruct the traumatic event as a recitation of fact. Out of the fragmented components of frozen imagery and sensation, patient and therapist slowly reassemble an organized, detailed, verbal account, oriented in time and historical context. [...] the completed narrative must include a full and vivid description of the traumatic imagery. [...] The description of emotional states must be as painstakingly detailed as the description of facts. (1992: 177)

The purpose of such a narrative, Herman argues, is to 'integrate these experiences into a fully developed life narrative' (1992: 181, 184). What we see in the case of theatrical performance in Terezín, however, is a very different approach to the same goal. In the testimony we simply do not find accounts of performances that include detailed, emotionally engaged accounts of traumatic events in the ghetto. Perhaps because the prisoners knew that, even in the protected space of the theatre, they were not yet truly safe, they were not able to bear such narratives; as Herman emphasizes, 'approaching them [traumatic memories] too precipitiously leads to a...damaging reliving of the trauma' (1992: 175). What we do find, however, are performances that dealt indirectly with events in the ghetto, often through comic allegory. By creating psychologically manageable narratives that enabled them to engage with potentially traumatizing aspects of life in Terezín, the prisoners were able to begin to integrate those events into their own life narratives, even while those events were still taking place, without risking retraumatization.

Three performances that emerged prominently in the 1963 testimony, Karel Švenk's *Last Cyclist*, Frýd's staging of E. F. Burian's *Esther* and Gustav Schorsch's production of Gogol's *The Marriage*, engage with the ghetto in allegorical ways. To achieve what the survivors called 'meaning' or 'impact' – their way, I believe, of expressing what I am calling integration – performances needed to do more than simply engage with events in the ghetto. Emotional engagement, although traumatic emotional states are not represented in the plays, still seems to be necessary, but in a perhaps surprising way: the plays needed to be performed with enough aesthetic quality that they engaged the prisoner-spectators both emotionally and intellectually. The combination of relevant narrative content and emotional engagement enabled them to integrate conditions and events of the ghetto without reliving the trauma.

The Last Cyclist

One performance that appealed both to their political sympathies and their sense of humour was Karel Švenk's revue *The Last Cyclist*, a thinly veiled comic allegory in which the protagonist Bořivoj Abeles, a petty-bourgeois cyclist (read 'Jew'), is pursued and imprisoned by a gang of lunatics (read 'Nazis') who eventually attempt to shoot him to the moon on a rocket.

Švenk himself, an author, director and performer, is consistently recalled in survivor testimony for his ability to bring laughter and optimism into the ghetto and for his political commitment. In 1963, Reinerová named Švenk's cabaret as one of three performances that had 'political impact' in the ghetto.[6] As Jan Fischer recalled:

> K. Švenk had the ability to react to the situation suitably, not with straightforward agitation.... The action only loosely structured, cabaret features and politically oriented.... Švenk at first glance and also in character worked like a frightened little Jewish clerk; he had however a great capacity for dry humour. (1963)

Šedová, who characterized Švenk as 'a talented comic and author, active in a Communist cell', who was 'very specific politically', described details of *The Last Cyclist* that reveal his political stance (1963). Švenk not only incorporated many elements drawn from the prisoners' experience of the immediate pre-war years, satirizing the tiny Czech Fascist party and Nazi racial laws, but created a comic allegory for class tensions in the ghetto:

> Scene on the boat. The boat had two decks, on the upper deck were prominents, on the lower proletarians. An SS-man counts them on an abacus. Social tension: prominents – proletariats. (Šedová 1963)

In Terezín, a small number of prisoners were classified as 'prominents' – usually those who had enjoyed high-status positions before the war or had important Aryan relatives – and given preferential treatment, which understandably caused resentment among the other prisoners. By representing this tension according to the interpretive framework of leftists in interwar Czechoslovakia, as a 'bourgeois versus proletarian' opposition, Švenk imposed the prisoners' own pre-war patterns of meaning-making onto the events of the ghetto.

However, making political sense of events in the ghetto was not Švenk's only mission. Šedová described the comic ending of the play, in which Abeles saved himself by accidentally lighting the fuse of a rocket while the lunatics were on board inspecting it, and Švenk's intentions: 'The performance *Last Cyclist* had as its goal to give people a bit of optimism. The happy coincidence that saves Bořivoj Abeles' (1963). Thus Švenk not only interpreted the ghetto in a comic way through a particular pre-war political lens, but indulged in some optimistic wish fulfilment rather than engaging with the truth of their ongoing imprisonment. By staging a conclusion to the play that implied a happy ending for the prisoners, he encouraged his audience to focus on the longed-for future rather than the dismal present.

Esther

The script *Esther*, adapted by renowned interwar director E. F. Burian, was brought to the ghetto by Reiner and Frýd, who had collaborated with him before the war; as Frýd testified, 'Frýd and K. Reiner brought the text [*Esther*] to Terezín (both worked with Burian's theatre), they knew that theatre was being performed there' (1963). Reiner composed music for the performance and Frýd directed it in Burian's style. As Šormová noted in her interview with Frýd, 'even though Burian's script relatively exactly describes and in detail determines the actorly and directorly approach, Frýd applied his own directorly ideas, but he did not depart from Burian's overall concept'. Reiner, in his testimony, recalled that 'the play *Esther*, in its political stance and point of view, was the most engaged work in the repertoire of Terezín theatre'. This production was clearly effective for himself and Frýd, but the other survivors did not recall it as having the same degree of impact.

An examination of Burian's preserved script immediately clarifies why Reiner believed this production would have such impact (Burian 1938). The performance is based on a nineteenth-century Czech folk play that portrays events from the biblical Book of Esther: Esther, the young Jewish queen, reveals to her husband, King Ahasuerus, the nature of his minister Haman's plot against the Jews. The king declares that Haman will be executed and decrees that the Jews may fight back against their enemies; they emerge victorious. Burian's adaptation, performed in the style of naïve folk drama and including nineteenth-century peasant characters, embodied an optimistic ending to the prisoners' own plight and recalled Burian's own decision, during the dangerous days of the occupation, to prepare a script that declared the Czech people's historical affiliation with the Jews.

For the other prisoners, however, the production failed to make the script relevant to the world of the ghetto. As Fischer, who played the role of the peasant, recalled,

> Frýd's direction of the folk play *Esther* – the whole thing was an artistic enough affair which did not have social impact. A person did not feel it like a blow which would lift him out of his chair, like with Brecht.... Also some players made fun of Frýd's direction (he was no director).... *Esther* was, in the given situation, too little. It was perceived like a fairy tale on a great theme. (1963)

It seems remarkable that, considering the theme and evoked recollections of Burian's gesture of solidarity, Fischer would view *Esther* as 'too little', but Miška and Šedová apparently concurred. Neither described the performance as exceptionally meaningful. Miška remarked only that the performance demonstrated 'how people tried to find ... current-sounding texts, which were possible to relate in content to the present situation'. Šedová, who played the peasant woman, recalled mainly Frýd's use of Burian's signature stylized movement.

Why did this performance have so little meaning for Fischer, Miška and Šedová? It appears that, in order to generate the level of emotional engagement that enabled a Terezín production to 'have impact' for this group of survivors, a certain level of aesthetic quality was necessary. Perhaps, as Fischer suggested, Frýd really was 'no director'; artistic failings may have prevented the other prisoners from engaging thoroughly with the work. Thus, although this performance was tremendously meaningful for Reiner, who had worked personally with Burian and was perhaps able to see the potential of the performance rather than Frýd's actual end product, the others did not experience a subjective sense of connection with the work, nor the work's connection with the present of the ghetto.

The Marriage

Gustav Schorsch's production of *The Marriage*, on the other hand, left a deep impression upon this group of survivors. As Miška recalled, 'Schorsch very anxiously attended to the quality of the performance from the artistic side and, from the social point of view, that it had some meaning' (1963). Schorsch had managed to invest Gogol's dark comedy about an indecisive suitor, his rivals, and his vapid potential bride with intense significance in the ghetto.

One thing that apparently differentiated Schorsch's production from Frýd's staging of *Esther* and other works the survivors described as having 'little impact' was his strikingly original approach to the staging. Both Fischer, who played one of the suitors, and Šedová, in the role of the matchmaker, Fyokla Ivanovna, described a highly stylized performance. Schorsch's concept for Šedová's character 'was of a caricature, the crooked painted mouth should have symbolized the obvious deceitfulness of the character' (Šedová 1963). Fischer described Schorsch's directorial savvy in working around the limitations of his actors:

> The selected level of style: exaggeration, in which the lack of knowledge of the non-actors was not to be recognized.... The characters were not like living people, but clear-cut types. The performance was tuned like a concert. Schorsch literally drilled entrance after entrance. (1963)

Fischer located the heart of the performance in the characterizations, overtly comparing Schorsch's production with the fairy tale atmosphere of *Esther*: 'the suitors in *The Marriage*...were perceived as more...monstrous, aggressive.... [with a] rough edge of pathological behaviour.... Absolutely nothing darling about them' (1963). Miška pinpointed a specific moment where the comic façade dropped to reveal the darkness behind it:

> *The Marriage*: The emphasis was placed on the characters – they work comically. The rhythm of daily life of characters, who awaken only in one short moment, so that they become aware of the senselessness of their behaviour. Then they are carried away by the current of everyday life. (1963)

Based on these comments it is possible to imagine the vivid single moment when the absurd, intensely vain and self-centred characters, completely caught up in their petty pursuits, become conscious of their own monstrosity – and then return immediately to their unconsidered lives. Schorsch apparently managed to draw out both the comedy and the brutality of Gogol's work and make it speak to their lives in Terezín by critiquing the type of fundamental human failings that the prisoners witnessed daily. Selfish behaviour that might have seemed insignificant or even comic in another setting, however, could have grave consequences in the ghetto. Pilfering from the common food supply, for example, meant that other prisoners received less and placed the elderly, who received the lowest food rations, in danger of starvation. Petty corruption among those who worked to assemble lists for the outgoing transports could mean a prisoner's life or death. With *The Marriage*, Schorsch and his actors engaged with this aspect of life in the ghetto in a safe narrative form.

However, I argue that much of the production's meaning derived from its connection to a world much larger than Švenk's and Burian's politically inflected visions, much larger than the ghetto itself – a world that Kavanová gestured towards when she described the individual who became a subject again in the theatre:

> What he heard from the mouths of actors confirmed at the same time that, as a spectator, he shared in the fruits produced by thousands of years of civilization in culture, in art, in the development of thought. (1967)

That is, Schorsch's production engaged with what the prisoners might have called universal human concerns, even when they were faced every day with what their fellow prisoner Anna Auředníčková called 'the hardship of our banishment' (1945: 36). Schorsch, by staging a story that could have served as an allegory for human failings in almost any society, tied the actors and audience to, even implicated them in, a problem that extended far beyond the walls of the ghetto – as Frýd wrote of Schorsch, 'his theater was oriented towards "eternal values" ' (1963). Schorsch's aesthetically excellent and socially meaningful production, not limited to the time or place of Terezín, allowed the prisoners to say something that could have great significance on any stage in Europe; thus they not only 'shared in the fruits produced by thousands of years of civilization', but contributed to them.

Reconnection with self, others and one's world

According to Herman, traumatized individuals must overcome their feeling of isolation by reconnecting with themselves, with others and with their communities. Reconnecting with themselves, however, cannot be separated from reconnecting with others. Because personality development depends on a sense of connection with caring people, damaged subjectivity cannot be restored in isolation; 'that sense can be rebuilt only as it was built initially, in connection with others' (Herman 1992: 52, 61).

Theorists and mental health practitioners recognize narrative as the vehicle of that reconnection; trauma victims must be able to create a story of the traumatic event and address it to an empathetic witness in order to recover their subjectivity. Theorist Kelly Oliver, for example, in elaborating on her notion that 'witnessing', as the process of address and response shared with another, is in fact the fundamental structure of subjectivity, discusses psychiatrist Dori Laub's concept of the 'inner witness': traumatized survivors, by interiorizing the interpersonal dialogue shared with the therapist, regain their ability to connect with themselves (Oliver 2001: 85).

In Terezín, theatrical performance became a site of reconnection with self and others where narratives about their experience could be shared. According to survivors, the interaction between actors and spectators established a process of address and response that restored that sense of connection and thus individual subjectivity. I believe this is the process survivor Eva Kavanová described in an essay when she wrote:

> The interaction of creators and spectators actually created a mass reaction. That mass reaction brought apparently contradictory results: it awakened in the listeners consciousness that they perceived, understood, reacted individually, that they were capable of

other feelings than those the fascists forced upon them by condemning them to the herd. A mass reaction, although it sounds paradoxical, that strengthened the consciousness of the prisoner that, so far, he still existed as an individual. (1967)

Šedová expressed a related sentiment in an essay: that Terezín theatre managed 'to weld a series of nameless transport numbers into an enthusiastic human collective' (1965: 239). Prisoners who had been alienated from themselves by the Nazis' reduction of their identities to a single, racialized category – who had been, as Oliver states, 'denied individuality and access to meaning making by a culture that chain[ed them] to a group identity... in a dehumanizing or denigrating way' – were able to re-establish a sense of themselves as individual subjects through the responses they shared with their fellow prisoners during theatrical performances (Oliver 2001: 35). Since prisoners in Terezín could select from many different performances, each reflecting a different national and political point of view, spectators' presence in the theatre represented their own subjectivity-restoring act of agency: a personal choice of group affiliation rather than an identity imposed on them by the Nazis. By serving as witnesses to each others' act of agency, the prisoners confirmed the reality of that agency and thus their own threatened subjectivity.

Theatrical performance also enabled prisoners to connect with others and forge social networks that were not limited to the space and time of performance. According to the survivors' testimony, intense bonds of solidarity were established among members of groups who worked together regularly, and especially among those with strong leaders. The value of a strong sense of community in enhancing all of its members' efforts to cope with potentially traumatizing conditions has been demonstrated in a wide variety of circumstances. As Steven Southwick and Dennis Charney write,

> The strategies used by resilient soldiers and civilians to create health-promoting social bonds and to foster social support have been studied by researchers for many years; it is now well known that social isolation and low levels of social support are associated with high levels of stress, depression and PTSD. (2012: 91)

Similarly, psychiatrists Roy Grinker and John Spiegel observed that, with soldiers in battle, the most important factor in countering psychological breakdown was 'the morale and leadership of the small fighting unit' (qtd in Herman 1992: 25).

In 1963 Miška described how young director Gustav Schorsch created a particular kind of community:

> Schorsch, before he began to do theatre, organized seminars, where he wanted to bring all participants – future interpreters – to the same common spiritual basis, to reach the point where there was affiliation among them in their approach to the work, to the text. Maximal feeing of responsibility. (1963)

The survivors described the intensity of his emotional investment in those activities and in them as performers. As Šedová recalled,

> Schorsch was a very suggestive director, he lived through things with his actors, he went for a very concrete analysis of the role, he literally pumped atmosphere into the actors. (1963)

Frýd described Schorsch's directorial methods and their effect upon the actors: 'He tried to give beginners and inexperienced actors the feeling that they were good, that they would achieve a lot; he led them to his ideas without force. The actors loved him' (1963).

Under Schorsch's leadership, these young actors had apparently forged the type of social bonds that offered them a degree of psychological protection against the potentially traumatizing events taking place in the ghetto. Lest the scene appear unrealistically idyllic, however, solidarity sometimes crossed the boundary into cliquishness. This group's own sense of insiderhood had apparently developed in part through pointed criticism of outsiders, recalled even 20 years after the performances were staged. Šedová, for example, saw no redeeming features in the Terezín production of a play called *Camel through a Needle's Eye*, calling the actors a 'half-amateur second-class group'. Miška was even more critical of some of his fellow actors. Of Vlasta Schönová's performance in Cocteau's *The Human Voice* he said, 'She has a chesty voice, plays with technical effort, without deeper inward foundation. Declamation, pathos, dramatization' (1963). He objected even more emphatically to Terezín director Ota Růžička's interpretation of Chekhov's one-act plays: 'Until this day I don't understand what it was supposed to be about. Růžička did not understand Chekhov at all, it was something completely different than Chekhov' (1963). However, Miška also acknowledged the function of such criticism in establishing their own sense of superiority: 'we had a little bit of an elevated relationship to the rest of the groups because we were those who did art, while the rest were for us hams, boulevard actors.' Thus the 'solidarity of the small fighting unit' that developed among Schorsch's actors did not extend to all their fellow Terezín theatre artists, and not even all their fellow young Czech actors. But returning to the notion of the safe space, even if the theatrical scene did not always engender mutually supportive relationships, it did engender relationships that functioned according to normal, pre-war dynamics. That is, rather than being preoccupied with their pathological state of helplessness in the face of the radical power imbalance between themselves and the Nazis, these young prisoners were engaged in emotionally intense yet normal relationships of affection, of personal rivalry, of artistic disagreement, and competition. Rather than internalizing the Nazi view that the only thing that mattered was their group identity as Jews and thus inferior beings, they focused on stakes that mattered to them as individuals and that united the members of their 'small fighting units', such as the aesthetic quality and political impact of their own productions versus those of their peers.

Through performance and spectatorship, the prisoners also symbolically reconnected with communities outside of the ghetto to which they felt they belonged. For this particular group of survivors, one of those communities was the Czech nation. During the early 1960s they had to exercise caution when expressing Czech national feelings, for the Communist government frowned upon manifestations of 'bourgeois nationalism' that interfered with the international solidarity of the proletariat. However, in an era of political reform when Chairman of the Soviet Communist Party Nikita Khruschev was encouraging the countries of the Eastern Bloc to find their own paths to socialism, it was possible to express enthusiasm for specifically Czech culture during World War II. Norbert Frýd demonstrated the survivors' attempts to negotiate these pressures when he described the prisoners' emotional reaction to a performance of Bedřich Smetana's *The Bartered Bride*, considered by many to be the Czech national opera:

> It had nothing in common with nationalism. Few true Czech nationalists lived in Terezín; to the left-oriented majority they were laughable. But before Smetana and in that situation everyone bowed his head. (1965: 224)

Jan Fischer recalled recitations of Czech poetry in the ghetto by Gustav Schorsch, explicitly recognizing the significance of public performance:

> Schorsch's recitation evenings – Neruda, Dyk, Halas – a proclamation of Czechness, Czech poetry. Neruda, Dyk – poets with revolutionary content. To identify oneself publicly with these poets was a deed. (1963)

His mention of 'revolutionary content' points to the poets' political as well as national significance. Each poet belonged to a different generation and each, in his day, had resisted the Germanic oppressors of the Czechs.[7] For the Terezín prisoners, choosing to attend a reading of works by these poets allowed them to perform both their loyalty to the Czech nation and their attitude towards the present-day oppressors.

Within the overall framework of Czech national identity, this group of prisoners created theatrical performances that allowed them to reconnect with even more specific cultural and political communities by drawing upon both the archive and the repertoire of interwar Czechoslovakia.[8] Two Prague theatres had tremendous influence on the young Czech Jews. The Liberated Theatre of Jiří Voskovec and Jan Werich, directed by Jindřich Honzl and featuring music by renowned jazz composer Jaroslav Ježek, inspired numerous performances in the ghetto. Šedová, for example, mentioned their influence upon the revues written in the ghetto by prisoners Josef Lustig and Jiří Spitz:

> Lustig-Spitz: *Prince Bettliegend, Ben Akiba Lied* (after the example of the Liberated Theatre, a pair of clowns, dialogues in entrances onto the forestage).
>
> They wrote new song texts to Ježek's music for the revues of the Liberated Theatre, inspired by Terezín conditions and reacting to them. (1963)

Comic duo Voskovec and Werich had resolutely refused to affiliate themselves with a particular political party, but their views were clearly left-leaning. As Nazi Germany's power grew they performed a series of increasingly pointed yet optimistic satirical reviews that played to packed houses and reinforced audience morale with their faith in the strength of ordinary but united people (Burian 2000: 51). Regardless of the content of a performance, using Voskovec and Werich's performance conventions would have carried specifically political connotations, the style alone giving the performance a political valence immediately recognizable to the other prisoners.

Another influential figure already mentioned as the adaptor of the script *Esther*, director E. F. Burian, was a member of the Czechoslovak Communist party before the war. He pioneered a striking and complex style of choral recitation that he called by the English word 'voiceband'. Burian, who had founded his own theatre in the fall of 1933, reacted to the threat of German domination by drawing on specifically Czech themes, especially those of folk and peasant culture.

All of these artists had Jewish colleagues who brought these popular styles into the ghetto. As already mentioned, Frýd and Reiner brought E. F. Burian's script *Esther* to the ghetto. Reiner's wife Hana Reinerová also pointed out that

> Czech theatre in Terezín was strongly influenced by the work of E. F. Burian, Jindřich Honzl, and the Liberated Theatre. The influence of Honzl and the Liberated Theatre was mediated by the designer František Zelenka, who worked with that theatre. (1963)

Reinerová, a caretaker in a Terezín youth home, revealed how, even in performances for children, Reiner's influence brought Burian's style and political stance into the ghetto:

> The fairy tales of [nineteenth-century Czech author] Karel Jaromír Erben (*King Skunk*, *Little Otto*...) were realized by means of choral recitation, but on the theatrical side it was very humble – no costumes. The defeat of Little Otto symbolized Hitler; King Skunk also. The performance had a very current alignment. (1963)

Thus, in addition to enabling the Terezín prisoners to reconnect with themselves and with others in the ghetto, theatrical performance allowed them to reach beyond the ghetto and virtually reconnect with their national and political communities – the communities they hoped to rejoin after the war.

Conclusion

As we have seen, survivor testimony indicates that theatrical performance helped the prisoners cope with potentially traumatizing experience in the ghetto by enabling them to create a safe space, to express their experiences in the ghetto as manageable narratives, and to reconnect with themselves, others in the ghetto and their own communities in the wider world. This particular group of prisoners was fortunate in that, for those who survived, the affiliations they had carefully maintained through performance in the ghetto enabled them to establish continuity, not only from their pre-war lives into the ghetto, but from the ghetto into life in post-war Czechoslovakia: they were actually able to rejoin their national and political communities after the war.

The same was not true, however, of other groups. There was no place for German-language culture in Czechoslovakia after World War II, and Czech Jews were expected either to assimilate completely to Czech culture or to emigrate to Israel. As preserved scripts from the ghetto reveal, Czechoslovak German speakers and Zionists used similar strategies to continue to perform their own affiliation to their communities outside the ghetto, but the outcome was quite different. Although theatrical performance may have ameliorated their sense of loss while in Terezín, it left them, after the war, with a set of carefully maintained affiliations that no longer had a home.

Notes

1. The Czechoslovak state ceased to exist from 1939 to 1945. During this period Slovakia was an independent client state of Nazi Germany, and the occupied western Czech provinces from which most of the Czech Jews were deported were known as the Protectorate of Bohemia and Moravia.
2. For insight into this generation's complex relationship with communism see Kovály (1986).
3. I would like to express my gratitude to Dr Eva Šormová for her generosity in sharing her interview materials.
4. Jana Šedová was the post-war stage name of Truda (Gertruda) Popperová.
5. Fewer than 30 members of the SS were assigned to Terezín/Theresienstadt during the whole time of the ghetto's existence; the prisoners rarely encountered an SS officer (Fedorovič 2007: 236).
6. The other two, Bedřich Smetana's opera *The Bartered Bride* and E. F. Burian's play *Esther*, will be discussed later in this chapter.
7. Jan Neruda (1834–91), journalist and poet, inspired Pablo Neruda's pseudonym. A known Czech patriot, he was accused in 1871 of treason against the Habsburg empire. Viktor Dyk (1877–1931) was imprisoned for anti-Austrian resistance during World War I. František Halas (1901–49), a favourite of Fischer's generation, published a collection of anti-fascist poems, *Dokořán* (*Wide Open*), in 1936.
8. Here I draw on Diana Taylor's distinction between 'archival' memory embedded in documents, literary texts and other items supposedly resistant to change, versus the 'repertoire' of embodied memory: performances, gestures, orality, movement, dance, singing, etc. (2003: 19–20).

Bibliography

Adler, H. G., 2005. *Theresienstadt: Das Antlitz einer Zwangsgemeinschaft*. Göttingen: Wallstein.
Auředníčková, A., 1945. *Tři léta v Terezíně*. Prague: Alois Hynek.
Burian, E. F., 1938. *Esther*. Unpublished manuscript.
Burian, J., 2000. *Modern Czech Theatre: Reflector and Conscience of a Nation*. Iowa City: University of Iowa Press.
Caruth, C., 1996. *Unclaimed Experience: Trauma, Narrative, and History*. Baltimore: Johns Hopkins University Press.
Fedorovič, T., 2007. 'Neue Erkenntnisse über die SSAngehörigen im Ghetto Theresienstadt'. In J. Milotová, M. Wögerbauer, and A. Hájková (eds) *Theresienstädter Studien und Dokumente 2006*. Prague: Sefer, pp. 234–50.
Fischer, J., 1965. Personal interview with Eva Šormová.
Frýd, N., 1963. Personal interview with Eva Šormová.
Frýd, N., 1965. 'Kultura v předposlední stanici'. In F. Černý (ed.) *Theater/Divadlo*. Prague: Orbis, pp. 213–29.
Herman, J. L., 1992. *Trauma and Recovery*. New York, NY: BasicBooks.
Kavanová, E., 1967. Unpublished essay.
Kovály, H., 1986. *Under a Cruel Star: A Life in Prague 1941–1968*. Cambridge, MA: Plunkett Lake Press.
Miška, F., 1963. Personal interview with Eva Šormová.
Oliver, K., 2001. *Witnessing: Beyond Recognition*. Minneapolis, MN: University of Minnesota Press.
Reiner, K., 1963. Personal interview with Eva Šormová.
Reinerová, H., 1963. Personal interview with Eva Šormová.
Šedova, J., 1963. Personal interview with Eva Šormová.
Šedová, J., 1965. 'Terežínské divadlo'. In F. Černý (ed.) *Theater/Divadlo*. Prague: Orbis, pp. 213–29.
Šormová, E., 1973. *Divadlo v Terezíně 1941/1945*. Ustí nad Labem: Severoceské nakladatelství.
Šormová, E., 2004. Personal interview with Lisa Peschel.
Southwick, S. M., and D. S. Charney, 2012. *Resilience: The Science of Mastering Life's Greatest Challenges*. New York: Cambridge University Press.
Taylor, D., 2003. *The Archive and the Repertoire: Performing Cultural Memory in the Americas*. Durham: Duke University Press.
Weiner, E., 1999. 'Freizeitgestaltung in Theresienstadt'. In A. Goldfarb and R. Rovit (eds) *Theatrical Performance during the Holocaust*. Baltimore: Johns Hopkins University Press.

4
Imagining Theatre in Auschwitz: Performance, Solidarity and Survival in the Works of Charlotte Delbo

Amanda Stuart Fisher

> *'People did not dream in Auschwitz, they were in a state of delirium'*
> (Delbo 1995a: 168)

In 1941 Charlotte Delbo, then 27 years of age, was working as an assistant to the renowned theatre director Louis Jouvet (1920–51). The company was on a tour of South America when Delbo learned that a communist friend of hers, André Woog, had been executed by 'guillotine in Paris by Marshal Pétain's police' (Felstiner in Delbo 1997: xii). In South America Delbo was relatively safe from the war, but on hearing this news she decided to return to occupied Paris immediately. In her account of this moment of decision in her book *Convoy to Auschwitz* (1997), Delbo explains that the need to return was born of a feeling of solidarity with, and a commitment to, those who were sacrificing their lives in the fight against Nazism. Despite Jouvet's concern for her safety and his efforts to dissuade her, she was resolved to go. Her decision, it seems, was based on a profound sense of personal, ethical and political conviction. She said to Jouvet: 'I must go home. I can't stand being safe while others are guillotined. I won't be able to look anyone in the eye' (1997: 74).

As we shall later see, Delbo returned to these ideals in her post-war writing where she would reflect on what I will later describe as a *communitarian* concept of existence, drawing on this concept to shape her accounts of life and theatre-making in the camps. It is within these texts that we can begin to understand Delbo's strong fidelity to others. This sense of camaraderie and friendship and a profound sense of communal responsibility and commitment informs not only her theatre-making in the camps, but also the process by which she undertakes the action of remembering itself. The sense of *communitas* which bound Delbo and her comrades together did not emerge simply from common identities or shared life experiences. Rather, I will suggest, following Roberto Esposito's work in this area, that communitas in Delbo's work develops from the situation itself within the camps, emerging from a shared sense of obligation and indebtedness. After the war, this obligation can be found in the performance of acts of remembrance through Delbo's testimony, which ensured that her fellow prisoners were not forgotten and would 'survive' as historical subjects within her texts. Correlatively, in the camps themselves, theatre-making arguably became a means of survival for Delbo and her fellow prisoners because it generated a sense of communitas or a *togetherness* which, following Jean-Luc Nancy, I would suggest describes a mode of *being-with* and *being-for* one another that countered the camp environment, which was designed to destroy any sense of solidarity. Jean-Luc Nancy associates the sense of togetherness with the heritage and etymology of the political term *communism*, which for Nancy does not denote a particular political ideology or doctrinal meaning, but instead becomes an idea or a way of understanding the 'togetherness of people' (Nancy 2010: 147). It is in this sense that we shall understand the 'political' dimension of Delbo's work here as being 'communist' not in any doctrinaire sense, but rather as a valuing and pursuance of togetherness, friendship and a care for one another.

Delbo's 'concentrationary literature'

Delbo's commitment to friendship and solidarity is depicted vividly in her play about Auschwitz: *Who Will Carry the Word?* (1982). Here Delbo seems to suggest two things. Survival itself, first of all, should be conceived of as being interrelational: it is rooted in a sense of communality, of being with and living for others. But the play also comprises, secondly, a reflection on the labour and responsibility of witnessing itself. The character of Claire sums up this perspective when she says:

> Haven't you heard them, the dying, who all say, 'If you return, you'll tell'? Why do they say that? They say that because none of us is alone and each must render an account to all the others [...]

> You aren't free. Even if you are nothing but the smallest link, you are part of a chain that links all men – that links them far into the future.

80 Imagining Theatre in Auschwitz

No matter what you do, you are part of the human chain. You cannot exclude yourself. (Delbo 1982: 281)

Delbo's decisive act of solidarity – her return to France in 1941 and her reconnection with the Resistance – had life-changing consequences. In May 1942, several months after her return, Delbo and her husband, Georges Dudach, were arrested at their apartment for producing anti-fascist leaflets for the Resistance. Dudach was executed several months later and Delbo, with 229 other French women, was sent to the Romainville Fortress, a Nazi prison and transit camp just outside Paris. She was later transported with the other women, first to Auschwitz-Birkenau, and then to a series of other concentration camps until she was liberated by the Red Cross in 1945.

Delbo started writing about her experiences in the camps several months after liberation, but didn't publish any of these texts until 1965 when she felt they 'had stood the test of time' (Langer 1995: x). It is from our reading of these literary texts, and particularly two of the plays she wrote, that we begin to learn about the theatre-making Delbo initiated during her incarceration in Raisko, a satellite camp of Auschwitz, and Ravensbrück, a women's concentration camp in Germany.

Delbo's texts are, however, difficult to negotiate and interpret as they are neither directly autobiographical nor historiographical in form, style or approach. Delbo's testimony emerges indirectly, through a poetics of writing, where the 'facts' regarding these performances often surface only as fragmented memories. This is a partial and often elliptical account of a past, which eschews the detail that we would normally look for when researching theatrical performances. Details such as when and where the play took place and who performed it are often excluded from the text and are therefore unknowable.

The literary texts Delbo produced after the war about her experiences could perhaps be best defined as a form of 'concentrationary literature' (*littérature concentrationnaire*). This term arose to describe post-war literature which is 'neither pure documentation (testimony) nor fictionalisation' (Sellam 2008: 18),[1] but rather a genre of writing which should be recognized as an autonomous form. Sellam positions Delbo alongside other Holocaust survivor-writers such as Primo Levi, Robert Antelme and David Rousset, from whose seminal account of the camps the term '*concentrationnaire*' arose.[2]

In an interview with Jacques Chancel in 1974, Charlotte Delbo explicitly addressed why she chose to use theatre to represent her experiences in the camps. In the discussion of her play *Who Will Carry the Word?*, Delbo distinguishes between the written and spoken word of testimony, suggesting that written words (*les mots*) are encountered in a moment of solitude for the single reader, whereas the spoken word (*les paroles*) opens up a space for communitas with others. When asked by Chancel why she wrote her play, she says:

> It's more than not forgetting. It is a wish to bring to consciousness the... some facts that should remain as historical facts and not enter the status of myth [...] Because, massacres in general – and humanity and the history of humanity is full of them – but... they need to be talked about [...] So, bringing this particular play to the stage perhaps seemed... it must seem a difficult thing to take on, but in fact it was the one thing that came to mind quite naturally because it is on stage that we hear the words pronounced out loud, whereas in a book we are alone, we read and reread... we can be touched by words but [...] it seems to me that we are less affected. I mean, in books we have words [*des mots*] and on the stage we have spoken words [*des paroles*]. (Delbo 1974)

Here Delbo seems to suggest that theatre, more so than literature, has the power to open up precisely the kind of communal space necessary for testimony to emerge. In this way, she positions testimony as a communal act that not only binds herself (as the witness) to the past and to those who supported her in the camps, but also to a community of listeners who are called upon to emerge in the now and to carry this story into the future.

What is so interesting – and even unique – about Delbo's accounts of theatre-making within the camps is that she provides an insight, not only into the function and meaning of theatre-making in moments of great suffering, but into how the particular style of acting and characterization she was interested in functioned within such performances. By interrogating her accounts of theatre, we can begin to understand how this specific theatrical genre opened up the possibility for communal activity to emerge in a context where community was not permitted to exist. Furthermore, what is perhaps most striking is that (to our contemporary perspective) Delbo's vision of theatre appears to be highly anachronistic: the theatre she describes is text-based and classical in form. This stands in stark contrast to more improvisatory approaches to theatre-making today, such as devised theatre, which we might expect

82 *Imagining Theatre in Auschwitz*

to see emerging in a context where theatre was being produced by non-actors – or, to use Delbo's terminology, by a group of 'modest interpreters' (Delbo 1995a: 171).

With the re-enactments of the classical French texts which Delbo and her comrades performed, they did not endeavour to reinterpret or represent in any way the day-to-day reality of the women's lives. In this sense it was the playwright's text, rather than the 'real lives' of the women who were performing it, that had primacy. Here Delbo might be simply following in the footsteps of her mentor, Jouvet, who summarized this approach to theatre and the influence of the playwright's text upon the actor:

> To direct a production means serving the playwright with a devotion that makes you love his work [...] In reality, a play stages itself; the only necessity is to be attentive and not too personal in order to see it take on its own movement and begin to manipulate the actors. (Jouvet in Cole and Kirch Chinoy 1983: 228–31)

However, there is something else at stake in Delbo's approach. In her text *Phantoms, My Companions* (1971) we begin to get a clearer picture of what acting and characterization meant to Delbo in the context of the camps. Here she evokes a number of 'characters' who emerged at different points during her incarceration.

Phantoms, My Companions (*Spectres, Mes Compagnons*)

Presented in the original French text as a fictive letter to her mentor Jouvet,[3] *Phantoms, My Companions* (1971)[4] is one of Delbo's lesser-known texts, but one which offers her most sustained consideration of theatre-making. Here Delbo explores not only her vision of theatre, but the distinction she makes between the 'novelistic' and the 'dramatic' character and why she feels that it is the dramatic rather than the novelistic character that is more capable of living in the concentrationary world. While the novelistic character is, she argues, 'somewhat rigid' and too knowable, remaining confined and 'trapped in the patterns of his complex existence' (Delbo 1971: 14), the 'dramatic character', by contrast, retains 'the mystery of the unknown'(14), leaving us 'to the discovery of their motivation' (13). Similarly, while the novelistic character acts only according to what we know about his past because he is 'followed all along the entire line of his existence', the dramatic character is constructed through decisive action.

He is, Delbo explains, 'caught in an action so arranged that he cannot escape' (13).

Written some 20 years after Jouvet's death, the text is both an autobiographical account of Delbo's experience in numerous concentration camps and, as Nicole Thatcher points out, an 'homage to Jouvet', reminding us of Jouvet's considerable 'importance as [Delbo's] literary [and theatrical] mentor' (2000: 72). Delbo conjures the presence of Jouvet within the text itself, enabling him to emerge both as a revenant and also an addressee for Delbo's testimony. In this way, Delbo's text attests to the labour of witnessing itself: specifically drawing on the image of Eurydice, who she pictures (in contrast to the original myth) as returning from the underworld, Delbo suggests that the act of witnessing requires that a journey be made. It requires a descent into a past which for Delbo remains haunted by Auschwitz and the 'stench of human flesh'(10).

Delbo begins her own journey into witnessing in *Phantoms, My Companions* by recalling conversations she had with Jouvet in Vallauris, France in 1939. Throughout the text she stages a series of these remembered conversations until finally, when Delbo's narrator arrives at Auschwitz, Jouvet merges with the character of Alceste from Molière's *The Misanthrope* and disappears. While the relationship between Alceste and Jouvet is not indicated within the text, we might assume that the character of Alceste has some resonance with Jouvet because his theatre troupe performed the first act of *The Misanthrope* in South America, shortly before Delbo left for Paris (Knapp 1958: 200). Throughout *Phantoms, My Companions* Delbo conjures a series of other 'phantoms', revenants from French literature, including both 'novelistic' and 'dramatic' characters such as Fabrice Del Dongo from Stendhal's novel *The Charterhouse of Parma* (1839), Racine's *Phèdre* (1677) and Ondine, the eponymous heroine of a play by Jean Giraudoux (1938).

Fabrice Del Dongo is the first to emerge and appears before Delbo's narrator when she is imprisoned in what we assume is La Santé Prison when she manages to get hold of a copy of Stendhal's novel from an inmate housed in the cell below. Fabrice is described by Delbo as 'handsome and somber' (1971: 18), but while he provides a degree of divertissement, he ultimately proves to be a somewhat aloof and limited companion. 'He hardly spoke,' Delbo tells us, and 'did not seem to enjoy much of anything, avoided questions and never gave himself away' (18). Fabrice also appears to possess very little imaginative potential for our incarcerated narrator: 'His face, his eyes,' she tells us, 'were empty, unvisited by thought' (17). The limitations of the spectre of

Fabrice are contrasted with the 'dramatic character' of the ghostly water sprite Ondine who, like Delbo, must kiss her husband goodbye before his death. Within her prison cell, Delbo tells us, Ondine not only has more 'life' than the novelistic Fabrice, but also the capacity to connect with Delbo's own real-life experience. For unlike Fabrice, who remains detached from the narrator, the dramatic character Ondine maintains an openness which allows for a sense of communion with the narrator while she endures her own period of mourning. Ondine's husband, Hans, blends with the image of the narrator's own husband, and when (in Delbo's text) the narrator must say farewell to her husband, just before his execution, it is the spectral Ondine who accompanies and reassures her. Delbo writes:

> The presence of Ondine assured me of my own presence by carrying me along with her into the supernatural. It was not a game, it was real. Hans was going to die – not a stage but a carnal death. Hans was bidding me farewell, his voice darkened by advancing shadows. (20)

It is Ondine who enables the narrator to discover that 'a dramatic character could live in prison' (20). While novelistic characters possess a closed and solipsistic quality, limiting the capacity for empathic connection and the imaginative potential necessary for their recreation in a prison, Delbo suggests that it is the sense of mystery evoked in the dramatic character which brings Ondine to life. Crucially, Delbo does not suggest this mystery can in any way be resolved by the representation of the character or by the labour of acting itself. On the contrary, she argues that the dramatic character always remains the creation of the playwright, and therefore maintains an objective and separate presence both to the narrator in her text and also, of course, to any actor who endeavours to represent her (or him). Delbo explains that there should be no psychological fusion between the actor and the dramatic character. Instead she suggests that it is the actor's work to bring the playwright's creation to life. The dramatic character, she argues, will always exist separately and autonomously from the actor:

> The dramatic character may exist to some extent through the actor, but he possesses an autonomous existence as well. He is a phantom to whom the actor must give greater or lesser reality. (14)

There is an interesting resonance here with Louis Jouvet's own philosophy of acting. Jouvet, like Delbo, argues that acting is not about the self-expressive fulfilment of the actor's internal life, nor is it reducible to the emotional work of the actor. Instead, acting, for Jouvet, is concerned with using 'the work of the author as the basis of performance' (Carlson 1993: 373). Jouvet often uses the term 'spiritual' to describe his approach to theatre-making. This is not in relation to a transcendental truth that exists within the psyche of the actor, but is, on the contrary, used to describe an evocation of the authorial vision in the moment of performance itself where the actor almost becomes a conduit for the words of the playwright. Theatre, Jouvet argues, should 'elevate the rights of the spiritual over those of the material, the word over the action, the text over the spectacle' (Jouvet in Carlson 1993: 373).

Yet, interestingly, this comment by Jouvet alludes to a slight, but perhaps significant, point of departure from Delbo's own theorization and practice of theatre. In her account of the dramatic character in *Phantoms, My Companions* Delbo offers a reframing of Jouvet's belief in the spiritual essence of the authorial word. While still advocating the primacy of the text over the invention of the actor, Delbo suggests that at times action is more significant than words.

Delbo uses a critique of the novelistic character to make this point. Although the novelistic character is a product of the imagination of the reader, she argues, it is also, paradoxically, too knowable to have any existence beyond the solitary act of reading as determined by the structure of the novel: the novelistic character, in short, can have no 'imaginative life' beyond the pages of the book. By contrast, the dramatic character remains a mystery, retains its objectivity or distance, and yet is also created through an interdependency between the playwright and the actor, and between the other characters on stage and the audience. Indeed, it is only through this process of *existing-with-others*, or so Delbo seems to suggest, that the dramatic character is 'unveiled'. It is only through the decision to 'act', she explains, that the character emerges:

> The dramatic character is caught at that moment of his life when he discovers himself [...] When the dramatic character begins to act, he is forced to unveil himself, both as character and hero, in self-surrender. He becomes his action, and, in turn, his acts serve to define him. (13)

I would suggest that here, in the demand placed on the dramatic character to unveil himself, to surrender himself, Delbo begins to draw an important parallel between a conception of action and the dramatic character, and what we might call 'good' character or acting in 'good faith'. And what, I think, is at stake in that parallel can be read into the decision Delbo made to leave Jouvet in South America to return to Paris, with the subsequent outcome of that decision, and her suggestion that it is through decisive action that the dramatic character 'begins to act' and 'is forced to unveil himself'. If we extend this further we might suggest that here Delbo is making a comment about what it means to exist *authentically* in the world. By authenticity I do not mean to suggest that Delbo associates authenticity with concepts such as self-realization or self-expression; instead I would argue that for Delbo authenticity is about owning up to one's existence and owing a responsibility to others – where existence is conceived as communitarian, wholly *being with* and *for* others. This resonates with a Heideggerian account of authentic existence which philosopher Taylor Carman interprets as '*owning up wholly* – that is, *wholeheartedly* – to [oneself] in [one's own] existence' (2003: 276).

We shall return to the question of authenticity later on in this chapter, but first let us consider how Delbo's theorization of theatre and characterization informed the theatre-making she facilitated in the camps and how this helps us to develop an understanding of the relationship between theatre-making and survival in Delbo's texts.

Theatre-making in the camps

As we have seen in *Phantoms, My Companions*, Delbo conceptualizes the dramatic character as communally created through the playwright's text and the imaginative labour of the actor. Unlike the novelistic character, who Delbo suggests is recreated subjectively within the solitary experience of the reader, the dramatic character emerges collectively through action and decision and therefore possesses a 'universality' which Delbo argues allows for the possibility of presence or a *life* beyond the confines of the play. This 'universality' is not born of recognition or familiarity; Delbo does not suggest that we recognize ourselves in the dramatic character through self-identification or a detailed knowledge of the character's day-to-day 'personal characteristics' (1971: 13). On the contrary, she conceptualizes the dramatic character as possessing an 'abstract' universality which emerges precisely because we do not and cannot fully know him or why he makes the decisions he does. 'The dramatic character,' she argues, 'is an abstraction of the human' (18) and he 'defies analysis, retaining the mystery of the unknown. This lends him a quality of plasticity, and affords the actor who must interpret him a measure of freedom' (14). Yet, when Delbo arrives at Auschwitz, Molière's Alceste, the last remaining dramatic character to accompany her on her journey, simply disappears. This leads Delbo to assert that the dramatic character cannot live 'so far from other men, from the human' (1971: 28–9) because, she argues, 'where human beings suffered and died, dramatic characters could not live' (29).

The disappearance of Alceste in the second half of *Phantoms, My Companions*, at the gates of Auschwitz, signals a shift in Delbo's relationship with the dramatic text. As she bids farewell to the ghostly revenant of Alceste, who here merges with the figure of Louis Jouvet, the narrator simultaneously welcomes her more 'earthy' companions, the French women in her convoy, whose presence we see emerging as a constant source of support throughout the *Auschwitz and After* trilogy. Significantly, when we refer back to Delbo's original French text we note a deliberate linguistic shift occurring at this point in the text. Rather than using the term *'amis'* to describe the women who she had travelled with on the convoy to Auschwitz, she instead shifts to the more politically nuanced term *'camarades'*. Rosette C. Lamont, who translated Delbo's *Spectres, Mes Compagnons* (*Phantoms, My Companions*), chooses to adopt the English words 'friends' and 'companions' to mark this shift in the English text, but arguably this does not fully capture the political nuance of a term such as *'camarades'*, which, while certainly meaning 'companion', also references comradeship – a term which is adopted by communism and many other left-wing political movements across the globe to describe a form of friendship based on solidarity and communitarian ideas. In Lamont's English text, this shift in terminology is presented in the following way:

> Alceste had disappeared. I never found him again throughout this sojourn in hell. Nor did I find any of his friends [*amis*], or my former friends [*amis*] [...] I acquired companions [*camarades*]. These women had the solid, fraternal qualities needed for such an unequal fight. (1971: 29)[5]

In order to think further about the meaning of theatre for Delbo in the concentrationary world, let us examine her accounts of theatre-making in the camps, asking what acting meant to Delbo and what it was that connected the actors – the women prisoners – with the dramatic enactments that took place.

Delbo wrote two plays which allude to her experience of theatre-making in the camps. These are *Who Will Carry the Word?* (*Qui Rapportera*

Ces Paroles?), published in 1974,[6] and *The Men* (*Les Hommes*), an unpublished play written in 1978 and set in the Romainville Fortress where Delbo was incarcerated for several months before being transported to Auschwitz-Birkenau (Schumacher 1998).

The first act of *The Men* focuses on the women's preparations for the staging of *Caprice* (*Un Caprice*), a comedy by Alfred de Musset (1843), which is to be performed at Romainville with Françoise as the director and the other women as actors and stage designers. Françoise appears in several of Delbo's literary works and, as Schumacher indicates, is perhaps best understood as a kind of 'double' who represents Delbo's perspective (1998: 218, 225).

The production of *Caprice* is rehearsed and prepared in *The Men*, with careful attention to detail: Françoise is 'a very meticulous director' who 'like her mentor Louis Jouvet [...] has the greatest respect for the author and his text' (Schumacher 1998: 221). Just before the final performance is about to commence a number of the women are called away to bid goodbye to their loved ones who are about to be executed. When they return, they are encouraged to continue with the performance and *Caprice* – the play within the play – is finally performed as a 'mime' with 'actors' who are now, however, very much distracted and dispirited. Delbo's stage directions read as follows:

> The actresses act without uttering a word. They mime *Caprice* without making a sound. They are withdrawn into themselves. But there is applause when Gina and Yvonne enter, the only interruptions to the monologues. (Delbo quoted in Schumacher 1998: 222)

A different kind of theatre-making is presented by Delbo in *Who Will Carry the Word?*, a play that draws on her experiences of Auschwitz-Birkenau and/or Raisko. Here, the characters do not stage a full-length play, but instead we learn that Françoise and her comrades recite plays to the others. The character Renée tells us about this:

> Stand up straight Marie. If we find a little dry corner to sit down during the break, we'll ask Françoise to take us to the theatre. What program will we ask her for? She tells it so well and she does all the voices. You would think you were hearing the actors. (Delbo 1982: 308)

The descriptions of theatre-making in *Who Will Carry the Word?* resonate with Delbo's earlier accounts of theatre in *Useless Knowledge* (1995a), the second text in the *After Auschwitz* trilogy. Here Delbo tells us that having spent six months in the 'death camp' Auschwitz-Birkenau, along with a small group of other women, she was moved to another camp which we can reasonably assume to be Raisko. Here, Delbo tells us 'the work was not as hard' (1995a: 167) and the improved conditions enabled the women to 'regain human appearance' (167), not least because for the first time they had 'hot showers, straw mattresses on individual beds, and toilets' (Delbo 1997: 10). With this renewed health, Delbo explains, they began to 'think of theatre'. She writes:

> One of us recounted plays to the others, who managed to work close to her, digging with their spades or hoeing. They'd ask: 'What are we going to see today?' Each telling was repeated several times. Each one wanted to hear it in turn, and the audience could never exceed five or six. However, the repertory was beginning to be used up. Soon we started considering 'putting on a play'. Nothing less than that. Without texts, without the means to get some, with nothing. (167)

When they do eventually 'put on a play' they opt for a classic text, enacting Molière's play *The Hypochondriac* (*Le Malade Imaginaire*). Delbo takes the role of the director and 'Claudette' reconstructs the script from memory, while the others work on the set and props or take on the playing of the different characters.

Arguing that imagination should be understood as the 'first luxury' of a nourished body, Delbo suggests that theatre-making in Raisko became possible because the women's physical health improved, saying:

> You may say that one can take away everything from a human being except the faculty for thinking and imagining. You have no idea. One can turn a human being into a skeleton gurgling with diarrhoea, without time or energy to think. Imagination is the first luxury of a body receiving sufficient nourishment, enjoying a margin of free time, possessing the rudiments from which dreams are fashioned. (Delbo 1995a: 168)

Yet while it is clear that the change in the physical conditions made it possible to 'think of theatre' (167), Delbo's account of this time does not help us to understand the full *meaning* of these theatre-making activities nor does it allow us to understand how theatre might have related to her own survival. To examine this further, we must examine more closely what survival meant in the concentrationary world and, specifically, to Delbo and her comrades.

Theatre and survival

The concepts of survival and resistance within the camps are much contested and debated in Holocaust studies. Some scholars suggest a correlation, for instance, between survival and the forms of aesthetic activity that occurred in the camps such as theatre-making, arguing that the suffering and inhumanity of the concentrationary world could be ameliorated – temporarily perhaps – through an engagement with certain cultural activities, such as theatre and the creative arts. In *Theatrical Performance During the Holocaust* (Rovit and Goldfarb 1999), Rebecca Rovit suggests that during the Holocaust '[m]usical and theatrical creation seemed to give people some sense of humanity' (Rovit 1999: 10). Performance, she argues, generated a kind of 'spiritual resistance' which 'helped inmates retain their sense of humanity amid the most inhumane circumstances' (5) of the camps. In his essay within the same book Alvin Goldfarb suggests that the theatre returned a sense of *normality* to those who were incarcerated:

> If the outside world provided no support or substance, theatre was another attempt by the victims to sustain one another and to try to preserve a semblance of normality in an obscenely abnormal universe. (Goldfarb 1999: 124)

An alternative and contrasting perspective would be to suggest that it was simply not possible to escape the brutal reality of camp existence, nor was it possible therefore to create any 'semblance of normality' in such a place. After all, it is arguable that the concentrationary world was, to draw on David Rousset's terms, utterly *ubuesque* – a 'totally enclosed' and 'strange realm' which was a 'world apart' from anything resembling normality (Rousset 1965: 36). Lawrence Langer, for example, argues that to speak of the possibility of a 'spiritual resistance' existing in the camps is to overlook the absolute and oppressive violence of the Nazi regime. According to Langer, in the camps, 'dignity and choice had temporarily lost their traditional meaning' (Langer 1980: 222). Here Langer uses the term a 'choiceless choice' to describe how the normative values of cause and effect no longer make any sense in the concentrationary world. In this context, he argues, what people chose to do or how they chose to act reflected no volition in any normative sense and 'critical decisions did not reflect options between life and death, but between one form of 'abnormal' response and another, both imposed by a situation that was in no way of the victim's own choosing' (Langer 1980: 224).

To be sure, negotiating these different perspectives of survival in relation to Delbo's experiences within the camps is not an easy task, not least because we do not have access to the 'Delbo' who lived at that time. All we can rely on is her own remembered accounts of her incarceration and her descriptions of the theatre-making she experienced there. Nevertheless, from my reading of the way theatre emerges in her texts, I would argue that, for Delbo and her comrades, the act of making theatre was not an attempt to escape (in either a psychological or spiritual sense) the day-to-day brutal existence of the camps. Like Langer, I do not think this was a possibility that was available to Delbo and her comrades. However, contrary to Langer, I would suggest that the decision to create theatre was a volitional act and, furthermore, one that was deliberately framed to forge a mode of being-with-the-other that resisted the absurd and *ubuesque* environment of the concentrationary world, which, through its use of kapos[7] and the indiscriminate violence of camp life, sought to set inmates against each other and destroy any sense of solidarity or communitarian existence. For Delbo, I would suggest, survival was due to the dependence of the prisoners on one another, a sense of fidelity to friendships that had been formed, and the general camaraderie that existed between prisoners incarcerated in the camp – a camaraderie, however, that extended beyond the camp, to shape and inform not only how Delbo chose to be with 'the others' while she was there, but also how Delbo chose to exist 'after' Auschwitz. Survival, for Delbo, should not be perceived as a physical or even psychological act of enduring the horror of the camps, but rather as the capacity to live on afterwards and to exist in such a way that honours those who did not survive. In this way, I am suggesting that the concentrationary world continues to exist beyond the temporal space of incarceration and that Delbo's accounts of theatre-making attest both to the spirit of solidarity which fostered communitas and survival *within* the camps, and to the continuing act of *witnessing* itself, with its imperative to remember those who did not return and who are remembered in Delbo's writing after the war.

Certainly, in Delbo's writings we see the theme of witnessing and remembrance returned to repeatedly. There is a sense that, even during their internment, Delbo and her comrades were focused on a futurity that they understood would always place a demand upon them: that they must remember the past and those who, while perishing in the camps, 'carried' and supported the women 'psychically, morally and physically' (Patraka 1999: 25). We see this reflected in an exchange that takes place in the final scenes of Delbo's play *Who Will Carry the Word?*, where the women reflect on their commitment to those who did not survive:

> *Françoise*: What of those we'll leave behind?
> *Gina*: We won't leave them, we'll take them away with us, in us.
> *Denise*: You mean, Gina, that we won't ever forget them? There are some of them whose names I didn't even know.
> *Gina*: Even without a name they'll be in us. We will restore them with a look, a gesture. Maybe in our dreams. (Delbo 1982: 318–19)

Delbo's concept of fidelity to 'the others' through witnessing is perhaps performed most clearly and painstakingly in *Convoy to Auschwitz: Women of the French Resistance* (1997). Here Delbo recounts the biographical detail revealed to her about each woman she met while on the convoy – the 229 women who, along with Delbo, were 'deported from Compiègne to Auschwitz on January 24, 1943' (Felstiner 1997: 1). Most of the women in the convoy were 'involved in resistance against the Nazis' (ibid.), yet Delbo chooses not to structure this text to tell stories of individual bravery and survival. Instead, each deportee is listed simply under the heading 'The Women' and given a short profile outlining her life before, during and, where possible, after Auschwitz. Delbo also places herself on the list, under her married name, 'Dudach'. In this way, I would suggest that she shifts the concept of survival away from the realm of the individual and indeed away from a narrative of psychological 'trauma' and instead reconfigures it so as to focus on the collective. The survivor does not emerge as independent and singular, but instead exists *for* and *with* others. Similarly, for Delbo, remembering the past becomes an ongoing labour of witnessing where the past is not overcome or 'worked through' in a psychological sense, but rather *held* open.[8] By this I mean that not only does the past remain unforgotten, but that it also does not overwhelm the present. Delbo's continual act of remembrance is arguably an act founded on a decision born of political ideals. It is an act that retains the past insofar as it expresses her commitment and fidelity to the others; in other words, it survives with her, and testifies to her own survival, rather than being a symptom of individual psychical trauma, as some commentators have argued.[9] We might also note here that Delbo continues this concern for justice for others in her other literary works. For example, in her text *Les Belle Lettres* (2012), Delbo comments on the treatment of Algerians in the French Algerian War and considers the significance of the emergence of French 'camps' in Algeria.

Given the politics of Delbo's literary work after liberation, we might reflect on the kind of theatre she created during incarceration and question the extent to which this had a political dimension. Certainly, the choice of plays may be somewhat surprising as they bear little or no relation to the situation the internees in Auschwitz faced in their day-to-day reality. Yet I would like to suggest that the enactment of these very literary plays was a kind of political act, albeit a subtle and not overtly explicit one. My use of the term 'political' here references the values and the 'idea' of communism and borrows from Jean-Luc Nancy who asserts that 'communism has more than, and something other than a political meaning' (2010: 148). I would suggest that for Delbo *the political* comes to mean a mode of *being-together* and a feeling of *togetherness* which was pressed forward through the act of theatre-making. Nancy's articulation of communism, which draws on Heidegger's concept of *being-with* the other (*Mitsein*), conceptualizes *togetherness* as an essential feature of human existence and this then enables us to describe communism in existential terms, as belonging to the *essence* of the human.[10] I would argue that this account of togetherness, which defines the political as an essential mode of togetherness, certainly resonates with the ideals of obligation and solidarity which we observe both in Delbo's accounts of her relationships with her 'comrades' in the camps and in her activism and resistance activities before, during and after the war.[11] In this way, arguably, Delbo's theatre-making became a means of politically redefining the women's collective existence in the camps for two reasons: firstly, because this activity was something *chosen* freely by the internees, and, secondly, in a world which destroyed all possibility of imagining an alternative world, and foreclosed the possibility of dreaming, this kind of theatre-making facilitated a mode of *being-with* one another which generated communitas and a creative togetherness. Indeed, while the concentrationary world prohibited imagining and dreaming it nevertheless could not entirely destroy the desire for collectivity and solidarity. Delbo's plays were not about escaping the camps, but bearing the suffering 'together' within them. In this way, arguably, Delbo and her fellow inmates bore the anguish of the concentrationary world as a *collective subject*. These acts of togetherness became forms of resistance to the model of the concentration camp, which sought to set its inmates against one another and close down any possibility of solidarity. In the last section of this chapter, then, I would like to look more closely at what we know about the choice of the texts Delbo and her comrades staged in the camps and explore what this style of theatre might tell us about the possibilities for communitas in the violent and hostile environment of the concentrationary world.

A literary theatre: text, authenticity and a theatre of communitas

As we have seen, the theatrical texts that Delbo and her comrades chose to enact recreated a very different reality to the concentrationary world. Furthermore, Delbo seems to suggest that a theatre which imitates life might actually have a deleterious impact on those interned in the camps. In *The Men*, we discover that prior to choosing to stage Musset's *Caprice*, the women had wanted to stage a play about their own situation. An exchange between Cécile, the wardrobe mistress, and Françoise reveals the reasons why such a realistic representation was to be avoided:

> *Cécile*: To stage our predicament: women locked up in a fortress, waiting to be deported… women who make superhuman efforts to avoid thinking about the death threat they, or their husbands, or their brothers, are under… […] No, this was not a suitable scenario, not now, even if the action had been set in Antiquity… not one of us could have played her own role. It was too hard.
> *Françoise*: That's precisely why I can't write it. Playing our own roles would have made us so acutely aware of the terrible reality of our situation that no one could have endured it. Neither the actresses, nor the spectators. (Delbo [1978] cited in Schumacher 1998: 224–5 [his translation])

An imitative form of theatre in the context of the concentration camp, Delbo seems to suggest, ultimately risks simply reflecting and reaffirming the hegemonic ideology of violence of the concentrationary world. Equally, however, to suggest that theatre-making, as Rebecca Rovit implies, 'transcended time and place and [created] a buoyancy of mind and spirit' (Rovit 1999: 9) also feels somewhat simplistic, particularly if we conceive of the concentrationary world not just as a series of individual places, but as a system or 'world' which enforced and upheld a violent and inhumane regime. Arguably, we might suggest that it was precisely because the inhumanity of the concentrationary world was so insidious and inescapable that a literary theatre became a necessity.

Rather than facilitating a sense of escape from the reality of the camps, then, I would suggest that for Delbo these theatrical enactments produced a creative space where existence was – temporarily at least – no longer focused solely on the act of survival itself, but on the collective process of putting on a play. In this sense theatre created a moment of communitas where the women experienced a mode of being-in-the-world together that was about interrelational connections and care for one another. Roberto Esposito's theorization of communitas is useful here. He develops a definition of communitas that challenges the conventional reading of community, which, he argues, is usually defined as *a property* that is held in common with others:

> a 'property' belonging to subjects that joins them together: an attribute, a definition, a predicate that qualifies them as belonging to some totality, or as a 'substance' that is produced by their union. (Esposito 2009: 6)

In contrast to this, Esposito's conceptualization of communitas distinguishes the *common* from the individual or the particular. Communitas then becomes a relational mode of being, rather than something 'possessed' by a particular group of people who share the 'same' attributes. Drawing on Neo-Latin etymology Esposito suggests we should conceptualize communitas as standing in opposition to what is 'proper' and arguing it denotes 'subjects of community [who] are united by an "obligation" in the sense that we say "I owe you something" not "you owe me something" ' (6).

In this sense, I would argue that the communitas that emerges in Delbo's accounts of theatre-making in the camps should be understood as the performance of a shared sense of obligation and care towards one another. Delbo describes the emergence of this theatre as 'miraculous' and by this I think she refers not only to the miracle of the possibility of theatre existing in such a place, but also how this communal act of working together creatively enabled, albeit momentarily, an *authentic* mode of being in the world that offered some resistance to what the philosopher Giorgio Agamben describes as the 'bare life' of the camps: the radical instrumentalization of existence within the concentrationary world, where lives could be extinguished with impunity (Agamben 1998). Delbo writes:

> The curtain rises. It's magnificent... It's magnificent because some of Molière's lines, having surfaced intact in our memory, come to life again... It's magnificent because each one of us plays her role with humility, without trying to push herself to the foreground. Perennial miracle of modest interpreters. The miracle of an audience having suddenly recaptured childhood's purity and resurrected the imaginative faculty. It was magnificent because, for the space of two hours, while the smokestacks never stopped belching their smoke of human flesh, for two whole hours we believed in what we were doing. (Delbo 1995a: 171)

The authenticity of being-with-one-another that this moment of communitas evokes is not akin to an escape or transcendence of the horrors of the camp; after all, as Delbo points out, the 'smokestacks never stopped belching'. Instead, theatre-making, it seems, facilitated a different mode of being, where interrelationality and dependency forges a *being-with* and *being-for* the other which itself opens a space of resistance that is irreconcilably at odds with the bleak and brutal instrumentalizing inhumanity of the Nazi's concentrationary world.

Through my reading of Charlotte Delbo's testimonial texts, her accounts of theatre-making and life within the camps, I have begun to piece together some proposals about what survival and theatre meant for Delbo in the context of the concentrationary world. Theatre-making, I have argued, facilitated a mode of togetherness and a *being-with* and *being-for* the other which countered, if not resisted, the brutality of the camp environment which sought to eliminate any possibility of solidarity or care for others. This sense of togetherness, I have suggested, was rooted in the political as it emerged within the values of communism which – for Delbo – are framed around a sense of communitas, solidarity and indebtedness to others. While *Auschwitz and After* (1995a) is Delbo's most well-known text and is much cited within Holocaust and trauma scholarship, *Phantoms, My Companions* (1971) has received far less critical attention. Yet, as we have seen, it is through Delbo's analysis of how theatre and acting operates in this text, that we are able to understand Delbo's relationship to theatre and what it meant to her within the concentrationary world. Theatre-making contributed to Delbo's capacity to redefine her relationship with her 'comrades' and this, I have argued, contributed to an existential process of survival by establishing communitas and a sense of solidarity amidst the harsh and unrelenting environment of the camps. Yet, Delbo's sense of indebtedness and obligation to the women she was incarcerated with arguably exceeds the temporality of the camps and re-emerges in the performance of remembrance within the testimonial texts she produces afterwards. Survival then – for Delbo – becomes not only an existential or biological process, but a form of commitment. That commitment led Delbo to continue to honour the women who cared for and supported her during her time in the camps. In this way, I would suggest that Delbo's testimonial work becomes not only an act of witnessing and remembering, but also an act of solidarity and a labour of care in itself as well.

Notes

1. All translations from the French are my own unless otherwise indicated. I am indebted to Karine Friez and Stephanie Laurent for their assistance with this.
2. In his book *L'Univers Concentrationnaire*, written in 1945, Rousset argues that the 'concentrationary world' should not be seen as an 'unexpected consequence of war', but as an almost absurd or 'ubuesque' society of 'inverted values' (Copfermann 1965: 14).
3. The French version of the text published by Berg International (1995b) opens with the words '*Cher Louis Jouvet*'.
4. Delbo's original French text, *Spectres, Mes Compagnons*, was first published in France in 1977 and republished by Berg International in 1995. In this chapter I will, however, quote from Rosette C. Lamont's translation, which appeared in the *Massachusetts Review* in 1971.
5. Delbo's original French reads as: 'Alceste avait disparu. Je ne l'ai point retrouvé pendant tout ce long séjour aux efers. Retrouverai-je jamais personne de ses amis ni de mes amis anciens? J'aurai maintenant des camarades. Elles on des qualities solides et fraternelles qui sont celles dont a besoin dans un combat aussi inégal' (Delbo 1995b: 43).
6. According to Robert Skloot, the play was written in 1966, but it was not until 1974 that the text was published in Paris by Editions Pierre Jean Oswald (see Skloot 1982).
7. A 'kapo' was a prisoner in a concentration camp who was given the task of carrying out certain guard duties. Delbo describes the kapo as 'a prison guard often recruited from the inmates and having a reputation for extreme cruelty' (Delbo 1982: 285n).
8. In *Writing History, Writing Trauma*, Dominick LaCapra writes about Freud's theory of 'acting out' and 'working through' in the context of writing about the Holocaust (2001). He argues that the trauma of the Holocaust means that some people can get caught up in an involuntary process of 'acting out' the past, unable to separate themselves from the traumatic events they narrate.
9. Geoffrey Hartman (1996) and Dominick LaCapra (2001), for example, interpret Delbo's literary work as symptomatic of trauma.

98 *Imagining Theatre in Auschwitz*

10. Nancy sums up this position when he argues that: '*Communism* is togetherness – the *Mitsein*, the *being-with* – understood as pertaining to the existence of individuals, which means, in the existential sense, to their *essence*' (2010: 147).
11. We know, for example, that Delbo was a member of the young Communists prior to the war and, certainly, her involvement in the Resistance was also linked to Communist organizations. For an illuminating discussion about how Delbo's testimonial work can be viewed as providing a political intervention in the politics of decolonization in France in the 1960s (when her memoirs were first published), please see Michael Rothberg's excellent article *Between Auschwitz and Algeria: Multidirectional Memory and the Counterpublic Witness* (2006).

Bibliography

Agamben, G., 1998. *Homo Sacer: Sovereign Power and Bare Life.* Translated from the Italian by D. Heller-Roazen. Stanford: Stanford University Press.
Carlson, M., 1993. *Theories of the Theatre: A Historical and Critical Survey, from the Greeks to the Present.* Ithaca: Cornell University Press.
Carman, T., 2003. *Heidegger's Analytic: Interpretation, Discourse and Authenticity in Being and Time.* Cambridge: Cambridge University Press.
Cole, T., and H. K. Chinoy (eds), 1983. *Directors on Directing: A Source Book of the Modern Theatre.* New York: Columbia University Press.
Copfermann, E., 1965. 'Préface'. In D. Rousset, *L'univers concentrationnaire.* France: Pluriel.
Delbo, C., 1971. *Phantoms, My Companions.* Translated from the French by Rosette C. Lamont. In *Massachusetts Review*, 12: 1, pp. 10–30.
Delbo, C., 1974. Interviewed by Jacques Chancel. *Radioscopie*, broadcast 2 April.
Delbo, C., 1982. *Who Will Carry the Word?* In R. Skloot, *The Theatre of the Holocaust.* Wisconsin: University of Wisconsin Press.
Delbo, C., 1990. *Days and Memory.* Translated from the French by Rosette C. Lamont. Illinois: Marlboro Press/Northwestern University Press.
Delbo, C., 1995a. *Auschwitz and After.* Translated from the French by Rosette C. Lamont. New Haven: Yale University Press.
Delbo, C., 1995b. *Spectres, Mes Compagnons.* Paris: Berg International.
Delbo, C., 1997. *Convoy to Auschwitz: Women of the French Resistance.* Translated from the French by Carol Cosman. Illinois: Northwestern University Press.
Delbo, C., 2012. *Les Belle Lettres.* Paris: Les Éditions de Minuit.
Esposito, R., 2009. *Communitas: The Origins and Destiny of Community.* Translated by Timothy C. Campbell. Stanford: Stanford University Press.
Felstiner, J., 1997. 'Introduction'. In C. Delbo, *Convoy to Auschwitz: Women of the French Resistance.* Translated from the French by Carol Cosman. Illinois: Northwestern University Press.
Goldfarb, A., 1999. 'Theatrical Activities in the Nazi Concentration Camps'. In R. Rovit and A. Goldfarb (eds) *Theatrical Performance During the Holocaust: Texts, Documents, Memoirs.* Baltimore: Johns Hopkins University Press.
Hartman, G., 1996. *The Longest Shadow: In the Aftermath of the Holocaust.* New York: Palgrave.

Jouvet, L., 1993. 'The Profession of the Director'. In T. Cole and H. K. Chinoy (eds) *Directors on Directing: A Source Book of the Modern Theatre*. New York: Columbia University Press.

Knapp, B. L., 1958. *Louis Jouvet: Man of the Theatre*. New York: Columbia University Press.

LaCapra, D., 2001. *Writing History, Writing Trauma*. Baltimore: John Hopkins University Press.

Langer, L., 1980. 'The Dilemma of Choice in the Deathcamps'. *Centrepoint*, 4.

Langer, L., 1995. 'Introduction'. In C. Delbo, *Auschwitz and After*. Translated from the French by Rosette C. Lamont. New Haven: Yale University Press.

Nancy, J., 2010. 'Communism, the Word'. In C. Douzinas and S. Žižek (eds) *The Idea of Communism*. London and New York: Verso.

Patraka, V., 1999. *Spectacular Suffering: Theatre, Fascism, and the Holocaust*. Indiana: Indiana University Press.

Rothberg, M., 2006. 'Between Auschwitz and Algeria: Multidirectional Memory and the Counter Public Witness'. *Critical Inquiry*, 33.

Rousset, D., 1965. *L'Univers Concentrationnaire*. France: Pluriel.

Rovit, R., and A. Goldfarb (eds) 1999. *Theatrical Performance During the Holocaust: Texts, Documents, Memoirs*. Baltimore: Johns Hopkins University Press.

Rovit, R., 1999. 'Introduction'. In R. Rovit and A. Goldfarb (eds) *Theatrical Performance During the Holocaust: Texts, Documents, Memoirs*. Baltimore: Johns Hopkins University Press.

Schumacher, C., 1998. *Staging the Holocaust: The Shoah in Drama and Performance*. Cambridge: Cambridge University Press.

Sellam, S., 2008. *L'Ecriture concentrationnaire ou la Poétique de la résistance*. France: Editions Publibook.

Skloot, R., 1982. *The Theatre of the Holocaust*. Wisconsin: University of Wisconsin Press.

Thatcher, N., 2000. *A Literary Analysis of Charlotte Delbo's Concentration Camp Re-presentation*. New York: Edwin Mellen Press.

Part III
Tactics and Strategies: Dissent under Oppressive Regimes

5
Swazzles of Subversion: Puppets Under Dictatorship

Cariad Astles

Second World War: Mr Punch appears in battledress and gas mask performing to British troops; Jack Ketch, the hangman, is transformed into Hitler and is duly hanged by the ingenious Mr Punch.[1] Carnival in Viareggio 1991: carnival elsewhere in Italy has been 'cancelled'. The floats are ready to parade in the streets despite the threat of the first Gulf War. Giant puppet figures of Saddam Hussein alongside world leaders adorn the floats, emphasizing the absurd politics of the international crisis. June 2013: anonymous Syrian puppeteers lampoon the dictator through satirical protest in an effort to drum up peaceful protest. Assad is a gross caricature. The artists hope that, by using puppets, they will be able to remain anonymous.

Puppets occupy a peculiar and distinct place in relationship to dictatorship. The metaphor of puppetry suggests ultimate control and power over a lesser being. The puppeteer has frequently been cast as a control freak; in Paul Gallico's book from 1954, *Love of Seven Dolls*, for example, he exercises supreme power over a community of characters, controlling their actions, desires and fates: a dictator in a small world. But puppetry is peculiar and unsettling also because, conversely, puppets represent the struggle for freedom; there are numerous examples throughout literature and film which metaphorize this relationship between control and freedom.[2] The popular puppet, moreover, is one that traditionally represents the absolute refusal to conform: cousin to the Commedia zanni, s/he subverts authority through trickery, ignorance, naivety, or simple blatant insubordination. Puppets emerge at times of political crisis in many guises: appropriated by all sides of the political spectrum, they have been used variously by national governments to bolster their political or moral ideologies;[3] by protesters using the 'otherness' of the puppet to represent the ludicrous nature of dictatorship; and by people wishing to escape censorship, blaming their actions on the puppet.

They have been used not only as instruments in the hands of ideologists, but also as vicious and sharp satirical voices. Balfour notes that theatre 'flourishes' and has a particular function for society during times of crisis (Balfour 2001: 1). Puppetry occupies a specific place in collective and individual consciousness during political crisis, which we can assume dictatorship to be. Puppeteers, as socially engaged artists, respond to the political conditions of the time; their constructed objects are material representations of a particular moment. Puppets also have a historical role in popular culture as purveyors of news, and as social or political commentators. They have often continued to do this under dictatorship; the distancing effect of the puppet in performance enables artists to view and open up their 'moment of crisis' to scrutiny. On a more fundamental level, the making of and performing with puppets seems to respond to a very basic desire to create, play with and critique representations of human life. There are numerous examples of puppets made from the simplest and basest objects by prisoners of war in concentration camps, by political prisoners and those in refugee camps around the world: evidence has been found of puppets made from towels and handkerchiefs[4] in the trenches of World War One; from rags and dry bread in World War Two; from their own clothes by political prisoners in Chile. In some cases, puppets have been made to entertain and to tell stories; in some cases for prisoners to entertain their children. There is something in both the power offered through the act of puppeteering and in the capacity of the puppet to capture the synthesized essence of a popular response to a political moment. This chapter explores the uses of political puppetry in three different contexts of dictatorship: Czech 'daisy' shows performed in Prague under Nazi occupation; as a farewell to the dictatorship of General Franco in Spain; and as a means to explore collective guilt and loss experienced by survivors following the dictatorship of Pinochet in Chile. All three examples are direct manifestations of collective responses to dictatorship, and all respond to a clear need to process and engage with the effects of dictatorship. All offer, therefore, different perspectives on the power of puppets to address, recall and evoke trauma. The chapter seeks to explore the suggestion by Wolfgang Kayser, in his study of the grotesque, that art created under obscene, manipulative or oppressive circumstances employs the grotesque to articulate the absurdity of the contextual circumstances, whether they are political, social or cultural (Kayser 1981: 29). The grotesque has greater freedom to challenge and undermine hegemonies of oppression due to its expansive and ludic nature. It does not function merely as a critique of inhumanity, but actively engages with the inhumanity, obscenity or oppression to change it in some way through an unsettling of its effects.

Puppet theatre in many ways lends itself quickly and easily to fulfilling the aspirations of the grotesque. Within the grotesque, the body is usually the primary focus.[5] Puppets, as constructed images of humans, animals and other living beings, foreground the sign-ridden body as site of investigation. Carnival puppet figures draw attention to those parts of the body which demand derision, or which call on the ritual and life-giving aspects of life to celebrate fecundity and excess. As noted by Kenneth Gross, they are inherently 'uncanny' in that they occupy perpetually the space between life and death (Gross 2011: 4). The grotesque teases both form and content; frequently the source of laughter, it also, through exceeding its boundaries, enables critical commentary of those boundaries. This feature of the grotesque was analysed by Kayser, who noted that: 'While the laughter of the grotesque might be radically innocent for its creator, it is never innocuous... the corruption of the natural order is likely to be associated with a satanic intrusion of pandemonium in the world...' (Kayser, cited in Harpham 1976: 463). Noting its potential for ambiguity, confusion and declassification, Kayser offers the perspective that the grotesque can be invoked for a sharp analysis of conditions, since it is an unstable form; this instability offers the reader or viewer a means to view the world as a changing entity, where morality and hegemony are questioned. Of particular interest for this chapter is the idea suggested by Harpham that the grotesque is employed to suggest the absurdity and irrationality of the outside world:

> ...no longer is the grotesque a method of portraying only the distorted inner landscapes of the diseased or neurotic imagination... in a bomb-dominated, anxious time, objective reality, revealed to man by his most reliably 'realistic' methods of observation, provides the stimulus for the grotesque. In addition, the neurotic himself, or at least the outsider, has come to feel himself custodian of the height of reason... So not only has the neurotic asserted himself as the standard of sanity... but the world has itself become more and more hallucinatory. (Harpham 1976: 467)

In a world of political absurdity, which is the context for the examples discussed in this essay, the world is represented as a 'hallucinatory' environment and there is thus an implicit criticism at work.

The first of the examples to be discussed dates from Czechoslovakia under Nazi occupation. Czech puppetry prior to the Second World

War had gone through an energetic process of artistic recognition and development by artists, intellectuals and academics. During the 1920s a specialist centre for puppetry was set up and a Puppetry Council gave official status to its members. The researchers of the 'Prague Circle' were fascinated by the stylization of the folk puppet and one of its members, Otakar Zich, wrote a document on the psychology of puppet theatre, in which he emphasized the dual nature of puppet theatre: its ability to present as 'dead material' and its simultaneous search for lifelike characteristics to give it the illusion of life (Jurkowski 1996: 113–14). In 1936, 1,350 amateur puppet companies were counted in Czechoslovakia. The traditional puppet was a rod marionette, operated from above with a fixed metal bar to its head. The theatre director Josef Skupa (1892–1957) became fascinated by the Czech folk character, Kašpárek, investigating his potential and presence in the avant-garde and developing his character as a puppet. Skupa's experimentations eventually led him to the creation of a new puppet character, derived from Kašpárek, but called Spejbl. Spejbl was presented in 1920, first as a trapeze artist, but later a talkative and irritating middle-class figure, much given to ineffectual and long-winded speeches. Spejbl was an outcry by Skupa against philistinism, narrow-mindedness and officialdom. Skupa then developed a second character, and six years later Spejbl was joined by Hurvínek, who became cast as Spejbl's son (Jurkowski 1996: 93–5). These two formed a double-act in which Spejbl would spout prejudice and ignorance, while Hurvínek expressed dissent, enquiry and energy. The dialogue between the two gradually became a means to debate political and social morality, and they became known for their biting and satirical comments. Over the 1920s and 30s these characters gained popularity throughout Czechoslovakia; the shows were dominated by dialogue; elaborate and complex discussions were enacted through comic repartee and misunderstanding. Hurvínek constantly questioned authority and rules and Spejbl continued to uphold old-fashioned and illogical ideas. Their comments focused on day-to-day aspects of life in Czechoslovakia. The polarization of characters offered excellent scope for a critique of the Nazi occupation and responded to the need within Czech society to condemn the dictatorship.

There had previously been a tradition in Czechoslovakia of radical outspoken puppetry. During the nineteenth century, the puppeteer Jan Nepomucky Last'ovka voiced political opinion through the mouthpiece of Kašpárek, escaping censure and punishment through blaming his puppet (Blumenthal 2005: 167). This model for comic social commentary became widespread and in the years leading up to the Nazi occupation puppetry became associated with Czech dissent, as well as with a representation of identity. The traditional puppet show was often staged as a cabaret or circus act with acts performed by the puppets. Political figures, contexts and stories from the Czech national scene became commonplace in the shows. As the threat of invasion came closer, the puppet figures became more outspoken (Blumenthal 2005: 168).

The role of Skupa in providing an example for Czech puppeteers to respond to political events cannot be underestimated. As events in Europe reached crisis in the late 1930s, he created two puppetry performances in response to the threat of occupation: *Jdeme do sebe* ('All Together Now') and *Kolotoc o trech poschodich* ('The Three-tiered Carousel'). The latter was an allegory of European political events in the form of fairy tale in which Hitler himself was lampooned (Jurkowski 1996: 97). This play was written by the puppeteer Jan Malík, who was active against the Nazi occupation. It is a comedy about a house with rooms for rent; new tenants move in and demand a better room with an eastern view, trying to take over the house overall. Later shows included allegories about the hope that life would improve (*Long Live Tomorrow* in 1941 and *Everyday Miracles* in 1942). The use of allegory to indicate political oppression was used increasingly by puppeteers and, following the invasion, many of these artists went underground. All theatre became subject to censorship and the Nazis began shutting down puppet theatres from early on in 1938, recognizing the power of puppetry to represent Czech political dreams. In 1939 the puppetry magazine *Loutkář* was also banned as, with its emphasis on Czech identity through puppetry, it was seen to be threatening to Nazi aspirations.

Skupa was by now working and performing in Pilsen. During the occupation the company was regularly harassed by censors, and the performances were subject to frequent criticism from the occupying authorities. Jan Malík cites from the pro-Nazi *Prague Voice* that the characters of Spejbl and Hurvínek were referred to as follows: 'There is no more exact caricature of the degenerate Jewish mongrel than these two idiotic figures, spreading abroad the vainglory of their despicable blood' (Malík, cited in Jurkowski 1996: 175). Skupa's performances frequently referred to the place of puppets as controlled beings; the puppeteer, however, refuted accusations of political dissent, insisting on the artistic autonomy of his puppets for many years. In 1944, however, he was arrested by the Gestapo and sent to a concentration camp in Dresden, from where he escaped following the bombing of the city by Allied troops.

Puppetry continued throughout the Nazi occupation in Czechoslovakia. Underground performances reminded people of their heritage. Kiki Gounaridou notes that, 'When a nation seeks to be reconnected with a sense of national identity, its cultural celebrations often express nostalgia for a past that defines a cultural high point in its history' (Gounaridou 2005: 1). This nostalgia could be seen through performances which had not long previously occupied a significant 'cultural high point'. A wave of puppet shows, performed secretly during the occupation in people's houses, bars and basements, voiced anti-fascist sentiment and kept Czech popular culture alive. These lively performances were not usually scripted (Jurkowski 2013: 98) and indications of their popularity can mostly be found in eyewitness accounts and stories.[6] The performances involved improvised dialogue between the popular characters of the Czech puppet stage – circus and cabaret performers, and Spejbl and Hurvínek – in which the puppets became increasingly critical of the occupation. The puppets themselves were operated on tables or makeshift stages, from above, with an improvised curtain masking the puppeteers. The performances were dialogue-based, using local vernacular and jokes understood by the listeners; repartee was tossed between the puppets and the audience which questioned the role of the citizen and artist under occupation, discussed the latest reprisals and rules, and also the collaborating authorities (Jurkowski 1996: 98). The shows themselves were comic and designed also to provide some relief from the anxiety felt under occupation. There is no doubt, however, that the puppeteers knew what risks they were taking, and that these performances were direct political actions against the occupying forces.

The shows performed secretly during these years were known as 'daisies', thus named partly because the name sounded innocuous; and also, symbolically, because daisies are believed to be able to grow in the dark, and to be able to push their way up through cracks in concrete to flower in the most difficult circumstances. The 'daisy' shows were carefully planned and coordinated by puppeteers, notably Malík, cited above. They were always performed in Czech. Numerous puppeteers were involved in this activity, despite the risk of arrest; over 100 Czech puppeteers are believed to have died in concentration camps. Many, however, continued their art in the concentration camps, making shows for their fellow prisoners and driven by the same impulse: to maintain freedom and art in the face of annihilation. There are records of these puppet shows in the concentration camps of Terezín and the women's concentration camp Ravensbrück, where in 1944 Czech puppeteers set up a puppet theatre for the children of the camp and other inmates using glove puppets made from stockings. In Terezín transit camp, puppets were allowed for a period between 1942 and 1944 and shadow and string puppet shows were reportedly performed by prisoners before their transferral to Auschwitz (Jurkowski 1996: 184). Ironically, puppetry was appropriated simultaneously by the Nazi regime to further its political purpose and promoted in occupied Prague: the traditional German puppet Kasperle was used to expound the virtues of the Aryan race and puppet heads were even x-rayed to determine whether their heads were sufficiently 'Aryan' in design (Blumenthal 2005: 163). In this political context, therefore, puppets were used for three main purposes: firstly, for the Czech nation to recall its cultural identity and take heart in the performance of its own stories; secondly, as a symbol of rebellion and freedom; and thirdly, to provide escape, entertainment and hope for the imprisoned, both children and adults. The eventual repression of Czech puppeteers by the Nazis was, however, brutal, and performances were increasingly and more ferociously stamped out and forbidden. The considerable efforts and dedication of Skupa, Malík and other Czech puppeteers under these dreadful circumstances have been recognized throughout the world. In 1999 the virtuoso Canadian puppeteer Ronnie Burkett created an extraordinary one-man show in homage to Skupa and his contemporaries: *Tinka's New Dress*. The poignant and political string puppet performance drew from Skupa's 1937 performance *The Three-tiered Carousel* and the figures of the Czech puppet cabaret; the performance recalls the events of the 1930s and 40s in occupied Prague. Burkett has since renamed his theatre 'The Daisy Theatre', further recognizing the impact of the Czech artists in speaking the unspeakable in situations where it was dangerous to speak.

Czech puppetry under Nazism is marked by political commentary under the guise of entertainment. The second example to be discussed in this chapter similarly critiques dictatorship and celebrates popular identity, albeit through very different stylistic devices. This example is drawn from Catalan puppetry, and is characterized by the raw and rough performance of *Mori el Merma* by the Catalan visual theatre company La Claca. This dynamic company emerged during the late 1960s during a revival of Catalan puppetry, emanating from the cultural hub of Barcelona. Catalan puppeteers were at the forefront of cultural resistance to Franco and through the late 1960s and 70s there was a growth in performances which celebrated the popular roots of Catalan culture. Traditions were often shown through puppet shows which sought to take back the right of Catalans to perform their own culture. Performances began to take place in Catalan (previously fiercely repressed), and popular forms, including street festivals with processions of giant puppets, began to emerge once more. Catalan puppetry, like that of Czechoslovakia, had also had a significant history; puppets had played a part in the popular theatre revivals of the nineteenth century, and puppets were used to relay news on street corners. More recently, the puppet had been the subject of modernist experimentation in Barcelona and several puppet plays were written by twentieth-century writers, including Jacinto Grau and Santiago Rusiñol. During the second Spanish Republic, between 1931 and 1939, puppetry was promoted as a means of education. Catalan puppetry, however, was repressed under Franco, as the policy of centralization controlled all cultural products. The puppeteer Joan Baixas was instrumental in the revitalization of the popular puppet in Catalonia; his company, La Claca, which he founded with Teresa Calafell in 1967, drew definitively, noisily and vigorously on the popular tradition. During the 1960s the company began to travel through Catalonia to recuperate popular and folk forms; Baixas was aware that these were in danger of disappearing and his research was an active and conscious attempt to ensure that the traditions were remembered, and also used as part of an assertion of identity. This defiant and assertive stance was followed by other puppeteers and companies; significant among these were Pepe Otal and Jordi Bertran, for whom the reclamation of street performances was a significant contribution to anti-Franco sentiment. Other companies included Marduix, who made performances of Catalan literature; Binixiflat, who performed Catalan folk tales; La Fanfarra, who reclaimed and reinvented the Catalan traditional glove puppet; and Els Comediants, a carnivalesque troupe performing spectacular outdoor performances using the Catalan festival as their main artistic source. During the early 1970s, a wave of visual and physical theatre exploded in Barcelona and surrounding territories. The performances celebrated the communal and the participatory, and avoided the use of Spanish (the language of domination). They also used scatological and grotesque imagery. This was the background for the performance created by Baixas's company in 1978, three years after the death of Franco. The use of the carnivalesque (after Bakhtin's theories of the carnivalesque as a radical and subversive form) in this work is powerful. Government suppression of cultural forms had relaxed during the 1960s and the mood of the people was angry at the years of repression, and celebratory at the dawn of a new political reality. The performances that emerged during these years poked fun at the dictatorship and, through making it grotesque, made it ridiculous. This use of puppetry bade farewell to the 'old order', rejecting all that it stood for and marking the moment of change as Spain moved towards democracy. It responded to a growing urgency in the population to articulate the need to close the door on a particular political chapter and to point the way to the future. This iconic use of puppetry to note, take stock and move on is profound; in Catalan performance history there is perhaps no similarly significant moment of change represented in theatre so visually and dramatically. *Mori el Merma* is the performance which crystallizes most clearly this response and marks the rupture in Catalan political history most clearly.

Several years earlier, La Claca had been approached by the painter Joan Miró, who wished to create a co-production to purge the excesses of the dictatorship. The project was from the start a vehemently political action; but rather than enact a political protest, the artists wished to use puppets to mock the past, making it thus less important:

> We began by talking about the famous and despicable Mr Ubu, whom Miró had come across in Paris. He loved this ridiculous, extravagant and energetic character, who he saw as representing many of the excesses he observed around him... This Ubu that we shared with Joan Miró was really none other than Franco, who had died a year before the beginning of our collaboration. We envisioned the piece as our Requiem Mass for Francoism...' (Baixas 2000: 16)

Mori el Merma ('Death to the Monster') was a performance without dialogue which included the procession, stomping around and physicalization of a grotesque, exaggerated, giant monster, which attempted to control all other puppet characters on stage through force. The monster is clearly Franco (and indeed all grotesque political dictators). During the performance, the monster attempts to scare the audience and other figures, but is mocked and satirized, eventually leading to his death. Little dialogue was used in the performance, and verbal interaction was performed through grunts, cries and incomprehensible comic outbursts of sounds rather than words. The puppets were huge, papier mâché painted figures, distorted with overgrown, shapeless bodies, chaotically and hopelessly trying to take control of the stage as political arena, but failing to. Miró's intentions were explicit:

> ... [My intention is]... to exorcise fears, dispatch the aggressors and their followers who had silenced the ideas and the voice of a whole people, to expel anger and bitterness, and, above all, to show the face

of the tyrant, turning him into an established symbol... [the performances] should be a riot of images made up of colours, forms and gestures of immense expressive force, arranged in a hypnotic balance of scenes that swing between the lyrical, poetic and intimate and the turbulent, frenetic and even brutal. (Fundació Miró 1996: 354)

This performance had huge repercussions nationally and internationally, and comments came from all sides of the political spectrum. Critics of the performance denounced its lack of narrative and dialogue. Those who supported the performance noted clearly its powerful satirical stance and laughed at the vision of the dictatorship.

Most of all, the performance marked definitively the end of the dictatorship and any lingering respect for it. Baixas and Miró make use of the carnivalesque grotesque to unleash collective rage in an atmosphere of laughter. Operating still in a climate of political tension in the period of the transition, the spectacle opened up discussions about political and artistic freedom. It made it acceptable to perform critical performance and it paved the way for the further development of Catalan visual theatre, exemplified in the later celebratory performances of Els Comediants, who made Catalan theatre famous during the 1980s and 90s. This use of the puppetry grotesque as a response to political oppression and trauma is therefore a form which openly satirizes, critiques and protests, while simultaneously asserting collective identity, optimism and artistic autonomy. Although comic, it forced people to question and repudiate the grotesque circumstances they had been living through, opening up spaces for new political ideas. The particular circumstances of Baixas's performance in the late 1970s were what made the performance notable; the temporality of the carnival space as a rite of passage from a distorted and unnatural order moving to a new world of democracy. Unlike the Czech puppeteers, Baixas and his company were able to critique in a celebratory sense and the metaphors were unlikely to be misunderstood.

The two examples discussed thus far have shown puppetry under dictatorship itself, and puppetry during the transition between dictatorship and democracy. The third example is of puppetry created after dictatorship, as a response to the past. The examples are all linked by their use of the grotesque in puppetry to disturb and critique political reality; this last example uses puppetry to critique people's own responsibility in allowing dictatorship to happen. The context is Chile, following the dictatorship of Augusto Pinochet. Puppets here play a different role from those expressed earlier. Rather than representing popular manifestations of repressed culture, they express absence and trauma.

Although there are traces of indigenous effigial forms and masks from pre-Colombian cultures in Chile, the puppet tradition in the country is largely derived from the European colonial influence, with the glove puppet figure of Don Cristóbal being widespread during the nineteenth and for much of the twentieth century. Puppetry increased from the 1950s onwards, becoming commonly used in education. During the Socialist president Salvador Allende's brief period in office, fervent interest in puppets as a popular form grew significantly, perhaps as part of the new government's dedication to the use of traditional arts as part of the country's cultural heritage. University theatres began to offer courses in puppet theatre and there was a renewed revitalization of the form. It was relatively rare, however, for them to be used in adult theatre.

During the period of the dictatorship itself, many artists, writers and performers went underground, were imprisoned or in exile. Due to censorship, and the overbearing fear of arrest, torture and imprisonment, artistic activity was severely dampened and in most cases under fierce control by the military government. Catherine Boyle has extensively documented much of the live theatre that took place during and just after the dictatorship, with detailed commentaries of how the military controlled artistic production.[7] The coup took place in September 1973; during the first few years, the country was in shock. From 1975 onwards, a number of puppet companies were set up, but they were exclusively for children's entertainment, and political puppetry was virtually unknown in the country until the 1980s. Ana Maria Allendes staged a marionette version of Lorca's *Mariana Pineda*, a direct critique of the military government which slipped through the censor's net under the guise of innocuous puppetry, but this is a lone example. A number of Chileans in exile used puppetry to show what was happening back home. The details of the atrocities committed under the dictatorship are well documented; briefly, around 3,000 people were 'disappeared' and around 40,000 tortured or abused, with the military retaining fierce control over the workplace, economy, press, the arts and business.[8] Pinochet remained in power until 1990; during the 1990s many Chileans earlier forced into exile returned, and Chilean society began to return to a semblance of democracy. During the 1990s, interest grew in puppetry and visual theatre as powerful forces to represent psychological trauma. This use of puppetry reflects on and analyses the deep and lasting effects of dictatorship on a society. The situation that is responded to in Chilean puppetry is the sense of a society haunted by absence and by the figures of the disappeared. The leaders of the dictatorship never really acknowledged the atrocities committed; to this day, there are still military figures awaiting trial for human rights abuses, disappearances and torture; most of these keep a deliberate silence and it is therefore likely that some of the disappeared may never be found or their deaths acknowledged. As late as 2013, eight former members of the military government were found guilty of 14 executions without trial during the infamous 'Caravan of Death', a death squad which visited towns through Chile during the first month of the dictatorship.[9] The trauma of losing family, colleagues and friends during the dictatorship, and, above all, the refusal by the military to release information relating to the disappeared, has left Chile a society with unresolved questions. While it is publicly known and internationally acknowledged that torture and execution took place, many families have been left without bodies to bury and without the truth being admitted by those who caused the disappearances. There is thus a feeling of lack of closure and a sense of absence. Further to this, as is common in situations of extreme atrocity, the survivors are often haunted by a sense of guilt at being left behind; of having survived where others have not.[10] Recent political history in relation to themes of trauma suggests that for a productive process of reconciliation to take place, truth needs to be acknowledged.[11] Dramatists in both Argentina and Chile, who deal with aspects of memory, disappearance and torture, return time and again to similar narratives: people wishing to have their stories told. Diana Taylor in particular has noted the potent theme of memory which runs through late-twentieth-century performance of Latin America (Taylor 2003: 35). The softly-softly approach taken by the newly elected government after 1990 was careful not to incite further internal turmoil; democracy was welcomed, but disappointment on many fronts ensued: the ruptures and tears within Chilean society were hard to heal. The performances discussed here therefore respond to the need within the society to understand the effects of the disaster of the dictatorship, and also, in a context where the truth often remained hidden, for the trauma to be acknowledged. Theatre in this context thus provided a space for both statement and therapy; the past could not be changed, but it had to be shown in some way. Taylor notes that in the absence of 'official records', the 'repertoire' – in this case, live performance – serves as a means to remember and to show 'evidence'. Its ephemerality does not make it in any way less valid as knowledge (Taylor 2003: 193). Puppetry, dummies and objects are used to symbolize ghosts, memory and the past, mostly within adult theatre.

Juan Radrigán is one of Chile's foremost twentieth-century playwrights. His plays urge people to bear witness to the truth of Chilean political history and to acknowledge that dictatorship does not end with the formal passage to democracy, but that it causes scars in people's memories and consciousness, in that dictatorship itself is an aberration of the human condition. Radrigán's 1988 play *La Contienda Humana* ('Human Strife') used a puppet/dummy to represent an-Other of the central character, Eladio, a writer. Closeted within his own studio, and unable to write, Eladio is physically trapped in a small room, and symbolically trapped inside himself; the dummy is a facet of his personality that he would like to get rid of, but cannot. It is the truth he cannot forget or purge. It thus represents, in a complex iteration of present and past, both Eladio's own voice tormenting him that he did not save those lost, and also the presence of others in himself – they are eternally present in him through his inability to forget. It is a ghost of the past, but also a visual and material representation of the traces, or scars, of others within himself. The one-person drama shows Eladio in conversation with the dummy and/or with himself, multiple voices from the past/from himself arguing, discussing and in strife about what to do, or what to think. The restrictions of the room itself evoke the situations of the disappeared who were incarcerated in darkened rooms, unable to get out, or to hear the truth about what was happening, with no idea about what would be likely to happen to them or to others. In this representation of the past intersecting with the present, the dummy is not manipulated like a figurative puppet; it hangs, occasionally operated by Eladio as he attempts to bring life to it, and to gain some freedom from its oppressive presence, but unable to do so. Here we see a different view of the puppet: the puppet does not refer directly to the dictator himself, but instead becomes an internal figure within the character's psyche. The distorted form of reality which presented politically under the dictatorship is seen as enacted upon the memory and consciousness of the individual. In doing this, the recurrent theme is twofold: in political terms, it is a reminder that political actions are both affected and effected by the actions of individuals within society; furthermore, it notes that this distortion of reality remains inscribed in the memory and consciousness of those who have experienced it, becoming a part of their ongoing identity. Haunted by the voices from the past, Eladio turns in on himself until he tries to destroy the dummy, finding he cannot do so. Marvin Carlson has noted the 'haunting' effect of theatre productions, where the past is evoked through performance in the present.[12] The Chilean theatre discussed here is haunted by the memories of the lost, and those taken and 'disappeared' continue to enact their presence through the memory of the survivors.

The director Jaime Lorca, co-founder of the physical theatre company La Troppa, gained international recognition in 2004 with a performance of *Gemelos*, based on a novel by Hungarian writer Agota Kristoff, *The Notebook*. Lorca studied at the University of Chile during the years of the dictatorship and was repelled by the stodgy curriculum he and his peers were given. Following his graduation, he wished to separate himself from classical, text-based drama and pursue new theatre forms, in a deliberate attempt to separate himself from all that was repellent about the dictatorship, including dominant hegemonies of theatre. La Troppa was set up as a devising collective with no director; the choice to work in this way directly reflected the company's wish to refuse to follow 'official' processes, as officialdom was associated with the government. The company turned to visual imagery as the best means to express their ideas; words were part of the 'official' hegemony and so physical theatre in the form of masks, puppets, animated objects and physical devising formed the backbone of the company's work. Lorca has consistently used literature over plays to set the context for his performances because he believes it offers more questions, whereas scripted plays already offer the answers; for Lorca, freedom in all contexts distanced him from the military government. Even the name of the company ('The Troop') was an attempt to subvert the use of military terminology to mean something enjoyable, rather than something associated with terror. The context for *Gemelos* was the Second World War: 'One of the things that attracted us was the climate of war...there is an obvious parallel...' (Olavarría 1999: 10). In this performance twin boys explore themes of cruelty and reconciliation during the war when they are mistreated by their grandmother. Puppets are used to represent figures created by the war that people would rather forget: a dead soldier, the suffering figure of the mother, a deserter from the army tortured by the police; and to represent the internal thoughts of the twins. The puppets are operated by human actors in view of the audience in a style which points to their 'uncanny' (after Gross) status between life and death: they are both performers and objects. They are brought onto the stage to tell a particular part of the story, and then discarded, referencing their status as mere objects.

Lorca went on to found a new company, El Viaje Inmovil ('The Motionless Journey'), which explores the relationship between the actor and puppet on stage. In his work, puppets continue to represent hidden aspects of the human psyche. His performances foreground the internal and psychological experience of the individual. Lorca is eloquent on the effects of dictatorship on the artist: 'You are alone, and there is no help available, which obliges you to develop muscles...in the sense that everything comes from inside, you can't look for anything, because the enemy is outside' (García Silva 2010: 412). Lorca believes that theatre offers a kind of therapy to work through trauma; he comments that trauma is inherited through the family, and that since 'Chile [can be seen as] a family',[13] therapy is needed in order to revisit and revise the traumas of the past. Puppets in his work speak the voices of the disappeared, lost, or uncover stories previously hidden. A 2008 production, *The Last Heir*, sets its story in a Chile attempting to gain independence from the Spanish crown; once more puppets perform alongside actors as ghosts of the past. This recurrent theme can also be seen in other work, again using classic texts to explore the trauma of the individual psyche; in *Gulliver* (2006), puppets represent the oppressed people under dictatorship who should be saved by Gulliver.

Both Radrigán and Lorca are prominent examples of an interest in puppetry within adult performance to show hidden voices, and ghosts from the past. The use of puppets and animated objects to tell hidden stories was also seen in performances by the companies El Equilibrio Precario, Periplos and La Luciernaga, which were set up in the late 1980s or 90s. These artists shared an interest in using animated objects, puppets to show 'other' voices, and to working through stories of the past in Chilean history. They use historical events and traditional forms to examine the Chilean character post-dictatorship. Puppets, therefore, in post-dictatorship Chile, often appear to indicate both *absence* of others, and *ghosting*, where the memories of those lost are continually invoked through the actual *presence* of the dummy, effigy or puppet. As a political metaphor this is potent, and is a means to link past, present and future in untangling questions of truth, testimony, identity and memories. Lorca's statements about theatre as 'family therapy' testify to the need to heal through opening up dialogue.

All three examples cited in this chapter note very different ways in which puppets have responded to dictatorship. Under Czechoslovakian occupation, puppetry offers a voice of popular opinion, resistance to the occupation, and the hope of survival. Puppet performance here is twofold: firstly, the *act* of performing itself is important, as it was banned, and thus in itself provides an act of resistance; secondly, the *content* of the performances offers a critique of Nazi occupation and a reassertion of Czech culture. It shows performance as reflecting people's need to perform themselves to themselves in times of crisis; a fundamental way of showing that they are still alive. Following the death of Franco in Catalonia, puppetry represented an enormous collective and carnivalesque sigh of relief at the passing of the dictator, and a comic rejection of everything he had stood for, as well as a powerful and dynamic reassertion of Catalan identity; again, it marks a moment in history where history can be seen to change radically. The opening up of new performance modes offered the way forward for Catalan theatre to take its place on the world stage. Chilean puppet theatre during the 1980s and 90s used symbolic means to channel trauma left by the unanswered questions following the dictatorship. It therefore provided a means for people to speak the truth and to acknowledge the losses, and, further, to acknowledge the scars left on the present by the past. It functions here as a kind of collective therapeutic response to abuse.

All the examples suggest that puppets have a very particular role to play in showing the need for people to play out their collective anxieties and responses to political crisis, and to enable people to materialize those anxieties through performance. The metaphor of the puppet in times of political extremity is potent; it expresses complex aspects of the human psyche. It can be seen as a desire for humans to make sense of their own narratives. It also grapples with the essential paradox of the human condition: not, perhaps, the question of whether we are able to control our own fate, but how far we are able to have a say in the way our lives unfold. Beyond this, puppetry is also often more than the individual voice; frequently, it is the voice of the group, uttering the collective hopes, fears and celebrations of a group of people brought together by history, experience or identity. The desire to make, and to perform, images of the human appears in all cultures; whether this is to acknowledge the power of life itself beyond the individual, or an attempt to represent oneself, it is a remarkable and persisting desire. It is therefore to be expected that puppets in situations of dictatorship have something very clear and powerful to say about the nature of power itself, and about the vitality of the human spirit under such conditions.

Notes

1. See: http://www.vam.ac.uk/content/articles/t/thats-the-way-to-do-it!-a-history-of-punch-and-judy/, accessed 15 July 2015.
2. The most famous image of this in popular literature and film is Collodi's *Pinocchio*, but a more recent example can be seen in Eva Weaver's *The Puppet Boy of Warsaw* (2013). The struggle for freedom of the puppet has also been theorized, notably by Vladimir Sokolov (cited in Jurkowski 2013: 3), who suggests that puppets were created as artistic freedom for the creative will. Conversely, the power of the director to control puppets as opposed to unruly and unpredictable actors has also been much noted by Jurkowski, who cites Lemercier de Neuville and Eleanore Duse lamenting the ease of the puppeteer in contrast to the director in live theatre (Jurkowski 2013: 5).
3. Examples of this, such as the appropriation of Kasper in Germany in the 1930s to bolster Nazi ideology, Mr Punch during World War Two to antagonize Hitler, and the Spanish national puppet, Don Cristóbal, being

used during the Spanish Civil War on both sides of the political spectrum, Nationalists and Republicans, are described by Jurkowski in *A History of European Puppetry: The Twentieth Century* (1996).
4. An exhibition of these is open at the German Historical Museum in Berlin at the time of writing.
5. For further definitions of the grotesque and its manifestations in literature and culture through historical and artistic movements, see Philip Thomson, *The Grotesque*, London: Methuen, 1972.
6. Evidence of eyewitness accounts, drawings of puppet shows in concentration camps and some of the puppets actually used can be found in the Holocaust Museum in Washington (www.ushmm.org).
7. See Catherine Boyle, *Chilean Theatre 1973–1985: Marginality, Power and Selfhood*, Madison: Farleigh Dickinson University Press, 1992, for accounts of repression and censorship of theatre during Pinochet's rule.
8. There are many accounts of the events during the dictatorship, including reports of the abuses from human rights organizations, but for an overview of the abuses, see Alexander Mikaberidz, *Atrocities, Massacres and War Crimes*, Santa Barbara: California, 2013.
9. See: www.bbc.co.uk/news/world-latin-america-25499373, accessed 15 July 2015.
10. The term 'survivor guilt' is defined by Davidson as 'existential guilt and anxiety at surviving in the face of others' deaths' (Shamai Davidson, in Israel Charny [ed.], *Holding onto Humanity: The Message of Holocaust Survivors*, New York: New York University Press, 1992, p. 187). Davidson also notes that survivor guilt is a key element of the reconstruction of human identity after witnessing dreadful events, and is part of the return to a sense of individuality after being part of a faceless community (as treated by others), and is necessary in some way for the restoration of lost human values.
11. See Pierre Hazan and Sarah de Stadelhofen (eds), *Judging War, Judging History*, Stanford: Stanford University Press, 2010, for discussions on the operation and effects of Truth and Reconciliation Committees around the world.
12. While Carlson discusses the experience of the spectator in viewing theatre performances, as an effect of 'déjà-vu', in which the spectator recalls their memory of previous shows, which informs their reading and reception of the one they are seeing, here I use his idea of 'haunting' to suggest that performance invokes the idea of figures from the past in real life. Theatre can thus be seen as an act of haunting in itself, in which the memory of those present informs the recollection of the past and its effect on the present.
13. See: www.revistanos.cl, accessed 15 July 2015.

Bibliography

Baixas, J., 1989. 'Miró, Saura, Matta y el "Teatre de la Claca"'. In *Puck No. 2: Las Marionetas y las artes Plásticas*. Charleville-Mezières: Institut International de la Marionnette.
Baixas, J., 2000. 'Sang, miel, fumée, sable'. In *Puck No. 13: Langages Croisés*. Charleville-Mezières: Institut International de la Marionnette.

Balfour, M. (ed.), 2001. *Theatre and War 1933–1945: Performance in Extremis*. Oxford: Berghahn Books.
Blumenthal, E., 2005. *Puppetry and Puppets*. London: Thames and Hudson.
Carlson, M., 2001. *The Haunted Stage: The Theatre as Memory Machine*. Michigan: University of Michigan Press.
Cramsie, H. F., 1984. *Teatro y Censura en la España Franquista*. New York: Peter Lang Publishing.
Delgado, M., 1998. *Spanish Theatre 1920–1995: Strategies in Protest and Imagination*, Contemporary Theatre Review, Vol. 7, Part 2. London: Routledge.
Dubatti, J., 2007. 'Títeres en la Argentina: cambios conceptuales en la postdictadura'. In Gilmar Moretti and Valmor Nini Beltrame (eds) *Móin-Móin Year 4*, Vol. 4. Jaragua do Sul: SCAR/UDESC.
Fundació Joan Miró, 1996. *Miró en Escena*. Barcelona: Fundació Joan Miró.
García Silva, P., 2010. *Una Mirada a la compañia 'La Troppa'*. Santiago: Universidad de Chile.
George, D., and J. London (eds), 1996. *Contemporary Catalan Theatre: An Introduction*. London and Sheffield: Anglo-Catalan Society.
Gounaridou, K. (ed.), 2005. *Staging Nationalism: Essays on Theatre and National Identity*. Jefferson: McFarland & Co.
Gross, K., 2011. *Puppet: An Essay on Uncanny Life*. Chicago: University of Chicago Press.
Harpham, G., 1976. 'The Grotesque: First Principles', In *Journal of Aesthetics and Art Criticism*, 34: 4, pp. 461–8.
Jameson, F., 1981. *The Political Unconscious: Narrative as a Socially Symbolic Act*. London: Routledge.
Jané, J., 2001. *Les arts escèniques a Catalunya*. Barcelona: Cercle de Lectors/Galàxia Gutenberg.
Jurkowski, H., 1996. *A History of European Puppetry: Volume Two: The Twentieth Century*. Lewiston, NY: Edwin Mellen Press.
Jurkowski, H., 2013. *Aspects of Puppet Theatre*, 2nd edition. Basingstoke: Palgrave Macmillan.
Kayser, W., 1981. *The Grotesque in Art and Literature*. New York: Columbia University Press.
Martín, J. A., 1998. *El Teatre de Titelles a Catalunya*. Montserrat: Publicacions de l'Abadia de Montserrat.
Minguet Batllori, J., 2000. *Joan Miró: l'artista i el seu entorn cultural*. Montserrat: Publicacions de l'Abadia de Montserrat.
Nuñez-Parra, M., and A. E. Puga, 2008. *Finished from the Start and Other Plays*. Evanston: Northwestern University Press.
Olavarría, P., 1999. 'Trabajamos en base a la libertad y a la imágen absoluta'. In *Vistazos*, 20. Santiago: Ediciones División de Cultura del Ministerio de Educación.
Taylor, D., 2003. *The Archive and the Repertoire: Performing Cultural Memory in the Americas*. Durham and London: Duke University Press.
Villegas, J., 1998. *Propuestas Escénicas de fin de siglo*. Michigan: Gestos.
Zegers Nachbauer, M. T., 1999. *25 Años de Teatro en Chile*. Santiago: Ministerio de Educación, División de Cultura.

6
Against Order(s): Dictatorship, Absurdism and the Plays of Sony Labou Tansi

Macelle Mahala

> Theatre leaves us ample space while the world around us unrelentingly seeks to take it over. (Sony Labou Tansi)

Congolese playwright, director and novelist Sony Labou Tansi created a large body of work during his most prolific period, the late 1970s to mid-1990s, while living through a series of political coups and authoritarian governments.[1] For two decades, Tansi's plays, novels and essays offered an array of diverse forms of resistance to dictatorship. Alternately celebrated for his international success,[2] harassed by state authorities,[3] and posthumously accused of ethnic factionalism,[4] Tansi's career is a searing example of an artist writing through authoritarian conditions and political upheavals. Educated under a repressive colonial system, Tansi witnessed independence and the establishment of a Marxist state, participated in political efforts that brought about the creation of a new constitution and the emergence of an ostensibly multiparty democratic system in 1992, and suffered from the state of violence and chaos into which the Congo was plunged after the parliamentary elections of 1993 were contested and the nation entered a prolonged period of civil strife that eventually escalated into civil war. At the end of his life Tansi suffered personally for his political activities when his passport was revoked; the medical treatment he sought for himself and his wife in France for their AIDS-related illness was fatally delayed and they both died upon their return to the Congo in 1995 (Thomas 2002: 57; Kirkup 1995: n.p.). Thus, when Sony Labou Tansi wrote about dictatorship and authoritarianism, he did so from the perspective of one who had lived his entire life under a series of repressive governments. His works express both the will to survive and the difficulty in doing so under such repressive circumstances.

Tansi also engaged directly in a variety of political activities. After participating in the effort to institute multiparty elections, he served as an elected representative of the Makélékélé neighbourhood of Brazzaville (Thomas 2002: 56). In his most overtly political piece of writing, the 1990 essay 'An Open Letter to Africans c/o the Punic One-Party State', Tansi denounced the Marxist rhetoric of his nation's one-party system as a mask for dictatorship:

> We deluded ourselves into believing that the single party was sufficiently revolutionary to become the manufacturing site of national unity... How childish to have sought to resolve the problem of national unity by the simple and shameful negation of our differences. (Tansi 2007: 271)

This letter did directly, in the political arena, what the author had been doing indirectly in his novels and plays for well over a decade: it decried the abuse of state authority. For instance, Tansi makes essentially the same point in the following passage from his 1979 debut novel, *Life and a Half* (*La vie et demi*):[5]

> Dictatorship is not a revolutionary weapon but a means of oppression just like moral and physical torture... You can't fight fire with fire. You can't burn the dictatorship; it's the dictatorship that burns... There is no softer form, only steps, that swallow you... no, we did not burn hell. (Tansi 2011: 95)

The similarity of these two passages reveals the overlap between Tansi's artistic work and his political practice. Both passages express the desire to speak directly to the national crisis. Tansi did not, however, see himself as politically didactic in his art. In the 'Warning' (preface) to *Life and a Half*, he wrote:

> As Ionesco said, I don't teach, I invent... To those who seek an engaged writer, I offer an engaging man... *Life and a Half* becomes this fable that sees tomorrow through today's eyes... The day when I'm given the chance to speak about any present day whatsoever, I will not take a thousand paths to get there, in any case, not a path as tortuous as this fable. (2011: 3–4)

Here, Tansi veils his critique of contemporary politics in the assertion that the book is a work of fiction that depicts a dystopian future. Tansi claims, in this passage, that he does not want to be an *écrivain engagé* (engaged writer), a term which, in the original French, implies a certain degree of political posturing and armchair intellectualism.[6] By rejecting this label Tansi sought to protect himself from both censorship and the pejorative connotations associated with being a political writer. The 'inventedness' of his work served him well in both of these arenas; he was not heavily censored or politically persecuted until the end of his life and he gained international acclaim as a writer whose novels and plays both spoke to and transcended the specifics of national politics.

Tansi's works perform survival in two specific ways. First, his early novels and plays functioned as forms of thinly veiled dissent that foreshadowed his later political writing. The fact that Tansi was able to express dissent through fictionalized satires and fables a decade before he felt comfortable speaking directly to the political situation in the Congo supports an interpretation of his artistic work as a 'rehearsal for the revolution' (Boal 1985: 155). Second, and to my mind more complexly, all of Tansi's theatrical works are, in essence, anti-authoritarian because they express a wild creativity that is implicitly resistive to a single way of living or viewing life. This kind of subversive creativity flourishes under dictatorships precisely because it affirms a complexity of being that authoritarian regimes, as a rule, seek to disallow.[7] Tansi's plays remain uniquely creative responses to authoritarian and postcolonial repression drawn from ancient Greek drama,[8] traditional Kongo theatre practices and religious traditions (Tansi 1996a; 1996b), Afro-francophone interpretations of absurdism (Kesteloot 1996: 4–13), and his own wild imagination. The multidimensionality of his plays transgressed the status quo of both the political and literary contexts out of which they emerged.

Two of Tansi's most transgressive plays are *La parenthèse de sang* (*The Parenthesis of Blood*) (1981)[9] and *Qui a mangé Madame d'Avoine Bergotha?* (*Who Has Eaten Madame d'Avoine Bergotha?*) (1995). These two plays use innovative theatrical forms to express resistance to authoritarian control. While Tansi's work has been described as a literature of pessimism,[10] these two plays reveal the 'absurdity of hopelessness' that seemed to sustain Tansi in the midst of repressive circumstances. In *Life and a Half* he describes himself as 'me, the one who speaks to you about the absurdity of the absurd, me, unveiling the absurdity of hopelessness' (Tansi 2011: 3). As this passage illustrates, Tansi saw hope as a critical component of his artistic expression. Therefore I do not find the characterization of Tansi's work as Afro-pessimist to be a sufficient exploration of his dramatic ethos. Pessimism implies a defeated acceptance of the status quo, whereas the stage action in Tansi's plays always involves passionate struggle. Although their resistance is frequently expressed in ways that involve fantasies of retributive acts of physical and sexual violation, the farmers, soldiers, women and civil servants who resist authoritarian power in Tansi's plays never passively accept their oppression or act in ways that suggest that the environment around them is impervious to change. These characters struggle against large and petty injustices until they cannot go on,[11] and in some cases continue even after their lives have ended; there are instances in both *Who Has Eaten Madame d'Avoine Bergotha?* and *The Parenthesis of Blood* where characters *sauter la frontière* (jump the border between life and death) (Tansi 1995: 102) and continue their struggle in a kind of *neant* (void) (Tansi 1981: 63). These actions give a metaphysical and spiritual dimension to Tansi's plays; he depicts political and material struggles as part of a greater religious cosmology.

In her article 'The Turning Point in the Francophone/African Novel: Eighties to Nineties', Lilyan Kesteloot argues that Tansi and other African novelists of the time expressed 'the African absurd'. Kesteloot describes the defining characteristic of this genre as 'a metaphysical dimension which goes beyond their main topic and which can be measured by the malaise which they emit' (1996: 6). I see the metaphysical qualities of Tansi's plays as the expression of Kongo religious beliefs and these will be specifically discussed later on in this essay. The malaise that is prevalent in many of Tansi's plays, on the other hand, results from Tansi's use of violence as one of his dominant dramaturgical tools. There is a continuous threat of violence in both *The Parenthesis of Blood* and *Who Has Eaten Madame d'Avoine Bergotha?* that creates a pervasive sense of dread. In a 1993 interview (published in 1999) Tansi stated, 'I oppose violence because I find it absurd. Unfortunately, I live in a world where violence operates on all levels' (Herzberger-Fofana 1999: n.p.). The frenetic energy of Tansi's characters, who seek to survive in violent environments where nothing but the assertion of power makes sense, reveals the 'devaluation of ideals, purity, and purpose' (Esslin 1961: xix) common to many absurdist texts without ever expressing any kind of resignation to the extreme environmental conditions in which the characters find themselves.

While the characterization of Tansi's work as a work of the African absurd has shed a significant amount of light on the purpose and form of Tansi's oeuvre, I believe that this term needs to be retheorized in order to acknowledge and further explore the resistive and compelling aspects of both Tansi's work and our understanding of absurdism as a theatrical modality. In his book *Reassessing the Theatre of the Absurd* (2011), Michael Bennett claims that Martin Esslin focused too much on meaninglessness and hopelessness in *The Theatre of the Absurd* (1961), the seminal text that essentially defined the genre. Bennett claims that the power of absurdist theatre lies instead in how absurdist plays innovatively 'make life meaningful given our absurd situation' (4). I would similarly argue that the characterization of Tansi's work as Afro-pessimist and as part of the African absurd needs to be revised so that the emphasis is not upon pessimism or malaise per se, but rather on the ways in which Tansi showed the vitality of life amidst horrific circumstances. In *Contemporary Francophone African Writers and the Burden of Commitment* (2011), Odile Cazenave and Patricia Célérier describe the aims of Afro-pessimism as 'addressing and keeping in check a specific type of postcolonial domination…It constitutes all at once a reactive/adaptive/transgressive form of political resistance' (26). This articulation of the aims of Afro-pessimism is patently not pessimistic and might serve as fruitful ground for recontextualizing a particular vein of African literature that uses absurdist techniques to express a postcolonial response to dictatorship, corruption and other forms of political exploitation. For instance, while all of Tansi's plays express deep anguish and malaise, they do so in remarkably creative and resistive ways. The critique of dictatorship and the creative resistance to a repressive social order that is expressed in both *The Parenthesis of Blood* and *Who Has Eaten Madame d'Avoine Bergotha?* illustrates a unique application of absurdist theatre in a postcolonial context.

The Parenthesis of Blood is one of Sony Labou Tansi's most hopeful plays in that it depicts an inspiring and unequivocal resistance to authoritarianism. While the majority of Tansi's works feature dictators struggling to maintain power through whatever means are available to them, *The Parenthesis of Blood* stands out as a play that concerns itself primarily with the powerless – the family of a murdered revolutionary and the rank and file soldiers they encounter. Written for a drama competition sponsored by Radio France,[12] the play takes place in a village where the body of the murdered revolutionary, Libertashio, has just been buried. Libertashio's family members are not particularly political. Their intention is to mourn their relative and move on with their lives. A band of government soldiers who come in search of the dead rebel ironically end up revolutionizing the family and several other members of the village. The soldiers' cruelty prompts the villagers to perform a variety of resistive acts that range from coping mechanisms and survival strategies to direct acts of opposition and martyrdom.

One of the ways this play expresses resistance to state authority is by showing the injustice of being compelled to profess as true something that blatantly contradicts one's own lived experience. Tansi conveys this indignity with both humour and pathos in a scene between Libertashio's daughter, Ramana, and the soldier Marc. This scene is representative of the kind of dark humour that Tansi used to reveal the coping mechanisms of those living under authoritarian regimes where the official truth is obviously false to the populations that are required to adhere to it. When Ramana tries to tell Marc that the man he is searching for is dead and that she would be willing to go to the capital to testify to this, Marc replies:

> We've told the capital. It doesn't believe us. *(He drinks)* The capital doesn't have ears. It asks us to search, we search. Libertashios? We'll find fifty, we'll find a hundred. As long as the capital tells us to search, we will search. *(Pause)* We don't search to find; we search to search. *(Pause)* If you say that Libertashio is dead, it's you that must be killed. I, myself, don't have a death wish. (Tansi 1981: 21)

This scene exposes the tension between the official party line and the lived experience of the common people. The soldier has accepted the 'truth' of the capital as a survival mechanism and counsels Ramana to do the same.

Writing about how power influences and dictates societal understandings of truth, Michel Foucault asserts:

> Truth isn't outside power, or lacking in power... Each society has its regime of truth, its 'general politics' of truth: that is, the types of discourse which it accepts and makes function as true; the mechanisms and instances which enable one to distinguish true and false statements, the means by which each is sanctioned; the techniques and procedures accorded value in the acquisition of truth; the status of those who are charged with saying what counts as true. (Foucault 1980: 131)

As Foucault points out, cohesive societies have little need for censorship; they have subtler mechanisms that authenticate certain perspectives as true and others false. The fact that there is disagreement over what is true in *The Parenthesis of Blood* suggests that the government has failed to fully integrate the people into its 'regime of truth' and vice versa. The consequence of proclaiming Libertashio dead is so dire precisely because there is a conflict regarding social order and state authority. The actions of the soldiers underscore this schism. As the only onstage representatives of the government, even the soldiers cannot manage to adhere to the official party line. In a moment of forgetfulness, Marc admits that Libertashio is indeed dead, at which point his men assassinate him and appoint another soldier from among the remaining ranks to be their sergeant (Tansi 1981: 24). This same sequence of events happens to four different sergeants over the course of the play. The mechanical nature and rapidity of these 'promotions' renders these acts humorous, albeit grotesque. The ridiculousness of these acts allow the audience to reaffirm their belief in an alternate regime of truth while at the same time revealing the catastrophic consequences of speaking such a truth in an authoritarian environment that forbids such utterances.

It is the tension between these two competing regimes of truth that serves as the central conflict of this play. On one side, the government, referred to as 'the capital', has declared Libertashio a traitor, and as such, a valuable scapegoat and target who is not allowed to be dead. 'Libertashios... we'll find a hundred' (Tansi 1981: 21). On the other side, for the townspeople, Libertashio is a martyred revolutionary whose spirit lives on and serves as a source of inspiring courage and resistance to the illegitimate authority of the state. The most overt acts of resistance to violence and repression in this play involve characters who invoke Libertashio's name during moments in which they defy the authority of the state. It is significant that Libertashio's nephew, Martial, a character whose name is derived from the Latin word for war, is mistaken for his uncle, a character whose name clearly signifies liberty. Martial's transformation from political apathy to martyred revolutionary is depicted as an inevitable response to extreme repression:

> *Martial*: Do you know what is said deep down within me? Me, who never approved of my uncle? And now, on the eve of my death, it speaks: Long live Libertashio. It repeats, over and over. All of my insides are like a song: long live Libertashio. It escapes from inside of me. *(He shouts)* Long live Libertashio! Long live Libertashio! Long Live Libertashio!
> *Cavacha*: Cut off his right hand. Gouge out his right eye. Avoid unnecessary loss of blood. He must die by pieces. Cut off the ears. Cut off the nose.

> *Martial tries heroically to cry out but the pain vanquishes him.* (Tansi 1981: 43)

The articulation of Martial's cry of resistance as an insuppressible song is a beautiful metaphor for how acts of liberation can erupt out of even the strictest martial law.

Another example of a resistive act within this play involves the character Madame Portès. After being condemned to death by the soldiers, each member of Libertashio's family is given a last request. One of Libertashio's daughters, Aleyo, requests to be married before she is executed. The soldiers prepare the marriage feast, the priest is summoned, and Madame Portès arrives as one of the wedding guests. At first things go well, 'like it was real' (Tansi 1981: 47), but eventually each wedding guest becomes drawn into conflict with the soldiers so that, by the end of the party, everyone (including the priest) is imprisoned and condemned. After Madame Portès shouts 'Long live Libertashio' out of anger and frustration, all her subsequent speech becomes unintelligible to the other characters as well as to the audience:

> *Madame Portès*: No! It's too much! *(She shouts)* Long live Libertashio! *She shouts while running all over the place like a lunatic.* Long live Libertashio! Long live Libertashio! *She begins to speak an incomprehensible language.* Voueza nazo cala mani Libertana...
> *Cavacha*: What a funny language... Is she crazy? Too bad! We won't be able to understand her last request. (Tansi 1981: 54)

The linguistic and presumably mental schism expressed in Madame Portès's speech and actions simultaneously show the anguish of being subjected to authoritarian repression, an active resistance to that repression, and the difficulty of communicating a victimized subjectivity within the dominant regime of truth. It is significant that Madame Portès is rendered incomprehensible, not silent. I see this character's speech as an effort on the part of the playwright to express the difficulty of communicating subaltern subjectivities on the international stage. By depicting Madame Portès's speech as meaningful, but not comprehensible, Tansi is expressing through performance the issues Gayatri Spivak broaches in her seminal essay 'Can the Subaltern Speak?' (1988: 271–313). By shutting down the linguistic field, Tansi effectively illustrates that it may be impossible for an (often Western) untraumatized audience to fully understand the acts of victimization that his plays depict. By creating a distance between what is said and what is understood, Tansi highlights the limits of language as a form of communication that is always mitigated by the subjectivity of both speaker and listener.

While largely unintelligible, Madame Portès's speech is also clearly an expression of dissent. In one of the last documentaries made about the absurdist playwright Harold Pinter before his death (*Working With Pinter* 2007), Pinter's long-time collaborator Henry Woolf stated that, for Pinter, his characters' use of language was not for the communication of information or ideas, but rather to defend themselves within their given territory. Similarly, Tansi uses Madame Portès's speech, which is not part of any codified language and thus has no direct meaning, to convey a resistive and unique perspective that the actress who embodies the role must clearly demonstrate and support through body language and vocal utterances. In this way the performance of Madame Portès's speech expresses an absurdist sensibility through innovative (non)language created to reveal the character's struggle for personal autonomy while at the same time remaining sufficiently artistically abstract to suggest multiple meanings, psychological states and emotional resonances.

Madame Portès's speech is one example of how Tansi's dramaturgy was able to destabilize language in a way that created greater symbolic meaning and interpretative possibilities. Another example is the play's enigmatic title, *The Parenthesis of Blood*. This title is not only abstract and therefore open to multiple interpretations, but is purposefully incomplete: a single parenthesis, instead of enclosing a complete thought (which is the grammatical function of a pair of parentheses), is necessarily fragmentary. The formal prologue that begins the play highlights the purposefulness of this fragmentary use of language: 'It begins – in this painful century...this parenthesis of blood, this parenthesis of entrails. It begins, but it is not yet finished' (Tansi 1981: 5). Both the title and the prologue suggest that the play takes place in a moment of violent rupture that calls for a literary register that is similarly jarring and disjointed.

The significance of Tansi's experimentation with language becomes even more complex when one considers that Tansi wrote in French, a language that was imposed upon him in the particularly brutal manner of a colonial education. When asked in a 1993 interview (published in 1999) about the inspiration for his first novel, for instance, Tansi explained:

> I started my schooling in the old Belgian Congo and the instruction had taken place in the maternal African language. When I left

Kinshasa for Brazzaville, I suffered a shock. All new residents received a sort of baptism or how do you say it in English: 'tossing' [hazing] ... They were ingenious in their discovery of outlandish corporal punishments ... the students had instituted the custom of a 'symbol' for the recalcitrants that consisted of a big box of s[hit] that was attached to our necks. I was the preferred target of my fellow students, because I had only learned Kikongo, my maternal language. I was often obliged to lock myself in the bathroom to escape this kind of bullying. (Herzberger-Fofana 1999: n.p.)

As this passage shows, for Tansi, learning French became a matter of survival that involved frequent humiliation and victimization.[13] Perhaps because of this, Tansi often depicted himself as an author who was both alienated from and violently overtaken by the language he used to create his most masterful works. For instance, in *Nation-Building, Propaganda, and Literature in Francophone Africa* (2011), Dominic Thomas translated and referred to a published interview from 1986 between Ifé Orisha and Sony Labou Tansi in which Tansi famously stated:

I write in French because that was the language in which the people I speak for were raped, that is the language in which I myself was raped ... One must say that if between myself and French there is anyone who is in a position of strength, it is not French but I. I have never had recourse to French, it is rather French that has had recourse to me. (ix)

There is a survivor's tenacious spirit in Tansi's expression in the former passage; he implies that he has the right, the authority and the strength to write in French precisely because of, and not despite, the colonial victimization that he experienced. In this passage, Tansi positions himself very differently from postcolonial writers such as Ngũgĩ Wa Thiongo, who chose to reject their colonial educations and wrote and staged plays solely in their indigenous languages.[14] By writing in French and frequently collaborating with French artistic and cultural institutions, Tansi was able to reach an international audience and take advantage of the substantial resources available to him through the French publishing houses and theatre festivals with which he worked.

Tansi's assertion that he wrote in French because that was the language in which his people were raped supports my conception of his innovative linguistic forms as both a record *of* and a resistance *to* a legacy of colonial oppression. There is a distance in his plays between what is said and what is experienced that speaks both to the imposition of colonial languages upon colonized subjects and to the use of French in absurdist literature to depict the violence and emptiness of language as an always insufficient method of communication. Language is menacing in many absurdist texts and it is even more menacing in Tansi's work because of its association with the egregious colonial exploitation of the former French and Belgian Congos. In both *The Parenthesis of Blood* and *Who Has Eaten Madame d'Avoine Bergotha?* Sony Labou Tansi used his virtuosic command of the French language to critique the exploits and aftermath of French and English colonialism.

In *The Parenthesis of Blood*, the soldier Marc links his difficulty with speaking French to his country's dysfunctional attempts at democracy in the post-independence period. In the original French, Tansi played with the orthographic similarities between the words *urines* (urine), *urnaux* (urinals), and *urnes* (ballot boxes). The juxtaposition of 'urinal' with 'ballot box' is intentionally vulgar; the association of voting with urinating implies a corrupt and ineffectual political process. In the following passage, I have roughly translated these words as 'pissing', 'pisser' and 'polls' to express the orthographic similarities and approximate meaning of the original passage:

> *Marc*: When you are called to ... piss ... to the pisser, how do you say it in fluent French? When one chooses a ... There are moments where their French gives me a pain in the ass [...] There are words in their language that you can't ... you can't ... You can't come to say them like they say them. [...] So when you go to p ... to pis ... You, tell me that word again.
> *Soldier*: Polls.
> *Marc*: With the article.
> *Soldier*: The polls.
> *Marc*: When you go there, when you go to the (slowly) p-p-polls, you don't say: we don't want this type of guy. You choose the b-boss. We protect him for you. And after all that, you think we're cruel [...] In our country, that's democracy. (1981: 22–3)

Given the political history of the Republic of Congo and the coups, assassinations, exiles and executions of political leaders such as Alphonse Massamba-Debat, Marien Ngouabi and Pascal Lissouba during the late 1970s, shortly before this play was written, Tansi seems to be offering a critique of a post-independence period in which the contestation of presidential power fundamentally derailed both the socialist and democratic systems of government envisioned by the leaders of the independence movement. Tansi likens voting in such a dysfunctional system to 'pissing' in this passage, thereby expressing the frustration of voting in a democratic system where elections were frequently contested and leaders abused their authority. The brutality of the soldiers in the play coupled with their attempts to speak French 'correctly' suggests that the use of force to seize and maintain presidential power in what is now the Republic of Congo during the 1970s and 80s was both a reflection and amplification of the violence and repression used during the colonial period in which there were also egregious human rights violations and little democratic representation within the government.

Sony Labou Tansi would go on to create an even more abstract and extreme dramatic portrait of political dysfunction in his play *Who Has Eaten Madame d'Avoine Bergotha?* which premiered in 1989 during the sixth International Francophone Festival in Limoges, France. The play was developed and performed by Tansi's company, Rocado Zulu Theatre. Like many of his novels, *Who Has Eaten Madame d'Avoine Bergotha?* features the brutal dictator of a former colonial nation. As a part of his efforts to suppress any opposition, the play's main character has banished all men from the tropical island he rules with the exception of 'his immediate family members and those Inseminators of the Party appointed by him' (Tansi 1995: 35). The dictator's name, Walante, is a near homonym of the French word *volunté*, a word meaning the power or desire to make something happen. The entire play is a struggle between Walante's effort to force his will upon the people of the island and the efforts of those who seek to thwart him. The latter includes his daughter and nephew, who attempt to overthrow him in a coup d'état, and Yongo-Loutard, a man who, dressing as a woman named Madame Bergotha to avoid exile, uses the attractiveness of his 'feminized' body as a tool to survive and form allegiances with those on both sides of the political conflict. This complex plot interweaves the struggle for political power with sexual desire, filial obligation, infatuation and homoeroticism in a power struggle that never clearly resolves.[15] At the end of the play Walante ends up in the land of the dead, but it is unclear precisely how he got there. In many ways, *Who Has Eaten Madame d'Avoine Bergotha?* is a more experimental play than *The Parenthesis of Blood*, which, despite its allegorical nature and linguistic liberties, still communicates a succinct and understandable plot. The latter play, by contrast, contains 24 scenes (many of which are no longer than a paragraph) and a cast of more than 20 characters with names such as 'the criers who cry' and 'the man with the voice of the devil and all the devilish bankers' (Tansi 1995: 36). The dramatic scope of *Who Has Eaten Madame d'Avoine Bergotha?* is immense. There are scenes that focus on ordinary citizens, scenes that focus of the ruling party, scenes that focus on soldiers, and scenes that focus on the opposition. The stage action is ritualized and abstract. All these elements combine to form a fragmented, recondite parable that is open to many possible interpretations.

Although *Who Has Eaten Madame d'Avoine Bergotha?* is clearly an indictment of dictatorship, the play can also be read as an expression of cosmic justice grounded in Kongo religious beliefs and spiritual practices. In two essays posthumously published in 1996, Sony Labou Tansi wrote about his use of specific African performance conventions and religious practices.[16] These essays provide brief summaries of specific rituals for readers and scholars from other cultural traditions. As such, the essays provide insight into the role Kongo practices played in Tansi's dramaturgy. They are similar in both form and purpose to Wole Soyinka's seminal essay 'The Fourth Stage', in which the Nobel laureate offered a brief explanation of the traditional Yoruba beliefs and religious practices he incorporated into his plays (1988: 142). Tansi's essays on Kongo ritual practices reveal how Tansi tied the political criticisms implicit in *Who Has Eaten Madame d'Avoine Bergotha?* to larger understandings of cosmic justice and spiritual equilibrium.[17]

Two of the Kongo performance rituals Tansi calls attention to are *le théâtre des rois ou insulte publique* (the theatre of kings or public insult) and *le Lembe ou culte de la seconde naissance* (the Lembe or cult of second birth) (Tansi 1996: 353). These rituals are clearly evident in *Who Has Eaten Madame d'Avoine Bergotha?* For instance, one can interpret the many ritualized diatribes against the dictator Walante as an adaptation of the theatre of public insult. Tansi defines this tradition as follows:

> Public insult is a form of happening that takes place at *lumbu* (the royal court), notably by the princes, governors, ambassadors, and the opposition party just after the coronation of the king. Dissent is permitted. The representation lasts one or more days. (1996a: 354)

In Tansi's view, this traditional form of theatre operated as an expression of political opposition. Within the confines of the performance space, criticism of the new leader was encouraged during inauguration ceremonies that publically recognized the viewpoint of the opposition and presumably encouraged the new leader to be cognizant of these criticisms during his subsequent reign.

In Tansi's plays, where dictators silence and attempt to crush all opposition, these criticisms are broached in the absence of the leader. Scene two of *Who Has Eaten Madame d'Avoine Bergotha?*, for instance, begins with a group of citizens insulting Walante and criticizing his takeover of the political process:

> *Peasant A*: (Foolish laughter. He listens to his radio): Walante, your capital smells of sludge and rot. Ha ha hi ho hié![18] Your independence smells like it's burning! How can one call 'capital' these stones without soul that screw these stinking patches of sun? Party of flies, of cockroaches, and of dead rats! Walante! You are good to baptize 'capital' this river of filth that doesn't remain a river of filth, but a capital of stagnant quarantine. (Tansi 1995: 38)

This scene consists primarily of peasants heaping verbal abuse upon Walante and comparing the absolute power of the old colonial system to the newly seized power of Walante's government. Although the play is ostensibly set on a fictional tropical island, Tansi implicitly references the the Republic of Congo and the Democratic Republic of Congo by referring to a river that runs through the capital. This is clearly a reference to the Congo River, which separates Brazzaville from Kinshasa, the two capitals of the Congo nations. Using a fictionalized setting, Tansi seems to have adapted a traditional form of theatre that sought to reconcile opposing political parties and created a less conciliatory and more politically transgressive theatrical work.

As in *The Parenthesis of Blood*, in *Who Has Eaten Madame d'Avoine Bergotha?* Tansi links the use of language to the potential for bodily harm. The peasant farmer who rails against the dictator in scene two resorts to both figurative and literal uses of urine and fecal matter as he engages in a corporal-linguistic revenge fantasy. 'Walante, I piss in your throat! (He pees)... Walante pee-pee! Walante poo-poo! I shit in your throat!' (Tansi 1995: 38). This fantasy serves as an expression of rage from a person who is powerless within the socio-political structure of the play. The man's curses and urine are some of the limited ways he is able to literally 'mark' his dissent.

Tansi's fecal references also echo the liberal use of the word 'shit' as a (for 1896) shocking expletive in one of the earliest plays of the French avant-garde, Alfred Jarry's proto-absurdist text *Ubu Roi*. *Who Has Eaten Madame d'Avoine Bergotha?*, like *Ubu Roi*, liberally references bodily excretions and features an insatiable dictator who threatens to 'eat' his opponents. Tansi updates Jarry's use of such a threat as a metaphor for a despot's rapacious greed by adding a racial and colonial dimension that recognizes Walante's dictatorship as entwined with a parasitic colonial past. In scene 18, for instance, Walante dismisses the English envoy, Sir Birmingham, with the following words:

> We know how to die, Mister Birmingham. Over there, you don't have anything much to teach us. Convey my position to your country. Afterward, die miserably in some corner of their earth, for I take care to avoid poison by eating the most offensive guests. (Tansi 1995: 90)

By referring to cannibalism, Tansi references the colonial use of such racial tropes as justification for political and economic domination. In this play, however, it is the former colonial power that is depicted as the source of a malignant savagery. This point is reinforced when Tansi describes Walante as a mixed-race man of English origin, literally *a metis de souche anglais* (a mix from an English stump) (Tansi 1995: 35). This suggests that the absolute authority Walante wields is a result of his being an 'offshoot' of the former colonial power and of learning to deploy the apparatus of the state in similarly exploitative ways.[19] Through these references, Tansi portrays the civil rights abuses and anti-democratic tendencies of post-independence regimes as a kind of after-effect of colonial rule.

Walante is depicted as someone who not only 'eats' his enemies, but also eats his nation, his children and his people. For instance, Tansi frames the play as a battle between the dictator and his cook, Touma, when a minor character in the beginning of the play addresses the audience, stating: 'Walante, Touma, two names, two cuisines. Who will boil this night in the patriotic fabric of corpses?' (Tansi 1995: 37). Because Touma plans and executes a coup against him, Walante is also depicted as one who is eaten up by the power and wealth that consumes him. The title of the play is misleading. It is not Yongo-Loutard disguised as Madame Bergotha who is eaten, but rather Walante, who ends up in a kind of limbo, wandering aimlessly in the land of the dead. The headings of scenes such as 'Scene odor of onion' and 'Scene tomato sauce' reinforce the metaphor of the dictator becoming a kind of sacrificial meal (Tansi 1995: 57, 84).

Throughout the play, Tansi depicts the ruling party as both the preparer of the meal and its chief offering. This extended metaphor ties the postcolonial critique Tansi is making to *Lembe*, the religious ritual. The *Lembe* ritual served to reconnect a rich man to his community through a religious intervention in which members of the clergy spoke to the man in a sacred space about the nature and quality of his soul. The rich man figuratively 'died' during the ritual and was 'resurrected' by the savants (Tansi 1996a: 354). The performance of the ritual also presumably redistributed some of the man's riches among the community, for he was required to pay for the ceremony. I believe the ambiguity that closes *Who Has Eaten Madame d'Avoine Bergotha?* comes from Tansi's adaptation of this ritual. The woman Walante encounters in the land of the dead represents a *Lembe* savant, the one who shows the rich man the state of his soul. To the question, 'Why are you out at this hour, you must have a troubled soul?' Walante responds, 'I have killed all of those who have troubled my solitude. This night, I have a very troubled soul' (Tansi 1995: 100). After hearing this the woman tells Walante that they are alike, having both lost love. Before attempting to seduce him in a symbolic act of communion, she tells him the story of her lover, exiled by Walante's decree against men. After failing to pique his interest, the woman says, '[W]hat will it cost for you to kiss me, even with the other side of your soul...what do you have in the place of a heart?' To this Walante replies, 'An island, Madame, that eats me alive and kills me' (Tansi 1995: 102). Walante is unable to accept the woman's offer of salvation, which has both Kongo and Christian religious overtones, because he is being consumed by the nation he attempted to exploit.[20] Just as Tansi inverts the theatre of public insult to act transgressively rather than conciliatorily, he similarly inverts the *Lembe* ritual so that the main character is not redeemed, but clearly damned. This ending allows the audience to imagine spiritual retribution for those who perpetuate acts of egregious violence and repression. The religious components of this play also complicate previous understandings of absurdism as predominantly atheistic. In African theatre, absurdist works frequently incorporate both Christian and indigenous spiritual beliefs and practices as is the case in both *The Parenthesis of Blood* and *Who Has Eaten Madame d'Avoine Bergotha?*

Tansi's plays are pieces of theatre that act against order(s) in the sense that they depict a resistance to authoritarian control through innovative theatrical forms that express the condition of people who find themselves in extreme circumstances. The environment is in essence 'out of order' and the characters within this environment are in a continual state of misalignment even as some of them attempt to repair themselves and their body politic using both political and spiritual means. I have focused on competing regimes of truth in *The Parenthesis of Blood*, the frequent references to bodily functions as metaphors for ridding both the body and the body politic of contagion, the destabilization of language to create greater symbolic resonances, and the representation of the separation between life and death as porous in *Who Has Eaten Madame d'Avoine Bergotha?* as the culminating evidence of Tansi's depiction of a people actively struggling against political, social and spiritual schism. The resistive, redemptive and transgressive aspects of these two plays alongside their despair, anger and rage create an innovative absurdist register with which Sony Labou Tansi was able to reveal 'the absurdity of hopelessness' in plays that remain both disturbing and sustaining.

Notes

1. Sony Labou Tansi was the pen name of Marcel Ntsoni. Tansi chose his last name in honour of fellow Congolese poet Tchicaya U Tam'si, who also used a pen name meaning 'little leaf that speaks for its country' in Kikongo, the authors' native language (Taylor 2008: 784–5).
2. In addition to performing his plays in the Congo with his troupe, Rocado Zulu Theatre, Tansi presented work at many international festivals. His numerous awards included the Grand Prix de l'Afrique Noire, the Prix Francophonie and the Prix Ibsen, making him one of the most celebrated international Francophone writers of his time (Tansi 1995: 2).
3. In his essay 'Sony Labou Tansi: Commitment, Oppositionality, Resistance', Dominic Thomas (2002: 55) recounts how Tansi was transferred multiple times during his career as a teacher because of his political views.
4. In Phyllis Clark's interview with Jean Clotaire Hymboud (1998: 183–92), Hymboud suggested that Tansi became embroiled with ethnically based animosities during local municipal elections in the mid-1990s.
5. Quotations from this novel are taken from Alison Dundy's English translation. Unless otherwise noted, translations of all other works quoted in this chapter are my own.
6. See Cazenave and Célérier 2011:1 and Ndiaye 2003: 112–13.
7. For instance, writing about the varied artistic responses to the Brazilian dictatorship of the 1970s and 80s, Claudia Calirman states, 'Far from paralyzing the creative production of the country...a period rife with suspicion and censorship stimulated newly anarchic practices, at times aggressive and at other times disguised in subtler modes of artistic intervention' (2012: 2).
8. Tansi made a living as an English and French instructor and was thus well versed in Western classical literature, which he frequently made use of in his novels and plays. For example, one of the characters from *Who Has Eaten Madame d'Avoine Bergotha?* directly addresses the audience, proclaiming, 'I was raised in the cult of Sophocles and his company' (Tansi 1995: 38).
9. The English translation of this play is often referred to as *Parentheses of Blood* (Alexander 1986:1), but I prefer to use the literal translation of the French, *The Parenthesis of Blood*, because of Tansi's penchant for linguistic wordplay and idiosyncratic use of the French language.

10. 'Afro-pessimism took a number of forms, most tellingly a literature of experimentation in the vein of Sony Labou Tansi, provocatively exploring the possibilities of the grotesque' (Cazenave and Célérier 2011: 25).
11. Here I am referencing the end of Samuel Beckett's 1953 novel *The Unnameable* (*L'innommbale*): 'One must go on, I can't go on, I will go on' (216). This grim determination defines the ethos of many absurdist texts.
12. Both *The Parenthesis of Blood* (1981) and *I, Undersigned Cardiac* (*Je soussigné cardiaque*) (1979) were winning plays of the Concours théâtral interafricain, a competition sponsored by Radio France International for theatre in Francophone Africa (Tansi 1981: 2).
13. For another description of the humiliation Tansi was subjected to in his colonial school, see Thomas 2002: 86.
14. See *Decolonising the Mind: The Politics of Language in African Literature*, 1986.
15. While I refer to *Qui a mangé Madame d'Avoine Bergotha?* as it is commonly translated in English (Who Has Eaten Madame d'Avoine Bergotha?), avoine is the French word for oats. Therefore, another accurate translation would be *Who Has Eaten Madame Oats of Bergotha?* The reference to oats is just one of many culinary references in the play, and the title, when translated this way, also implies both an explicit sexual act and the more generic concept of sowing one's wild oats. All of these linguistic resonances are incorporated into the action of the play.
16. Phyllis Taoua discusses Tansi's status as an international figure writing for a Western audience in *Performing Identity: Nations, Cultures, and African Experimental Novels* (2001: 193–219).
17. Existing scholarship already details the ways in which *The Parenthesis of Blood* references Kongo religious practices and performance traditions (Nkashama 1990: 33–6; Kouvouama 1997: 95–106).
18. This appears to be onomatopoeia, perhaps a representation of something between a laugh and a cry.
19. See also Riesz 2000: 100–28.
20. The fact that Walante's offer of salvation is sexualized underscores the gender politics of the play, where men who cannot act politically are depicted as emasculated. For a fascinating treatment of gender politics and queer performativity in Tansi's work, see Julin Everett's Must *La Victime* Be Feminine? Postcolonial Violence, Gender Ambiguity, and Homoerotic Desire in Sony Labou Tansi's *Je soussigné cardiaque* (2013: 1–18).

Bibliography

Alexander, L., 1986. *Parentheses of Blood*. New York: Ubu Repertory Theater Publications.
Beckett, S., 1953. *L'innomable*. Paris: Les Éditions de Minuit.
Bennett, M., 2011. *Reassessing Theatre of the Absurd: Camus, Beckett, Ionesco, and Pinter*. New York: Palgrave Macmillan.
Boal, A., 1985. *Theatre of the Oppressed*. New York: Theatre Communications Group.
Calirman, C., 2012. *Brazilian Art under Dictatorship: Antonio Manuel, Artur Barrio, and Cildo Meireles*. Durham: Duke University Press.

Cazenave, O., and P. Célérier, 2011. *Contemporary Francophone African Writers and the Burden of Commitment*. Charlottesville: University of Virginia Press.
Clark, P., and J. C. Hymboud, 1998. 'Sony Labou Tansi and Congolese Politics: An Interview with Jean Clotaire Hymboud'. *Research in African Literatures*, 29: 2, pp. 183–92.
Dévésa, J. M. (ed.), 1996. *Sony Labou Tansi: Ecrivain de la honte et des rives magiques du Kongo*. Paris: L'Harmattan.
Esslin, M., 1961. *Theatre of the Absurd*. New York: Anchor Books.
Everett, J., 2013. 'Must *La Victime* Be Feminine? Postcolonial Violence, Gender Ambiguity, and Homoerotic Desire in Sony Labou Tansi's *Je soussigné cardique*'. *Research in African Literatures*, 44: 1, pp. 1–18.
Foucault, M., 1980. *Power/Knowledge: Selected Interviews and Other Writings 1972–1977*, C. Gordon (ed.). New York: Pantheon Books.
Herzberger-Fofana, P., 1999. 'A L'Ecoute de Sony Labou Tansi, Ecrivain: Un entretien avec Sony Labou Tansi, Ecrivain'. *Mots Pluriels*, 10, available online at http://www.arts.uwa.edu.au/MotsPluriels/MP1099slt.html, accessed 10 August 2013.
Jarry, A., 2012. *Ubu Roi ou les Polonais*. Hamburg: Tradition Classics.
Kesteloot, L., 1996. 'The Turning Point in the Francophone/African Novel: The Eighties to the Nineties'. In E. D. Jones and M. Jones (eds) *New Trends and Generations of African Literature*, Vol. 20 of *African Literature Today*. London: African World Press, pp. 4–13.
Kirkup, J., 1995. 'Sony Labou Tansi: Obituary'. *Independent*, 20 June, available online at http://www.independent.co.uk/news/obituaries/sony-labou-tansi--obituary-1587368.html, accessed 1 August 2013.
Kouvouama, A., 1997. 'Sony Labou Tansi ou l'utopie pratiquée'. In M. Kadima-Nzuji, A. Kouvouama, and P. Kibangou (eds) *Sony Labou Tansi ou la quête permanente du sens*. Paris: L'Harmattan, pp. 95–106.
Ngũgĩ, W. T., 1986. *Decolonising the Mind: The Politics of Language in African Literature*. Nairobi: Heinemann.
Nkashama, P. N., 1990. 'La mémoire du temps… Le temps de la mémoire dans le théâter de Sony Labou Tansi'. *Notre Librairie*, 102, pp. 33–6.
Riesz, J., 2000. 'From "L'état sauvage" to "L'état honteux"'. *Research in African Literatures*, 31: 3, pp. 100–128.
Soyinka, W., 1988. *Art, Dialogue, and Outrage: Essays on Literature and Culture*. New York: Pantheon.
Spivak, G. C., 1988. 'Can the Subaltern Speak?' In C. Nelson and L. Grossberg (eds) *Marxism and the Interpretation of Culture*. Urbana: University of Illinois, pp. 271–313.
Tansi, S. L., 1979. *Conscience de tracteur*. Dakar: CLE.
Tansi, S. L., 1981. *La parenthèse de sang*. Paris: Hatier.
Tansi, S. L., 1995. *Théâtre 1: Qui a mangé Madame d'Avoine Bergotha?, Qu'ils le dissent, qu'elles le beuglent*. Montréal: Editions Lansman.
Tansi, S. L., 1996a. 'Les Kongo: Cinq Formes de Théâtre Essentiel'. In J. M. Dévésa (ed.) *Sony Labou Tansi: Ecrivain de la honte et des rives magiques du Kongo*. Paris: L'Harmattan, pp.353–5.
Tansi, S. L., 1996b. 'Les Sources Kongo de Mon Imagination'. In J. M. Dévésa (ed.) *Sony Labou Tansi: Ecrivain de la honte et des rives magiques du Kongo*. Paris: L'Harmattan, pp. 359–62.

Tansi, S. L., 2007. 'An Open Letter to all Africans c/o the Punic One Party State'. In T. Olaniyan and A. Quayson (eds)*African Literature: An Anthology of Criticism and Theory*. Malden, MA: Blackwell.

Tansi, S. L., 2011. *Life and a Half*. Bloomington: Indiana University Press.

Taoua, P., 2001. 'Performing Identity: Nations, Cultures, and African Experimental Novels'. *Journal of African Cultural Studies*, 14: 2, pp. 193–219.

Taylor, J., 2008. 'Rereading Tchicaya U Tam'si'. *Antioch Review*, 66: 4, pp. 784–90.

Thomas, D., 2002. *Nation building, Propaganda, and Literature in Francophone Africa*. Bloomington: Indiana University Press.

Thomas, D., 2011. 'Introduction'. In S. L. Tansi, *Life and a Half*. Bloomington: Indiana University Press.

Working with Pinter: A Master Class for the Stage. 2007. [Film]. Dir: Robert Fox. New York: Films Media Group.

7
Surviving Censorship: El-Hakawati's *Mahjoob Mahjoob* and the Struggle for the Permission to Perform

Samer Al-Saber

The history of censorship in Palestine remains mostly undocumented and unstudied. Because the complex history of the land and its people spans from antiquity to the present, the periodization, scope and disciplinary orientation of most historical accounts on censorship would likely prevent an in-depth chronology in a single study. However, the emergence of the Israel/Palestine conflict at the end of the nineteenth century presents a compelling case for the examination of the topic. The foundation of Israel and the near eradication of Palestinian cultural production in 1948 have left a significant mark on the history of censorship of performed content in Palestine. The extensive record of controversial encounters between the Israeli authorities and Palestinian artists since 1948 suggests that Palestinians have contended with a constant stream of closures, bans and arrests (Slyomovics 1991: 18–35).[1] The struggle for the permission to perform, which serves as a reminder of the disparity in power between the occupier and the occupied, characterizes the relationship between the Palestinian theatre artists and the State of Israel. To perform, the artists had to survive the interventions of the Israeli office of censorship.

The legal necessity of obtaining a performance permit indicates that a state structure of institutionalized censorship prevents artists from physically presenting and publicly expressing their chosen message. This legally justified requirement institutionalizes the 'permission to narrate', a concept that Edward Said introduced in the aftermath of the 1982 Israeli invasion of Lebanon (Said 1984: 27–48). He suggested that

142 *Surviving Censorship*

the entrenchment of Zionist narratives in the Western public sphere served as a form of censoring Palestinian narratives. Thus, 'balanced' news reporting on Israeli issues in American news media disregarded the Palestinian experience as propaganda. He argued that the criteria of presenting the Palestinian story opposite the Israeli one created false symmetry and served as a form of 'democratic censorship'. In other words, he demanded a 'permission to narrate' the Palestinian narrative independent of the Zionist narratives which are prevalent in the West. Similarly, I suggest that, in the presence of a vast power disparity, a state can use legal means and military influence to suppress performed narratives. The idea of a 'permission to perform' adds a live bodily dimension to Said's idea of a 'permission to narrate'.

In its 1992 report on Israeli censorship in the Palestinian Occupied Territories (OPT), the London-based human rights organization ARTICLE 19 accounted for extensive Israeli controls over the dissemination of the Palestinian narrative in the press and human rights violations concerning academic freedom and artistic expression. In the section entitled 'Attacks on Artistic Freedom', the report states:

> Plays, art exhibitions and public dance and music performances have been restricted and censored. Many have been banned on the grounds that the military censor considered that they might incite rebellion, that they posed a threat to peace and order, or that they threatened the security of Israel. Palestinian artists who refused to comply with regulations have been arrested and detained or have been banned from performing or travelling. (Essoulami 1992: 26)

In reconstructing the performance conditions of El-Hakawati's production of *Mahjoob Mahjoob*, it becomes clear that the antagonistic relationship between the theatre artists and the Israeli authorities played a significant role in the development and, in some cases, the 'de-development' of Palestinian theatrical production.[2] Furthermore, the history of this production shows that the censorship of Palestinian content abroad occurred in the form of skewed media representations or acts of vandalism. As I reconstruct and document the history of this production, I rely on interviews with Palestinian theatre artists, the original unpublished text, and journalism of the period. I have also used previously unexplored censorship records from the Israel State Archive.

In 1979, El-Hakawati Theatre Troupe began their rehearsals of *Mahjoob Mahjoob*, which challenged the Palestinian image of heroic characters.[3] In the play, 'six characters, in their own spaces on stage and after their own purposes, had been isolated from the world and thus developed their own habits and traditions' (El-Hakawati 1980: 1).[4] The central character in the play, Mahjoob, is a Palestinian anti-hero who struggles with keeping his own traditions and nationalistic goals in the face of his desire to survive under occupation. The word 'mahjoob' indicates a person who is covered up, concealed, obscured or veiled. The title of the play suggests that Mahjoob has been isolated or veiled from reality. Although his naiveté causes him trouble on occasion, he attempts to survive by avoiding conflict. The play begins by introducing each major character in their specific area on stage: the bureaucrat Abu Hmayd stamps blank papers, the teacher dreams of creating his own newspaper as he sits behind a makeshift typewriter made of garbage, the merchant Abu Ali cleans his store and shouts for customers to buy cans of goods, Mahjoob cleans a table at his café and attempts to kill flies, Im Mustapha works her land as she reminisces about her pre-1948 home in Jaffa, and the young woman Lily Asfour stands on a ladder drawing images/messages of resistance on a large blackboard. In the opening of the play, the characters intrude on each other by throwing their garbage in each other's workspace, thus causing immense disorganization. Meanwhile, a dejected Lily Asfour works diligently to depict 'the Palestinian reality' on her blackboard. Breaking the monotony of everyday life, the characters call a meeting to solve the historical problems facing their people. The meeting satirizes the summits and elections of the Arab leaders of the twentieth century. The characters begin with a ritual election, which Abu Hmayd rigs to win 99 per cent of the vote for leadership. To protest the unproductive meeting, Mahjoob decides to die, signalling the absurdity of the character and the play. In the ensuing funeral, the characters place his body in a casket, from which he listens to their account of his personal history. His indigenous Palestinian biography provides an exemplar of the Palestinian struggle for self-preservation.

In the remainder of the play, a series of flashback scenes depict Mahjoob's struggle to survive as a Palestinian under occupation. Accompanied by the sound of an owl, he is born at midnight on the cursed day of 29 February, which arrives every four years. He also dies on the same date. After being dropped on his head as a child, he develops a physical disability characterized by his head swaying to the right as he walks. After asking too many questions in school, he argues with his teacher. As a result, he insults his teacher by calling him a 'donkey', then drops out of school. To sustain his lower-class living, he attempts to sell water, but fails. He also works in his uncle's shop. As a young adult, he demonstrates his love to a girl by unskilfully knitting her a scarf. After he enlists the help of Im Mustapha the girl accepts his marriage proposal because nobody refuses a request by this neighbourhood matriarch. His first struggle against the authorities occurs during the Jordanian rule of East Jerusalem before 1967 when he refuses to stand for the Jordanian national anthem. The Jordanian police attempt to arrest him, but he beats them up to the sound of admiration from the audience in the cinema. During the 1967 war, Mahjoob cheers for the successes of the Arab armies on the radio, only to learn that the Arab victory is an elaborate lie. A few days later, as Israeli soldiers demand his identification in a commuter taxi, none of his fellow Palestinians assists him. Needing sustenance, he works at an Israeli factory, but is fired because the police interpret the colours of his attire as a depiction of the Palestinian flag. After the 1967 war, he leaves the country as some of his countrymen have done, immigrating to America, where he works menial jobs. He saves his salary, and then pays an American woman to marry him on paper in order to obtain a green card. Having earned a legitimate identity, he returns home victorious.

During the Jerusalem Municipality elections, Mahjoob receives leaflets from various political factions. He joins the Histadrut (General Federation of Labourers in Israel), but leaves when fellow Palestinians call him an apostate and a traitor for participating in Israeli politics. Soon after, his friend Abu Hmayd pays him ten liras to vote in the Jerusalem Municipality elections. As a civil servant in the municipality, Abu Hmayd is required to vote, but he does not dare appear at the elections, which East Jerusalemites have boycotted to resist naturalizing the occupation (El-Hakawati 1980: 31). To appear at the elections constitutes character suicide among his family and neighbours. Under financial pressure, Mahjoob accepts the offer and goes in disguise. As the only Palestinian in the voting booth, Israeli television films him in the act. With cameras rolling, Mahjoob pretends to be a janitor, a believable function for an Arab in an Israeli establishment. A series of oppressive events leads Mahjoob to resist the occupation in unusual ways: he is arrested and imprisoned for attempting to help an activist, and then he is accused of possessing 'suspicious packages'. To retaliate against this accusation of terrorism, Mahjoob ridicules the police by planting 'suspicious' packages throughout the city, represented in the production by the auditorium. Towards the end of the play, he meets President Anwar Al-Sadat during Sadat's trip to speak before the Knesset in 1977. They discuss the problem of normalization with Israel and the negative image of the Egyptian president among the Palestinians. When Mahjoob speaks earnestly of the struggles under occupation, Al-Sadat leaves him behind, presumably heading to the Israeli Knesset for his historic speech. Finally, the cast of characters remembers Mahjoob's feeble attempt to become a police officer, which causes more traffic problems. When the characters complete their overview of Mahjoob's history, the casket explodes. All characters, including Mahjoob, fall to the ground. Then, Mahjoob appears to face their perceptions of his character, and challenges their own shortcomings. In the last image of the play, the cast leaves the stage, while Abu Hmayd carries on his pointless meeting by himself. In this ending, El-Hakawati satirically critiques the ineffective Arab summits concerning Palestine and provokes the audience to take control of their own destiny, breaking through the collective casket, which represents both the occupation and their own failures.

In the early 1980s, this production presented a departure for Palestinian cultural production. In a rare depiction, the character of Mahjoob represented not only the struggles of East Jerusalemites with sarcasm and self-criticism, but also with indirect satire against occupation. Inspired by timely local issues, the play aimed at challenging the colonial aims of the Israeli government in East Jerusalem. Since 1967, the Israeli government had taken systematic steps to annex the city, occupying it 'legally' by extending the sovereignty of the West Jerusalem Municipality over the demographically Arab East Jerusalem (Lustick 2008: 286). From the Israeli perspective, this occupation by municipal expansion became a fait accompli by 1980, when the Knesset passed the Jerusalem Law declaring 'undivided' or 'reunified' Jerusalem as Israel's capital. The de facto annexation may have functioned administratively at the Israeli state level; however, in the daily lives of the occupied Palestinians, both Christians and Muslims, the new political and bureaucratic realities translated into daily obstacles and questions of self-determination: how would the Palestinians communicate with the Israeli security apparatus? Who would collect their taxes and what services would they receive in return? What kind of representation would they vote for in elections, if any? What kind of identity paperwork would they present or honour? How would they preserve their Palestinian/Arab/religious identity in a self-proclaimed exclusively Jewish state? But most importantly, how would they survive a military occupation intent on transforming not only the physical and demographic identity of their city, but also their legitimate presence as Arab citizens to mere residents of the city?

Emerging from the onset of insecurity among Jerusalemites, *Mahjoob Mahjoob* merged the political struggle against occupation with the individual desire to survive in the character of the play's anti-hero. Director François Abu Salem critically evaluated the schism between the everyman figure and image of the national hero:

> The minute you create heroes within a national movement, you start to deviate slightly toward national chauvinism and racism. It makes you feel superior to others, more moral and just than others. But it's not true. We have a just cause, it's true, but as people we're just completely normal. (DeBare, Blum, and Abu Salem 1985: 232)

Mahjoob redefined the character of the typical Palestinian protagonist, who had often been presented as a heroic figure in contemporary poetry and folklore, as an everyman caught between the politics of the Jewish state and the demands of traditional Palestinian society. This naïve post-national anti-hero strives for normalcy. He yearns to fall in love, be married, start a family and work peacefully, but he is caught in unusual conditions that force him to behave like an accidental hero. When he fakes his own death, he becomes privy to the interpretations and analysis of his comrades in the struggle. While his intentions have never been heroic, his people construct a novel posthumous narrative that does not reflect his perception of his own life.

In spite of his complex post-national condition, Mahjoob was played with a clearly recognizable Palestinian identity. The production implemented a simplified local Palestinian dialect and common struggles in occupied East Jerusalem. Simultaneously, the narrative situated the character in relation to foreign situations. For example, Mahjoob's journey towards attaining an American green card represented the hopes of a colonized subject to realize the American Dream. His attempt to become a traffic cop showed his desire to earn a living at any cost, even if this employment could be interpreted as collaboration with the occupier's municipality. Thus, this everyman figure becomes a vehicle to represent less of the heroics of armed national resistance and more of the everyday strategies of 'making-do' in otherwise restrictive and usually unforgiving circumstances.

In order to reach a wide audience locally and abroad, El-Hakawati adopted a 'poor theatre' approach. Local critics responded to the simplicity of the production, which depended primarily on a set composed of chairs, a casket, a ladder and two platforms. Using a directorial strategy he developed while staging a previous play, *Al-ʿatma*, Abu Salem staged the events of the present on the first platform and the flashback stories on the second. Selective lighting and appropriate accompanying sound effects defined the space for each character.[5] Characters changed costumes throughout the play. Jackie Lubeck designed and wore the most elaborate costume as an American girl, standing tall in a direct allusion to the Statue of Liberty. In overt satire of popular American culture, she carried a Coca Cola can and wore a costume inspired by the American flag, roller skates and large sunglasses (Lubeck 2012).

On 7 December 1980, based on an application for a performance permit by Jackie Lubeck, the Israeli censorship committee approved the play.[6] In the file, an official's explanatory note indicates that Lubeck provided an English-language summary of the play and suggested that a group of Hebrew University students were to perform it at the YMCA in English.[7] Although the summary follows the events of the play almost verbatim, it intelligently presents a depoliticized text. For example, Mahjoob's retaliation against incessant police searches by placing suspicious packages throughout the theatre is described as 'Mahjoob has a difficult time throwing out his garbage. In response, he leaves garbage all over town'. The play's critique against participating in the West Jerusalem Municipality elections is described as 'Mahjoob goes to vote and is surprised when he is interviewed by television'. Mahjoob's fight against the Jordanian police is described as a fistfight with ushers. His argument over his identity with the Israeli army became 'he cunningly proves that he is who he is by pointing out his height and the colour of his eyes'. His interrogation over wearing what resembles the colours of the Palestinian flag became 'Mahjoob is questioned about the outfit he wears to work one day'. Lubeck's summary also codes the ending of the play by concealing its subtext. In the last paragraph of her summary, she describes:

> The play ends with some of the characters demanding a meeting to discuss if Mahjoob is alive or dead, while other characters refuse to join the meeting, and start pulling people out of [their] seats, and asking them to leave the hall.[8]

Despite this benign summary, on stage and in performance the characters symbolically called for revolutionary resistance by provoking the audience to break through the casket of occupation.

Opening in December 1980, the production of *Mahjoob Mahjoob* launched the troupe to local fame. After opening at the YMCA, the troupe toured to the villages of the Galilee. In his critical review, Talal Abu Afifeh stated, 'the play *Mahjoob Mahjoob* posed many issues people have lived for many years before or after 1967 under the Israeli occupation. The play showed people's suffering in the street, in school, at work, and at home' (1980). However, their successes were short-lived. A few hours before their performance in Nazareth on 16 January 1981, the Nazareth police delivered an order from the Israeli Ministry of the Interior to cease all performances because the troupe did not adhere to the text of the play. *Al-Itihad* newspaper reported:

> The audience of Nazareth, which came to watch the play, transformed the performance into a popular meeting of protest, in which a decision was made confirming that banning the play continues and escalates the policies of suppression in the Occupied Territories, the stalking of male and female students, and political assassinations. (1981: 6)[9]

Both the theatrical director and head of the Municipal Cultural Centre of Nazareth, Riad Massarweh, and the former Knesset member and prolific Palestinian author Emile Habibi condemned the ban, expressing anger at the double standards of 'Israeli democracy'.[10] In his word to the crowd, Habibi stated:

> Actually, the decision to ban the performance surprised us, not because we are naïve, but because we did not realize that the hostility towards democracy had reached this level. To reach the point of banning the performance of a play, a progressive one but still a play, indicates that the deterioration in Israel reached an unimaginable limit.

To appease the crowds' demands for a performance, the troupe improvised a new scene alluding to the suppression of the censorship. They sat on stage, physically tied to their chairs with their mouths taped shut (Muallem 2010). Under Habibi's editorship, *Al-Itihad* pronounced that El-Hakawati's alternate scene 'served as the funeral of Israeli democracy, which could not handle the play' (Habibi in *Al-Itihad* 1981: 6).

Without a doubt, El-Hakawati's presence in the city of Nazareth contributed significantly to the spirit of resistance on this fateful night. Since 1948, the city had become a political hub for Palestinian citizens of Israel, also known as the 1948 Palestinians. The Communist Party of Israel, to which the Palestinian political leadership belonged, became the only political platform for Palestinian participation and mobilization at the state level. Furthermore, in the arena of cultural production, resistance poets such as Mahmoud Darwish, Samih Al-Qassim and Tawfiq Zayyad had produced a model for cultural resistance through their publications in the party's Arabic newspaper, *Al-Itihad*, and public performances in Galilee. This model of resistance prompted the cultural critic and West Bank political activist Mohammad (Abu Khaled) Al-Batrawi to declare 'We are all the children of Nazareth', referencing the Nazarenes' assertion of their Palestinian identity on the 1976 Land Day demonstrations (Al-Batrawi 2010).[11] The presence of the Palestinian political and cultural elite at the performance of 16 January 1981 provided the support that both El-Hakawati and their audience needed to resist the orders to close the evening's proceedings. Although the troupe failed to perform the scheduled play, the series of improvised scenes and speeches of resistance, in lieu of the play, became a theatrical happening in itself.[12]

A letter dated 6 January 1981 caused these shocking events in Nazareth. Presumably sent by the Ministry of the Interior's censorship office, an official secretly reported on El-Hakawati's performance in the village of Iʿbilin. He analysed the play in 11 bullet points, each titled according to the site or his perception of the action in the scene: Checkpoints, Freedom, Colours, House Confiscation, Immigration to the United States, Municipality Elections, Campaign Episode, Coffee Shop, Explosive Materials, Sadat and Shekels. The description of the production appears sensitive to events concerning issues of oppression, the desire for freedom, the colours of the Palestinian flag, the allusions to soldiers and police, satirization of security procedures, and all events concerning political matters such as elections and President Anwar Al-Sadat. Although Israel was not explicitly mentioned in the play, the official reported an intention to disgrace the state. He also noted that the play empowered, incited and provoked the Arab minority towards hatred and division in the state of Israel through expressions or words invoking 'uprising'. He provides exemplary lines from the play: 'here, forbidden to ask questions', and the radio announcement of 'we won, we want freedom'. After his summary, he states: 'In my opinion, there was no justification to give the organizers a permit for this kind of play.'[13]

Internal correspondence among members of the censorship committee suggests that the letter prompted an internal investigation to determine how the troupe received the performance permit for *Mahjoob Mahjoob*. On 5 January 1981, the responsible committee decided to censor the play citing a significant difference between the English-language summary and the performed text. Believing they were misled by the application, they questioned the initial premise that a group of Hebrew

University students were to perform the play at the YMCA. One letter noted that the 'secret service agent' who wrote the initial report had indicated that the play was full of hatred towards the state of Israel. The events also prompted further investigation of troupe member Jackie Lubeck and her partner, François Gaspar, who had been reported to be the author of the play.[14] The investigation produced a magazine article by *Al-Yassar Al-Arabi* (*The Arab Left*), in which Abu Salem discusses the theatre in Palestine as an integral participant in Palestinian resistance against occupation. Providing an excerpt in Hebrew translation, this investigative report explained that the Beirut-issued weekly magazine was funded by 'the terrorist organization of George Habash and Nayef Hawatmeh', referencing the PFLP, the Popular Front for the Liberation of Palestine (Youssef 1981: 20).[15] Based on the article, a member of the council provided his personal opinion that François Gaspar and his wife, Jackie, both described as 'the motor' behind this company, had obtained the permit under false pretences. By playing in Arab villages, the production had realized 'the goals of terrorist organizations' that sought 'to undermine the existence of the state'.[16]

This tangential and inaccurate link between El-Hakawati and the PFLP proved to be a source of concern for the Israeli government and its office of censorship. From the late 1960s until the late 1980s, the PFLP had forced itself on the political scene as a powerful faction which adopted programmes of armed, cultural and social resistance to the occupation. The PFLP spokesperson, novelist Ghassan Kanafani, believed that cultural production was necessary 'to understand the land on which the rifles of armed struggle stand' (Kanafani 1968: 9).[17] Despite its influential civic engagement in the Palestinian struggle and its declared pan-Arab socialist ideological agenda, the PFLP gained a reputation for being a radical faction after a number of well-publicized guerrilla operations, including the hijacking of El-Al, TWA, Pan-Am, and Swissair planes. In Israel and the West, the faction's reputation became synonymous with terrorism, as did the Palestine Liberation Organization (PLO), which functioned as the umbrella organization of several Palestinian factions. Meanwhile, some operatives, such as the PFLP's Leila Khaled, became known as stars of Palestinian resistance, even during their captivity as convicted terrorists. Established connections to the Japanese Red Army and the KGB had made the PFLP and its splinters a significant enemy of the Israeli military apparatus.[18]

In an interview with the PFLP's newspaper, *Al-Hadaf*, François Abu Salem described the implicit connection between theatre and armed struggle in the aftermath of Black September, the name given to the battles between Palestinian militias of resistance fighters and the military forces of the Hashemite Kingdom of Jordan:

> September of 1970 was the spark that opened up many fields of resistance. When our people felt that armed struggle was struck down in Jordan in 1970, they had to create the conditions to assist resistance in all its forms. The theatrical movement was a facet of resistance, and an affirmation of the Palestinian national character. (Abu Salem 1982: 48)

Despite the absence of any proven financial or ideological links between the troupe, the play and the PFLP, the Israeli censors and their investigators believed theatrical activity posed a dangerous threat. For the censors, to undermine the 'existence of the state' suggested an act of treason by a fifth column of Palestinians. Without a doubt, El-Hakawati's critique of the policies of Israel and their open identification with the Palestinian cause of liberation provoked the censors to interpret their commentary in the press as being ideologically directed. In reality, connections between El-Hakawati and the PFLP did not exist in any official capacity beyond their shared goals of affirming Palestinian identity.

But the allegation of realizing the 'goals of terrorist organizations' became an underlying justification for banning the play. According to a Hebrew-language newspaper article included in the censorship file, the troupe requested a 'decree nisi' against the censorship decision and provided the council with a Hebrew-language translation of the text for further evaluation.[19] Upon review, a council member determined that the text had undergone a special process in order to 'look naïve'. Noting omitted elements and phrases from the performance in Iʿbilin, the member also questioned the continuity in the dialogue and 'illogical leaps' between topics. He summarized the case as a 'sophisticated act of fraud' and recommended continued censorship of the play. In a statement dated 26 January 1981, a second member of the council suggested that the full three-hour Arabic-language production contained implicit 'incitement' and 'ridicule' of freedom in Israel and the state's military. He agreed to permit only the Hebrew text, which El-Hakawati had provided as part of their appeal. By the end of January, *Al-Fajr* and the *Jerusalem Post* reported the lifting of the ban and the council's condition for the troupe to follow the approved text without further changes.[20]

In practice, the censors and the security apparatus could not enforce the restrictions in the permit unless the production was monitored at every performance. The troupe's improvisational style, coded language and indirect depiction of local issues presented a difficult interpretational challenge, especially for non-native informants. El-Hakawati's *Mahjoob Mahjoob* never depicted any slogans or political symbols. Rather, it represented characters caught in unusually difficult circumstances and their attempts to survive them. This strategic choice not only assured the production's survival under the watchful eye of the censors, but also creatively encouraged audiences to root for Mahjoob, the comedic anti-hero. For example, when Mahjoob is wrongly accused of terrorism, he retaliates by leaving 'suspicious packages' in various places in the city. Here, the play ridicules the orientalist stock character of the Arab as terrorist. In addition, the harmless packages represent physical and cultural Palestinian content, which is banned on grounds of 'state security'. Thus, El-Hakawati satirizes Israeli censorship's obsessive concerns with Palestinian theatre makers, who the Israeli establishment perceives as propagandists.

With the ban overturned, the troupe performed the play 36 times in 26 villages and cities in the West Bank, the Galilee and the Triangle area.[21] Despite the acquisition of the performance permit, the troupe continued to encounter further harassment, suggesting that legal permits did not assure the production's survival. In various towns such as Al-Lyd and Majd al-Kroom, they faced interruptions and threats of closure by the police, the secret service or local municipalities.[22] In the absence of well-equipped theatres, the production often played in the Arabic schools of Palestinian villages in Israel. Recalling this period, actor Edwar Muallem noted: 'Despite our permit, some school principals received threats... sometimes they allowed us to play in the school yard, sometimes they didn't' (Muallem 2010).

By the end of 1981, they had followed the initial run of the play with a European tour that included 61 performances in England, Poland, Belgium, West Germany, Holland, Sweden, Norway and France (*Al-Fajr* 1982: 14). In London, Ned Chaillet of *The Times* reported the uniqueness and purpose of the troupe: '*Mahjoob Mahjoob* is a new exception, the work of a Palestinian company called El-Hakawati, a group subject to Israel and Israeli censorship but clearly intent on speaking of that country's occupation of Palestine' (1981). The *Jewish Chronicle* reported 'a significant police presence outside the theatre' (1981a: 68). Rosalind Carne of the *Financial Times* explicitly outlined the anxiety underlying the troupe's presentation of their play in Europe:

> The Riverside Studios, mindful of Jewish backers, has reportedly stated that *Mahjoob Mahjoob* is not anti-Israel. This is bunkum.

Nobody mentions the PLO – but their spirit lurks behind the entire production. Mahjoob personifies a population crushed; his two failed attempts to escape from his coffin and his ultimate success can have only one interpretation. (1981: 22)

In addition to highlighting the English sensitivity towards the Jewish community, Carne accurately interprets that Mahjoob's attempts to escape the coffin indicate an effort to overcome the imprisonment of the occupation. Accordingly, his ultimate success suggested that the Palestinians liberate their nation. But her equation of Palestinian resistance with the PLO implied that El-Hakawati functioned as a politically motivated mouthpiece, serving the purposes of the period's leading national representatives, not their own.[23]

But the incorrect link drawn between El-Hakawati and the PLO placed the troupe at risk at home and abroad. Especially in this period, the PLO had situated itself as part of a worldwide anti-colonialist movement. In the West, the PLO and its guerrilla army, the PLA (Palestine Liberation Army), were synonymous with terrorism. Having created a stronghold in Lebanon after the expulsion of Palestinian resistance from Jordan in the events of Black September in 1970, the militarized PLO had established itself as a pseudo-state within a state in civil war-torn Lebanon. In 1982, Israel named the PLO presence as the pretext for invading Lebanon. Carne's statement that the PLO spirit 'lurks behind the entire production' placed El-Hakawati in the context of militarized resistance, contradicting the troupe's declared intention to present the Palestinian condition and everyday struggles, albeit using a satirical approach. Although interviews with members of El-Hakawati suggest that leaders in the PLO were aware of its activities at home and abroad, the troupe insisted on maintaining its financial and political independence during the period of its emergence on the scene in the late 1970s and early 1980s.[24]

Since the Palestinians and their political struggle had been unrecognized as a legitimate cause in mainstream international news, El-Hakawati's artistic message caused a crisis for Western journalists, who at times responded with sympathy and, often, with familiar orientalist tropes. For most critics, *Mahjoob Mahjoob* challenged common stereotypes by presenting the life journey of a defenceless man performing the everyday struggles of Palestinians under occupation. *City Limits* captioned one photograph 'From Jerusalem come the Palestinians of El-Hakawati in *Mahjoob Mahjoob*', a then radically positive equation of Palestine, Palestinians and the city of Jerusalem. Positively reviewing the play, Jonathan Keates of the *Guardian* touted the troupe's performance as vigorous and 'sinisterly charming'. He described: 'Put together by the 10 actors, the play blends circus, fable and polemic in the archetypal story of plucky scapegrace Mahjoob giving two fingers to the brasshats, bureaucrats and demagogues before going under' (1981: 11). On this tour, El-Hakawati delivered an inspiring, positive image of the Palestinian people. They were oppressed but peaceful, poor but creative and, most significantly, occupied but alive.

But underneath the positive reviews, an orientalist subtext positioned El-Hakawati as an exotic foreign presence on the European stage. The majority of the European press insisted on presenting the troupe, not only as accomplished artists with a just cause, but also as Arabs arriving from a violent 'Orient'. Stereotypical framing devices of Islam and the Arab world pervaded the European coverage of the troupe. For example, Ned Chaillet framed his review with the following statement: 'Islam is no respecter of the theatrical form. Form in general is unwelcome if it is an artistic representation, particularly where the human form is concerned' (1981: 22). A month before El-Hakawati's arrival, the *Jewish Chronicle* published a preview article entitled 'Anti-Israel Play Comes to London', a preemptive misrepresentation of the play and the troupe (1981b: 68). In some instances, local papers reached absurd levels of Orientalism. For example, the *Brentford & Chiswick Times* referred to Mahjoob and Im Mustapha as 'Widow Twankey and her lazy son Aladdin' (1981). The paper further reported that 'drama critics and their friends were being frisked by a muscular heavy at the door of Riverside Studios before being allowed inside', which emphasized the unusual presence of Palestinian Arabs and prefigured their reports of 'threats from someone who presumably wanted to stop the show' (*Brentford & Chiswick Times* 1981). On the week of the performance, a short announcement in the *Jewish Chronicle* simply stated in the title 'Arab actors in London', accentuating the identity of the troupe over the content of the production (1981b). These articles emphasized El-Hakawati as the 'Other' using the stock orientalist framework of Islam as an anti-theatrical religion, the presence of extremists in London, and being 'Arab' as being a natural enemy of Jews. Taking its cue from the *Jerusalem Post*, the *Jewish Chronicle* reported that the Israeli censorship board passed the play, thus implying that Israel was a mature democracy, while simultaneously suggesting that the play was anti-Semitic. Deeply influenced by an orientalist lens, these articles heightened El-Hakawati's foreignness at the expense of the troupe's adoption of familiar theatrical tropes and techniques.

Perhaps the French Montpellier newspaper *Midi-Libre* best reported the physical and verbal violence against El-Hakawati during the European tour. The newspaper reported the overnight systematic erasure of the word 'Palestinian' from El-Hakawati's posters, the breaking of the windows and door of their truck, and the breaking of the door of their accommodations at a local school. On the morning of their performance, an 'unknown' urinated on the troupe's flyers, which were placed on a table at the entrance of the TQM (Théâtre Quotidien de Montpellier). Strangely, although the contents of the truck were emptied or dumped, nothing was stolen. In closing, the unnamed writer of the article exclaimed at the level of intolerance towards Palestinians in Montpellier, suggesting that such actions were a stark reminder of humiliation under military occupation in Palestine (*Midi-Libre* 1981).

The *Mahjoob Mahjoob* spirit of survival, on and off stage, at home and abroad, solidified El-Hakawati's position as Palestine's leading theatre company in the 1980s. The banning of the performance in Nazareth and the ensuing censorship battle increased the troupe's popularity among Palestinian audiences and forced the Israeli news media and theatrical institutions to take notice of Palestine's cultural scene. For example, on 22 February 1983, El-Hakawati performed the play in Tel Aviv in a performance coordinated by the Birzeit Solidarity Committee and the leftist Israeli theatre Tzavta. The Arabic press referred to the event as the first occasion of a Palestinian theatrical troupe performing 'directly in front of the Israeli audiences' (*Al-Fajr* 1983). The event presented the troupe with an unavoidable political question: should Jerusalemites perform before their occupiers? For El-Hakawati, their mission comprised an educational dimension of 'introducing this audience to the truth of Palestinian civilization and culture as comparable to other sophisticated civilizations' (*Al-Fajr* 1983).[25] At the time, the troupe saw the Tel Aviv performance as an act of resistance, rather than an act of normalization.

The journey of El-Hakawati's *Mahjoob Mahjoob* from Jerusalem to Palestinian cities and villages to an international tour in Europe provides an example of the influential power of censorship on the history of Palestinian cultural production in general and Palestinian theatre in particular. But it also indicates that the Israeli censors' performance permit did not necessarily offer Palestinians the ability to perform freely. Official approval of the play became but one step in El-Hakawati's struggle for a more encompassing 'permission to perform', which could be defined as the guaranteed ability to legally, physically, literally and publicly perform the experience of the oppressed under a systematically oppressive structure. Beyond the experience of El-Hakawati at home, their performances abroad demonstrate that, even on the international stage, in free and democratic societies, the Palestinians have seldom had the privilege of such permission.

Notes

1. Scholars often recognize and mention the effect of the Israeli occupation, security apparatus and censorship on Palestinian theatre; however, detailed accounts of censorship remain absent in the scholarly literature. See, for example, the works of Hala Nassar, Reuven Snir, Mohammad Mahamid and Yasser Al-Mallah.
2. On the concept of 'de-development' in the Occupied Territories, especially in Gaza, see Sara Roy (1995). She argues that Israeli economic policies served as a means to de-develop, discourage or delay Palestinian economic growth. Similarly, Israeli censorship served as a means to control Palestinian theatre in the West Bank and Gaza.
3. El-Hakawati theatre troupe was founded in 1977, when it produced a play entitled *In the Name of the Father, the Mother, and the Son*. The original company members were François Abu Salem, Edwar Muallem, Jackie Lubeck, Adnan Tarabsheh, Jamil Eid and Talal Hammad.
4. The troupe created the play through improvisation under the leadership of the director, François Abu Salem. The original actors were Edwar Muallem, Jackie Lubeck, Muhammad Mahamid, Adnan Tarabsheh and Ibrahim Khalayleh. I obtained the unpublished text of *Mahjoob Mahjoob* from Edwar Muallem.
5. François Abu Salem was a founding member of the Palestinian troupe, Balalin. He collaborated with the Balalin troupe on devising *Al-'atma* (1972). The play employed a similar staging and flashbacks as a narrative structure. I learned about the staging of *Al-'atma* in personal interviews with Balalin company members Adel Al-Tartir (24 October 2010, Ramallah) and Sameh Aboushey (11 January 2011, Ramallah).
6. *Mahjoob Mahjoob*, File GL2431/21, Israel State Archive (Reading Room), 35 Makor Haim Street, Talpiot, Jerusalem. The censorship committee signed off on the approval in a meeting dated 15 December 1980.
7. Three troupe members, Edwar Muallem, Mahamad Mahamid and Adnan Tarabsheh, had been students at the Hebrew University at the time El-Hakawati produced its first production, *In the Name of the Father, the Mother, and the Son* (1977).
8. The document is found in the censorship file *Mahjoob Mahjoob*, File GL2431/21, Israel State Archive (Reading Room), 35 Makor Haim Street, Talpiot, Jerusalem.
9. For an Israeli source, see the *Jerusalem Post* 1981a.
10. Habibi served in the Knesset from 1951 to 1959 and from 1961 to 1972.
11. Personal interview with Mohammad Al-Batrawi on 24 October 2010 in Ramallah. See also Nida Shoughry's chapter '1976 Land Day' in her book *'Israeli-Arab' Political Mobilization: Between Acquiescence, Participation, and Resistance*. On 30 March 1976, Palestinian citizens of Israel declared a general strike and demonstrated in large numbers to protest Israel's expropriation of

Palestinian lands. Protests and demonstrations extended to the West Bank, Gaza and refugee camps in Lebanon.
12. See Reuven Snir and Hala Nassar for the importance of the Communist party to theatrical activity in the period 1948–67. Scholar Leena Dallasheh discusses the political realities of Nazareth in her dissertation *Nazarenes in the Turbulent Tide of Citizenships: Nazareth from 1940 to 1966*, New York University, 2012.
13. This letter and all subsequent letters are found in the censorship file *Mahjoob Mahjoob*, File GL2431/21, Israel State Archive (Reading Room), 35 Makor Haim Street, Talpiot, Jerusalem. For all the direct quotations from Hebrew, Dr Amal Eqeiq assisted in providing literal translations from the original Hebrew.
14. François Abu Salem's French birth name was François Gaspar. He was known in Palestine as Abu Salem. Although Abu Salem led the process as a director, the play was collectively created by the troupe.
15. The article in question was published in issue 29 in March 1981 of *La Gauche Arabe* (*Al-Yassar Al-Arabi*), pp. 20–22. Journalist Ahmad Youssef cites the function of the theatrical movement as resisting the occupation.
16. *Mahjoob Mahjoob*, File GL2431/21, Israel State Archive (Reading Room), 35 Makor Haim Street, Talpiot, Jerusalem.
17. As a member of the *Popular Front for the Liberation of Palestine*, Kanafani embraced both armed struggle and cultural resistance, together and separately.
18. For a detailed account of Palestinian armed resistance, see Section II, 'Years of Revolution, 1967–1972', in Sayigh.
19. *Mahjoob Mahjoob*, File GL2431/21, Israel State Archive (Reading Room), 35 Makor Haim Street, Talpiot, Jerusalem.
20. See *Al-Fajr* 1981; *Jerusalem Post* 1981b.
21. *Filastin Al-Thawra*, 17 December 1981, 'Palestinian El-Hakawati Troupe to Radio Monte Carlo'. See also *Al-Hadaf*, 30 December 1982, 'The Play "Mahjoob Mahjoob": El-Hakawati Troupe Penetrates the Zionist Siege'.
22. *Al-Fajr* (English), 17–23 May 1981.
23. According to my personal interviews with El-Hakawati members, including Edwar Muallem, Jackie Lubeck, Adnan Tarabsheh, Radi Shehadeh, Iman Aoun, Imad Mitwalli, Amer Khalil and other contemporaries, El-Hakawati did not function under the auspices of the PLO.
24. For a historical account of the PLO's activities during this period, see Cobban 1984.
25. Before the Oslo agreements and the building of the Wall, the movements against normalization and for cultural boycott were not yet defined or exercised en masse within Palestine. Although provocative in this period, many Palestinians considered playing in Israeli theatres to be a major breakthrough.

Bibliography

Abdel-Latif, H., 1982. 'Theatre, a Front of Resistance and Proving Palestinian Character, an Interview with the Palestinian Director François Abu Salem'. *Al-Hadaf*, 6 February, p. 48 (Arabic).

Abu Afifeh, T., 1980. 'Al-Hakawati's play *Mahjoob Mahjoob'*. *Al-Fajr*, 27 December (El-Hakawati archive) (Arabic).
Al-Batrawi, M., 2010. Personal interview. Interviewed by Samer Al-Saber, Ramallah, Palestine, 24 October.
Al-Fajr, 1981. 'The play "Mahjoob Mahjoob": The Censorship Committee for Plays and Cinematic Films Lifts the Ban on It'. 27 January (El-Hakawati archive) (Arabic).
Al-Fajr, 1982. 'El-Hakawati's 61 Performances: Palestinian Theatre Successful in Europe'. 15–21 January, p. 14 (English).
Al-Fajr, 1983. 'El-Hakawati Prepares to Perform "Mahjoob Mahjoob" in Tel Aviv'. 19 February (El-Hakawati archive) (Arabic).
Al-Hadaf, 1982. 'The Play "Mahjoob Mahjoob": El-Hakawati Troupe Penetrates the Zionist Siege'. 30 December (El-Hakawati archive) (Arabic).
Al-Itihad, 1981. 'After the Official Permit to Show the Play "Mahjoob Mahjoob", Authorities Return to Suppress and Stop Its Showing Arbitrarily'. 20 January, p. 6 (Arabic).
Al-Quds, 1983. '"Mahjoob Mahjoob" Performed Next Tuesday in Tel Aviv'. 19 February (El-Hakawati archive) (Arabic).
Al-Saber, S., 2013. *Permission to Perform: Palestinian Theatre in Jerusalem (1967–1993)*. Unpublished doctoral thesis, University of Washington.
Balalin Theatre Troupe, 1995. *Al-'atma*. In S. K. Jayyusi and R. Allen, *Modern Arabic Drama: An Anthology*. Bloomington: Indiana University Press.
Carne, R., 1981. 'Mahjoob Mahjoob'. *Financial Times*, 24 September, p. 22.
Chaillet, N., 1981. 'Mahjoob Mahjoob'. *The Times* (London), 23 September, p. 15.
Cobban, H., 1984. *The Palestinian Liberation Organisation: People, Power, and Politics*. Cambridge: Cambridge University Press.
Dallasheh, L., 2012. *Nazarenes in the Turbulent Tide of Citizenships: Nazareth from 1940 to 1966*. Unpublished doctoral thesis, New York University.
DeBare, I., L. Blum, and F. Abu Salem, 1985. 'Palestinian Culture Takes Root'. *Journal of Palestine Studies*, 14, pp. 230–34.
El-Hakawati Archive. Archived articles from local and international newspapers. Ashtar Theatre, Ramallah, Palestine.
El-Hakawati, 1980. *Mahjoob Mahjoob*. Unpublished manuscript provided by Edwar Muallem, Ashtar Theatre, Ramallah, Palestine.
Essoulami, S., 1992. *Cry for Change: Israeli Censorship in the Occupied Territories*. London: Article 19.
Filastin Al-Thawra, 1981. 'Palestinian El-Hakawati Troupe to Radio Monte Carlo'. 17 December (El-Hakawati archive).
Jerusalem Post, 1981a. 'Ban Lifted on Israeli West Bank Play'. 30 January (El-Hakawati archive).
Jerusalem Post, 1981b. 'Censors Ban Performance by Israeli-W. Bank Troupe'. 18 January (El-Hakawati archive).
Jewish Chronicle, 1981a. 'Arab Actors in London'. 25 September.
Jewish Chronicle, 1981b. 'Anti-Israel Play Comes to London'. 28 August.
Kanafani, G., 1968. *al-Adab al-Filasṭini al-muqawim taḥta al-iḥtilal, 1948–1968*. Bayrut: Mu'assasat al-Dirasat al-Filastiniyah (Arabic).
Keates, J., 1981. 'Mahjoob Mahjoob'. *Guardian*, 26 September, p. 11.
Lubeck, J., 2012. Personal interview. Interviewed by Samer Al-Saber, Jerusalem, 8 October.

Lustick, I., 2008. 'Yerushalayim, al-Quds, and the Wizard of Oz: the Problem of "Jerusalem" after Camp David II and the Aqsa Intifada'. In T. Mayerand and S. A. Mourad (eds) *Jerusalem: Idea and Reality*. London: Routledge.
Mahjoob Mahjoob. Israel State Archive (File GL2431/21) (Reading Room), 35 Makor Haim Street, Talpiot, Jerusalem.
Mallāh, Y. I. 2002. *Ṣafaḥāt maṭwīyāt min tārīkh al-masraḥ al-Filasṭīnī: dirāsah adabīyah*. al-Khalīl, Jam'īyat al-'Anqā' al-Thaqāfīyah.
M'Hamid, M. 1989. *Masīrat al-ḥarakah al-masraḥīyah fī al-Ḍiffah al-Gharbīyah, 1967–1987*. al-Ṭayyibah, Markaz Iḥyā' al-Turāth al-'Arabī.
Midi-Libre, 1981. 'Agressions contre la troupe palestinienne <<El Hakawati>>'. 27 November (El-Hakawati archive).
Muallem, E., 2010. Personal interview. Interviewed by Samer Al-Saber, Ashtar Theatre, Ramallah, Palestine, 26 October.
Nassar, H. K., 2001. *Palestinian Theatre between Origins and Visions*. Unpublished doctoral thesis, Freie Universität Berlin.
Rajjal, Y. I., 2005. 'Jerusalem: Occupation and Challenges to Urban Identity'. In S. K. Jayyusi, *My Jerusalem: Essays, Reminiscences, and Poems*. Northampton, MA: Olive Branch Press.
Roy, S., 1987. 'The Gaza Strip: A Case of Economic De-Development'. *Journal of Palestine Studies*, 17, pp. 56–88.
Said, E., 1984. 'Permission to Narrate'. *Journal of Palestine Studies*, 13: 3, pp. 27–48.
Sayigh, Y., 1997. *Armed Struggle and the Search for State: the Palestinian National Movement, 1949–1993*. Oxford: Clarendon Press.
Slyomovics, S., 1991. ' "To Put One's Fingers in the Bleeding Wound": Palestinian Theatre under Israeli Censorship'. *TDR*, 35, pp. 18–38.
Snir, R., 1998. 'The Palestinian al-Hakawati Theater: A Brief History'. *Arab Studies Journal*, 6/7, pp. 57–71.
Snir, R., 2005. *Palestinian Theatre*. Wiesbaden: Reichert.
Thaxter, J., 1981. 'Laughs after a Frisking'. *Brentford & Chiswick Times*, 25 September (El-Hakawati archive).
Youssef, A., 1981. 'Theatre of Resistance in Occupied Palestine: Defying Occupation, Backwardness, and Paralysis'. *Al-Yassar Al-Arabi*, March, pp. 20–21 (Arabic).

Part IV

Coming in from the Outside: Theatre, Community, Crisis

8
The Council Estate as Hood: SPID Theatre Company and Grass-roots Arts Practice as Cultural Politics

Katie Beswick

Introduction

In 2011, in the aftermath of the riots that took place in many of Britain's major cities, cabinet member for housing Jonathan Glanz released a statement:

> Social housing isn't a right, it's a privilege and if people abuse that privilege then in common with anyone else they should face the consequences [...]. We have a responsibility to our communities at large. Many people living in these communities are playing by the rules and were not involved in criminal activity over the last few nights. They wouldn't want to live next door to people who are getting away with bad behaviour and enjoying the privilege. (McCann 2011)

This statement was issued in support of Westminster City Council's announcement that they intended to evict social housing tenants involved in rioting. In Glanz's statement, as in much of the media response to the riots, residents of urban social housing estates (or 'council estates' as they are known colloquially) were positioned as central actors in criminal activity.

Glanz's reference to social housing residents is troubling, both because his statement was released before the identity of rioters had been established and because no similar threats of eviction were made towards private renters or owner-occupiers. Glanz's words reveal the conflation between deprivation, criminal activity and council estate residency that has characterized popular contemporary conceptions of the urban council estate environment. His statement, and the wider media response to the riots, which particularly implicated gangs of black males (Ball 2011), illustrates the enduring crisis of the council estate. This crisis includes the poverty and stigma that affects the day-to-day lives of individual residents (McKenzie 2009) and the related crisis of representation. This representational crisis is epitomized by the popular use of the phrase 'council estate' as a collective description for a variety of different and distinct spaces – connected because they were initially intended to provide mass subsidized rented housing provision for low-income households.[1] In its popular, representational incarnation, however, the council estate is a dysfunctional, deprived criminal breeding ground, which poses a threat to those both within and outside of it. Although the 2011 riots are not the central concern of this chapter, the media response to them, and in particular Glanz's warning to estate residents, is revealing in demonstrating the wider status of council estates in contemporary British life.

In this chapter, I argue that the council estate serves as the British incarnation of what Richardson and Skott-Myhre call the 'global hood'. I examine the way that SPID (alternately Specially Produced Innovatively Directed/Social Political Independent Direct) Theatre Company, a collective of professional film and theatre makers and professional and amateur performer-residents, located on the Kensal House estate in Ladbroke Grove, West London, has responded to the discourse of estate 'crisis' in popular representation.[2] I argue that SPID's work can be considered as part of an oppositional global culture; by framing the company's work as hood cultural politics and examining its complexities through this lens, I propose that its performance work operates through the habitus (Bourdieu 1977)[3] of those engaged in its practices via the making, performing and viewing processes. I argue that grass-roots artistic work taking place within urban council estates can be positioned as hood cultural politics, and therefore as part of a globally significant struggle for survival in the face of a neoliberal landscape that works to silence the voices of the marginalized.[4]

Global hood

In addition to the stigmatizing narrative inherent in Glanz's statement, his words also invoke an alternative conception of council estate space encompassing 'community'. Within popular discourse council estates are often subject to nostalgic narratives of community, which reference a fantasy idyll of working-class life where sociality and collective identity are associated with safety. Positive conceptions of community have been associated with council estates since their inception. The design of many modernist estates sought to incorporate a collective domain, which would provide areas of social interaction where neighbours might form relationships and forge networks of informal governance. Bauman (2001) has proposed that certain notions of community, however, can be dangerous; he suggests that negative perceptions held by outsiders have often operated to fracture and marginalize already marginalized groups further, as individuals accept external labels and form voluntary ghettos. Bauman's notion of community as a dangerous concept is useful in drawing attention to the way that Glanz's speech worked, paradoxically, to invoke nostalgic conceptions of working-class 'community' while, at the same time, positioning estate residents as (a potentially destructive) 'other' to non-residents.

The paradoxical narratives of the council estate invoked by Glanz's speech resonate with the definition of the 'hood' (an abbreviation of 'neighbourhood' often used in North American slang to refer to marginalized, residential areas of the inner city) offered by academics and former hood residents Richardson and Skott-Myhre, who argue that the term hood has come to embody

> [...] both the utopian and dystopian aspects of the low-income urban areas of large cities. It represents an awareness of community: an enclosed space in which residents are united in their daily struggles. It also signifies an isolated, marginalized, and often-criminalized space that appears frequently in popular media representations, legal discourses and public discussions. (Richardson and Skott-Myhre 2012: 9)

The 'hood', like the 'council estate', is a representational space of crisis, encompassing a set of diverse and divergent spaces.

Despite its association with North America, Richardson and Skott-Myhre define the hood as a multiple, shifting, global site of urban marginality. They propose that, because of the appropriation of North American hood culture globally, the 'global hood' has become a conceptual space, which comprises multiple sites of struggle and resistance in a variety of low-income urban areas. This conception of a shifting, global site of urban struggle resonates with Walter's notion of the 'dreadful enclosure', which, he argues, exists in all parts of the world and serves to identify areas and people as inferior and dangerous (Walter in Damer 1974: 221).

Unlike Walter, however, who suggests that the 'dreadful enclosure' is a limiting fantasy, Richardson and Skott-Myhre (2012) argue that the hood is a space that 'can be both liberating and limiting' (19). They argue that in its global incarnation the hood is defined by its residents' 'activism, art, personal experience and day-to-day living' and can serve as a site of 'liberation and revolution' as well as one of marginalization (19). Richardson and Skott-Myhre propose that the 'creative works within the hood and outside of it (re)present a cultural politics' (2012: 22). They highlight Nas's album *Illmatic* and the 1990s movies *Boyz in the Hood* (1991) and *Menace II Society* (1993) as defining examples of hood representation. These commercially successful examples illustrate how hood practices are almost always created by (or with) artists who might be positioned as 'authentically hood'. For example, Nas grew up in the Queensbridge Houses Project, a public housing development in Long Island City, Queens; *Menace II Society* was directed by the Hughes Brothers, half Armenian, half African-American twins who were raised by a single mother in Los Angeles and have suggested that the movie worked within a paradigm of 'art-imitating-life or life-imitating-art' (Takako 2014); and *Boyz in the Hood* stars rapper Ice Cube, who grew up in South Central Los Angeles, an area that was synonymous with gang violence and racial tension throughout the latter half of the twentieth century.

The creative activity of the hood can be positioned as political because it is commonly concerned with challenging existing systems of power and control in a specific spatial context – thus meeting Collini's definition of politics as 'the important, inescapable, and difficult attempt to determine relations of power in a given space' (Collini in Kelleher 2009: 3). The resistant potential of the hood's cultural politics hinges upon residents engaging in the production of creative works – through which they celebrate their marginalized position and survive in a culture weighted against them. The cultural politics of the hood can therefore be defined as a resistance 'against the forces of control and domination', where 'networks of self-production [are] no longer constrained by the axiomatic discipline of the dominant media, the state, or the market'. Importantly, these acts of creative resistance are produced 'within the bounded space of the hood itself' (Richardson and Skott-Myhre 2012: 19). According to Richardson and Skott-Myhre, it is from the located hood environment where residents are most effectively able to resist those dominant stigmatizing narratives produced about them by those outside of that environment.

Despite the parallels between the North American hood and the contemporary council estate, as Wacquant (2008) and Kitossa (2012) warn, direct comparisons between urban spaces 'run short of apprehending the distinctiveness of each of them' (Kitossa 2012: 127). While some of the appropriations of hood culture by British artists, discussed below, are undoubtedly rooted in local identification with global forms of resistance, there are marked differences between UK and US contexts. Therefore, the notion of the hood has the potential to work as a reductive, homogenizing fetishization. Kitossa proposes that in much the same way that colonial narratives existed to exoticize the East and create the orient as an oppositional 'other', so too contemporary neoliberal societies fetishize the hood (or 'ghetto') in order to create an 'objective structure' of difference in which 'the "non-ghetto" is neither in question nor problematic' (Kitossa 2012: 127). For Kitossa, global hood representation is exoticized and seductive (Richardson and Skott-Myhre 2012: 15); this seduction belies a capitalist violence in which the poor are deliberately marginalized in order to sustain existing distributions of power and wealth. His work points to the importance of the non-hood in the construction of global hood discourses, and suggests therefore that the 'non-hood' must feature in any useful consideration of global hood culture.

Understanding the council estate as an incarnation of a conceptual, global space, despite the problems with this approach as articulated by Kitossa, allows an international contextualization of the activities that take place there. These located, ostensibly local activities are part of a network of global, grass-roots practices that exist alongside the neoliberal, capitalist structures that create the conditions which necessitate their existence.

Surviving the hood

Couldry (2010) argues that voice, which he defines as the capacity to speak and be heard both within and beyond formal politics, is often obstructed in contemporary social life. He proposes that this is a direct result of market-focused neoliberal politics and that 'there is no shortcut to understanding neoliberalism's consequences for people's daily conditions of voice without listening to the stories people tell us about their lives' (114).

The voicing and listening process is essential for survival at a grass-roots level because, as Bauman points out, 'the articulation of life stories is the activity through which meaning and purpose are inserted into life' (2001: 13). Survival, in any incarnation of the global hood, requires residents to strive beyond the basic need for food and shelter.

As several sociological studies of urban council estates have demonstrated, residents have a profound need to narrate their lives positively and to resist the dominant stereotyping that works to structure and limit their life chances (Reay and Lucey 2000; Watt 2006). Couldry proposes that space is important in the struggle for voice, and that spaces and the people within them need to be regarded as part of the political landscape in order to effectively operate within that landscape (2010: 130). The hood, then, despite its limits, has the potential to serve as a conceptual, political space, through which individuals and communities across the globe, connected by their marginalization from neoliberal politics, can participate in the discourse that shapes and structures their daily lives. My analysis of SPID's work articulates the way in which one company operates as part of this global struggle for survival.

Council estate as hood

Council estates serve as radical sites for cultural intervention precisely because the experience of living on an estate – including being subject to stigmatizing narratives that have created these spaces as marginalized in British culture – profoundly structures and shapes the identities of residents. Indeed, negative depictions of hood spaces are absorbed and replayed by residents, which contributes to the continued marginalization of such spaces (Richardson and Skott-Myhre 2012). bell hooks asserts that the margin exists as more than a site of deprivation. It is also a site of 'radical possibility, a space of resistance' (hooks 1990: 149). Her work emphasizes the importance of located cultural practices in strategies for survival. As she argues, '[o]ur living depends on our ability to conceptualize alternatives, often improvised' (hooks 1990: 149).

Richardson and Skott-Myhre highlight young, energetic, predominantly black subculture – such as that presented via music, fashion and attitude in cultural forms such as hip-hop – as conventional features of hood representation, but acknowledge that the hood signifies much more than this in contemporary culture. While the hood is often associated with predominately masculine, African-American culture, in both its North American and its global incarnations these spaces now 'incorporate a plurality of ethnicities and subcultures', because 'global capital and new media technologies have collapsed previous notions of time and space' (2012: 9).

However, just as race remains a central, if complex, component of the North American hood, so too the distinct racial problematics of the council estate are a significant feature of its identity in popular representation. As Power proposes in her case study of Broadwater Farm estate, there is a common perception that race is a 'root cause and explanation of social problems' on estates (Power 1999: 5). Rogaly and Taylor (2011) point to the common imagery of the white 'chav' – often considered an acronym for 'council housed and violent'[5] – in representations of the council estate (3). They examine the intersection between race and class by arguing that representations of the British working class are dominated by depictions of whiteness, while ethnic minorities are defined solely by their ethnicity. However, I suggest that, although both nostalgic and derogatory conceptions of the term 'working class', and particularly the word 'chav', may be bound up with conceptions of whiteness, representations of the council estate, especially in popular culture, regularly engage with the mixed-race reality of these spaces. Indeed, particularly in contemporary London and other ethnically diverse cities, non-white groups are regularly implicated in working-class narratives of the council estate. In recent media and political discourse, representations of 'the underclass' have included depictions of black-on-black gang violence as well as the white 'chav'. Fictional representations based on such binary stereotypes – such as the predominately black gangs in Channel 4's drama *Top Boy* (2011 and 2013), or the white 'chavs' in the BBC's comedy sketch series *Little Britain* (2003–6) – become an easy way to offer superficial reflection on race and class. However, such representational stereotypes tend to separate the suburban white working-class experience (as seen in, for example, the television programme *Shameless* [2004–13] and the film *Fish Tank* [2009]) from the urban 'black' working-class experience, with representations of the latter often featuring a multicultural cast, but focusing on issues relating to stereotypes of black subculture, particularly gangs (*Attack the Block* [2011], *Sket* [2011]). While acknowledging that this division is due in part to stereotyping, I have chosen to focus on 'blackness' in my discussion of the racial aspects of SPID's council estate practices, both because the concept of black gang crime has become central to public understanding of urban social housing estates, and because the figure of the black male is problematically bound up with conceptions of the 'hood'.

There are many parallels between the North American hood and the urban council estate in popular representation. For example, the physical and socio-economic aspects of the hood are reflected in popular representations of council estate space as multicultural, marginalized from respectable, middle-class experience (McKenzie 2009; Skeggs 2005) and dangerous to outsiders. Many scholars[6] have pointed to the damaging effect that such stigmatizing narratives have on council estate residents. McKenzie argues that negative representations work as part of a series of structures that 'reify' the council estate as the space of the dangerous criminal 'other' (McKenzie 2009: 23). As theorized by Bourdieu (1977) and discussed in more detail later in this chapter, these structures also work as 'structuring structures' (Swartz 1997: 103), which contribute to individuals' 'habitus', that is their unacknowledged learned behaviour, in a way that works to limit the opportunities available to them.

In addition to negative depictions of estates, however, so too the 'spirit' of 'liberation and revolution' that Richardson and Skott-Myhre describe as a central feature of the cultural production of the hood has become an important feature of estate representation. One genre where the hood parallel is particularly striking is British hip-hop music, which draws upon a conventional genre within hood representation to politicize council estate space, celebrate estate culture and resist oppressive mainstream representations of estate spaces. Autobiographical (at least ostensibly) narratives of resistance in the face of poverty and struggle are significant features of British hip-hop music. Artists regularly refer to their personal experiences of living on council estates in their lyrics to suggest that such spaces, like the American hood, are identity-making 'spaces of creative force that [are] built on a certain kind of survivorship and mutual suffering' (Richardson and Skott-Myhre 2012: 19).

For example, British rapper Skinnyman's single and music video *Council Estate of Mind* (2004) draws on the conventions of hood culture to politicize the experience of living on a council estate. The music video for this track comprises intimate shots of the interior and exterior of a council estate from a first-person perspective. Affiliation with the American hood is suggested through shots of posters on the walls of the homes within the estate depicting the emblematic American rapper Tupac. The lyrics are darkly humorous and undercut with a sense of hopelessness and, like Tupac's music, can be read as a cry of despair or a call for political intervention (Richardson 2012: 198): 'I live amongst smashed syringes / squatters' doors hanging off the hinges / hookers looking money for Bobby / shotting their minges'. However, the lyrics also portray a sense of collective experience, of survivorship in the face of desolation: 'So these are lyrics for my people / living on the streets who / know they ain't got nothing else to retreat to' (Skinnyman 2004).

The history of the British adoption of hood culture, by both estate residents and outsiders, is arguably tied up with the globalization and commercialization of hood identity which has occurred through the successful marketing and distribution of the forms of cultural production mentioned above. The generic conventions of the hood and the youthful, revolutionary 'spirit' it embodies have been appropriated by global marketing and advertising campaigns, with prominent brands such as Adidas receiving endorsement from hip-hop artists such as Run–D.M.C. There are certainly ethical questions to be posed regarding this globalization of hood culture, such as who profits from such appropriation and how such profits are distributed. As Kitossa proposes, narratives of the hood are seductive and potentially dangerous. The British appropriation of hood culture, particularly via hip-hop music, has been subject to accusations of fuelling American-style gang violence. However, rather than focus on these negative aspects of hood appropriation, already well established in popular discourse (see, for example, Pogatchnik 2011), I am interested in the ways in which the global hood might have the potential to work as a resistant political space.

Situated on an urban council estate, SPID Theatre Company demonstrates how performance practices that engage with the spaces of marginalization, and which implicate both the hood and the 'nonhood', might give a voice to the marginalized and celebrate the creativity and dynamism that exist within cultures of urban deprivation. However, just as the hood is a paradoxical space, so too the work taking place in global hood spaces; work that attempts to offer participants strategies for survival, negotiates paradoxes and cannot be considered a straightforward, 'revolutionary' cultural politics – if, indeed, there is any such thing.

SPID Theatre Company

SPID Theatre Company was established in 1999 and has worked for a number of years to embed itself within the Kensal House estate. In 2005, after securing funding to renovate the dilapidated community rooms, the company moved permanently to Kensal House. Although originally established by a collective of artists from outside the estate, attracted by the performance potential of the community rooms, and perhaps also by the potential they offered to engage with fashionable urban culture, SPID's ongoing work on the site, including a youth theatre company, has led to a number of residents joining the company as professional members. All of the company's work is developed with residents and locals, who suggest subject matter for performances and work alongside professional company members to develop and stage performance works. The company's performance practices include film and theatre and intend to offer opportunities for participants to draw from real-life experience in the creation of work, and to use the performance process to transform the possibilities available to them within their home-space.

Although SPID engages in grass-roots practice, embedded within and driven by the local community, it is also an instrumental organization, seeking to foster positive relationships with and between the estate and its residents. SPID has also worked to foster institutional connections with a variety of stakeholders. Partner organizations include Kensal House Residents Association, Arts Council England, the Royal Borough of Kensington and Chelsea, Riverside Studios and Open House London. This network of partners offers not only avenues for funding, which are undoubtedly important for a small-scale company, but also a platform via which work can resonate beyond the immediate locational context of the estate and its residents.

However, despite the positive aspects of SPID's institutional practices, the inherent paradox of hood cultural politics, its 'limiting and liberating' nature, is present in the work. As Bharucha has suggested, the term 'community' has become particularly troubling in applied theatre practice, as it is often used in an uncritically celebratory manner, 'with scant regard for its inner dissonances and intolerances, assuming an implicit homogeneity' (Bharucha 2011: 370). It is important to acknowledge that SPID does not operate outside of problematic conceptions of community. Indeed, the company relies to some extent on the identity of the estate community as marginalized, and its own identity as an organization which uses celebratory arts practices to address such marginalization, in order to maintain the funding and the institutional partnerships outlined above. This is evident in the way that the company frames Kensal House in its corporate planning:

> [Our projects with youth residents] are our way of honouring architect Maxwell Fry's vision of the community rooms as a place where residents recognise their potential to help and entertain each other. Situated in St Charles Ward, which is amongst the top 10% of deprived wards nationally, the residents are a transient group including a high proportion of refugees and a diverse ethnic mix; drug use, violence and unemployment are rife. Using theatre as our tool, we see ourselves as catalysts for the regeneration of the community rooms and the estate itself. (SPID 2009: 8)

I draw attention to the above statement, not because I want to suggest it is a misrepresentation of the lived reality of the estate, but in order to highlight that this corporate framing of the company's work sits somewhat uncomfortably with the challenges to dominant estate representation that the company have made central to its practice. This demonstrates the complexities of undertaking located, socially engaged practice which attempts to address and remedy significant social problems.

Affected: hood imagery

SPID's 2011 film *Affected: Greed is Contagious* is set in an apocalyptic version of an unnamed London council estate, and the echoes of hood imagery in the film clearly position SPID's work within the cultural politics of the global hood. In *Affected*, the estate residents are depicted as violent zombies, slowly driven wild by consumerism and greed – traits personified by a mythical character, the 'tempter'. The threatening presence of the zombie-residents becomes increasingly menacing as two white, teenage, middle-class filmmakers navigate the estate in search of the 'tempter', leading to their inevitable demise. *Affected* presents a version of the council estate and its residents where both are corrupted by contemporary consumer culture – a vision which, a few months after the making of the film in 2011, was to be realized in the UK as a result of the riots. Unlike the media commentary surrounding the riots, however, which blamed the pathological nature of estate residents for their behaviour, *Affected* called the legitimacy of contemporary capitalism into question by positioning the residents, like the middle-class filmmakers, as victims of this culture.

Throughout the film there are references to hood culture, which work both to position the film within a global hood discourse and also to suggest that the homogenization of distinct spaces sets up expectations of residents' behaviour that do not necessarily equate with reality. For example, the film opens with a gang of men of different races burning a suitcase filled with cash. Off camera a voiceover asks: 'Are there any men here? Any real men?' Immediately the camera cuts to a teenage black boy on his mobile phone. In the short pause before he speaks he might be a gang member, coming forward to volunteer as a 'real man'. However, it quickly becomes clear that he is a young boy, frightened by the violent activity taking place in his home-space.

The concrete modernist housing block was the central location of the film, and was foregrounded in landscape shots, referencing similar shots of estates in films and music videos such as *Nil By Mouth* (1997) and *Council Estate of Mind* (2004). Although the architecture is different, this bleak, urban landscape with its burnt-out cars and lawless inhabitants is resonant of the kind of films Richardson and Skott-Myhre refer to as archetypal hood representations (*Boyz in the Hood, Menace II Society*). The home-made quality of the work – the hand-held camera, grainy shots and natural, often stark, lighting – serves, aesthetically, to suggest that the film is grass-roots practice. Through this cinematography *Affected* invokes and undercuts dominant estate narratives. The low-budget quality of the movie, the references to iconic images of urban deprivation and the oppositional message of the film channel the hood's energy of resistance and survivorship, while also suggesting that the neoliberal flattening of time and space that integrates the council estate into global narratives of urban poverty works to the disadvantage of council estate residents.

Habitus and reflexivity: *Sixteen* and the non-hood

Habitus, as mentioned above, is a theory that proposes social structures contribute to unacknowledged learned behaviour. Simply put, habitus can be thought of as the recognition that 'the human body always carries the effects of the society in which it grew and was educated' (Shepherd and Wallis 2004: 191). Habitus offers a theoretical model through which we can understand the ways that places inform the body and contribute to the opportunities and limitations that exist for individuals from particular places. SPID's live performance practices frequently implicate the bodies of both participants and audience members, and the narratives of the estate the company offer often attempt to challenge deeply inscribed behaviours, perceptions and prejudices.

As Richardson and Skott-Myre point out,

> The habitus of the hood plays a crucial role in teaching residents what is and is not acceptable, achievable, and dream-able. [...] Habitus can also make certain practices seem inherent to the spaces in which they occur, as if these practices were only possible in these neighbourhoods and all other possibilities are out of the question. This aspect of culture, as situated in geography, is often confused with nature. (Richardson and Skott-Myhre 2012: 11)

Richardson and Skott-Myhre also propose that the different habitus that exists in distinct class groups feeds into perceptions of artworks, and inevitably leads to different readings of a single representation (19). Thus the theory of habitus might also be used to explain the negative perceptions of marginalized spaces held by 'outsiders'. Although habitus is often conceived of as a fixed set of behaviours, shared by those from similar backgrounds, it has also been theorized as potentially malleable. This malleability means that individuals who are offered opportunities to understand how their behaviours are structured by habitus might access 'reflexivity' (Sweetman 2003); that is, they might become aware of the structures that limit their life chances, or the life chances of others, and work to restructure them. SPID's *Sixteen* involved a series of strategic interventions, conceived to reveal and subvert the audience's (assumed) prejudices, thereby drawing attention to habitual perceptions of estate residents by outsiders.

Sixteen was a professional performance developed by the National Theatre Studio and supported by the Gate Theatre, which was produced by SPID and set and performed on the Kensal House estate. The strategic interventions, designed to confront the perceptions and expectations of audience members, implicated the 'non-hood', as many of the residents, as the review in *The Stage* (Barnett 2009) suggests, were not estate residents. These interventions had the potential to interrupt habitus in a way that encouraged reflexivity.

A key example of such intervention happened before the performance of the play had begun. As the audience made their way through the estate, towards the community rooms where *Sixteen* was staged, they passed groups of rowdy teenagers, dressed in hooded tops and jeans or tracksuit bottoms – the quintessence of 'hood' youth. The teenage estate residents shouted abuse at the arriving audience in an attempt to dislocate them from the expected comfort and familiarity of the theatrical experience and confront them with stereotypes of the council estate environment. The staged nature of the encounter was not made clear to the audience until the performance began and the young performers appeared in the ensemble, establishing that the 'gang' were part of the performance collective. This was a deliberate intervention, enacted by performers who were estate residents parodying a media stereotype of their 'anti-social behaviour'. This uncomfortable encounter attempted to encourage audiences to confront the ways in which their own practices of space, and the expectations of others, were influenced by stigma regarding the danger of the council estate space. Of course, the usefulness of the intervention in this context is questionable; the spectators had decided to attend a performance on an estate, and so likely either did not have negative views of the estate or were willing to have their views questioned. I find this aspect of the performance particularly interesting, however, because of how it worked to highlight the complicity of those from the 'non-hood' in the creation of the council estate 'other'.

176 *The Council Estate as Hood*

In beginning the performance with a confrontation of audience members' (assumed) prejudices and then subverting them by revealing the 'gang' as part of the fiction of the play, the piece drew attention to the role of 'outsiders' in constructing dominant representations of estate residents. The intervention suggested that those from the 'non-hood' have a role to play in resisting the discourse of the council estate in crisis. This radically shifts established expectations of applied theatre, which is often concerned with the effects of practice on participants.

The extent to which this intervention worked on individual audience members is uncertain. Indeed, although one audience member I spoke with told me that the young 'gang' had forced him to question his initial reluctance to enter an unfamiliar estate, he also told me of another audience member who was 'so intimidated' that she had left the performance before the fiction was revealed. Nonetheless, for those who stayed, simplistic readings of the performance and its contents, which Richardson and Skott-Myhre might suggest would have occurred as a result of differing habitus on the part of the audience members, were made more difficult than they might otherwise have been; thus the interruption in expectation potentially interrupted the habitus of audience members, as the disjuncture between reality and representation required some reflexivity on the part of those watching the work.

Representation and reflexivity in *23176*

SPID's *23176* also operated strategically to encourage reflexivity. The play was performed by the youth theatre company in 2008. It was devised with 13–19-year-olds living on the Kensal House estate. *23176* is a secular reworking of the parable of the Good Samaritan, which SPID states was intended to appeal to a 'modern, local audience' (email exchange, 2010). The title refers to the number of sexual assaults recorded in the UK in 2008. The play tells the story of a group of young people who discover a woman who has been sexually assaulted on their estate and offer her support, acting against the expectations of the women on the estate – who, hidden in their homes, consider the young people gathering in the communal areas outside as a threatening and potentially violent gang. The play intended to reveal how young people are particularly implicated in negative hood discourse, and also demonstrated how negative discourse shapes and influences perceptions inside, as well as outside of, the estate.

The piece also attempted to reveal the agency that young people on the estate had to break away from the life imposed on them by deterministic representations, and to change the environment of the space they call home. Throughout the piece, the young performers played stereotypical representations of themselves; on stage they were depicted as part of a gang, loitering by the bus-stop that was a central feature of the set. Although subversion of expectations as the teenage gang comfort the assault victim is not, in itself, a revolutionary theatrical tactic, the twist in the plot alongside the use of intermediality in the performance created a platform where young people had the ability to voice their resistance against the kind of negative hood stigmas that create and sustain habitus.

The performance used a number of screens throughout, upon which various representations of the inner city were shown. The pre-recorded scenes included a duologue between two women, set in the kitchen of what appeared to be a flat on the estate. This scene, in which the women ruminated on the threat posed by the young people outside, referenced soap operas and popular drama – both in terms of the mid-shot camera angles used throughout the exchange and the realist, kitchen-sink setting. Another screen depicted a video game set in the urban inner city – referencing the global culture which council estates are part of. On another screen, in a scene that referenced the style of television documentaries, the young people directly confronted representations of themselves ever-present in the popular media. They spoke of their educational aspirations and argued that they had been regularly demonized by popular representation, which failed to acknowledge their individual potential.

The use of screens throughout the performance referenced the ubiquity of councilestate representation in screen media and also served to reveal the processes by which the estate is mediated. By revealing this mediation, the performers were able to draw attention to some of the social and institutional structures which operate to limit residents' life opportunities and through which their limited ability to participate obstructs voice.

However, the making process also importantly afforded the young people involved in it the opportunity to access processes of representation. They took part in filming, performing and scripting their own version of estate space. In this way, the performance process not only allowed the teenage estate residents a space in which to contest dominant narratives, but also an opportunity to experience how such fictional narratives are constructed in the media industry. Additionally, it equipped them with the skills and knowledge to create and disseminate arts practices beyond their work with SPID. Allowing young people to rehearse and improvise counter-narratives in a space where their habitus is structured is a potentially powerful way of offering them tactics for survival both within and beyond the estate. As hooks' 'politics of location' suggests, the fact that residents were able to creatively engage in resistance on the estate where they live gave the work extra potency. While the play itself did not mark a moment of long-term change in the way that council estates and their residents are represented, it did offer the possibility for individuals to engage in reflexivity; to understand the media structures that structure their identity, and that operate globally, which are potentially transformative. In *23176*, young people were able to safely capitalize on the potentially dangerous notion of community, in a site where they felt ownership, in order to offer an alternative conception of their collective identity: one that pushes against the dominant images they are shown of themselves.

Limits and liberation: race, SPID and hood culture

As I outlined above, race is a central feature of hood culture, and is significant in popular conceptions of council estate space. However, despite SPID's apparent commitment to confronting negative, dominant estate narratives, race is rarely confronted directly in its work.

The issue of race was directly acknowledged only once in *23176*, in a fleeting moment that took place during the filmed documentary-style scene where the young people confronted media representations of their identity. In this scene, improvised by the young company members, black members of the group described themselves individually and collectively as 'black', despite the fact that there were members of the performance collective from non-black ethnic groups. When asked 'how does the media see you?', replies from the young people included: 'The media sees me like I am a black guy who don't know nothing', 'as a young black hooligan', 'they think just because we're young, we're black, we're gonna start trouble on people. But we're not.'

While the individual young black boys who spoke these words were likely referring to their own positions as subjects of racism, the fact that they used the word 'we' in a context where they were collectively confronting media depictions of themselves potentially revealed racial dynamics beyond individual identity. On the one hand, the young people were voicing their own distinctive identities, while on the other hand the play, and particularly this specific filmed scene, worked to position the young people as part of a (global) collective. The use of the identity-marker 'black' through the term 'we' operated in performance to suggest that the young people were articulating a shared identity. While this perhaps points to a need for collective resistance in the face of ongoing, intersectional stigmatization, the performance moment also raised questions about how the articulation of their identity had been mediated during the performance-making process, and more widely by the global hood discourse filtered into everyday life via film, popular music and the newspaper press.

Alexander and Knowles argue that race is important in navigating the intersections between internal and external identity. They argue that the surface of the skin operates as a boundary where 'external constructions meet and intersect with internal processes of identity formation' (2005: 13). They articulate how racial identity is created through space as well as through and on the body: 'space is a physical environment that materially inscribes racialized meanings, exclusions and dangers; that is claimed and transformed through its use and reimagination' (2). The moment in *23176* where the young people describe themselves as 'black' reveals the process of identity-making that they are navigating and the difficulty they have in finding a language through which to describe their located and bodily, personal and collective identities. It points to the central struggle for survival implicit in grass-roots practices, which, as I point out above, is connected to residents' profound need to resist reductive stereotypes and positively narrate their lives.

Racial difference has been, and remains, a point of conflict in racially diverse communities (Pearce and Milne 2010: 2). Conversely, however, particularly in locations where the population has not remained largely white, adopting or affiliating with a non-white racial identity might also become a way in which white residents assimilate themselves into a community and through which the community finds an identity. McKenzie suggests that, by adopting the traditions and culture of the Jamaican diaspora, some white residents on the St Ann's estate in Nottingham forged a community with a distinct identity (McKenzie 2009: 98). She argues that on the St Ann's estate many white working-class women 'find value for themselves and their children with a local identity linked to the West Indian community' (349). I would like to draw a connection here between McKenzie's description of collective identity and the 'spirit' of the hood to suggest that collectively referring to themselves as black enabled the young people to articulate a shared, local identity, one 'built on a certain kind of survivorship and mutual suffering' (Richardson and Skott-Myhre 2012: 18).

However, although the pronunciation of this collective identity in performance can be framed as a celebratory moment, there is a troubling element to the lack of attention that this moment was afforded in the performance and to the lack of attention given to race in SPID's wider repertoire of work, where race and ethnicity are rarely mentioned directly.

Because, although it *can* be framed positively, the collective identification of the group as 'black' also invoked external, negative conceptions of young, economically deprived urban people often deployed in political and media rhetoric. By referring to themselves collectively as 'black' although they are not all, technically, black, particularly in a context where they are confronting the disjuncture between their external, media-constructed identities and how they see themselves, the performers unfortunately also hint at the loaded, pejorative language – 'gangs', 'ghettos' – that is lazily applied in various ways to council estate residents and which is related to hood culture and thus racially loaded. Such language serves to create and sustain stereotypes of the inner city by capitalizing on existing conceptions of urban youth and highlighting 'blackness' as a key feature of their supposed delinquency.

While the location of the practice allows the company to critique and unpack harmful estate dogmas that prevail in the wider culture, and while certainly these critiques implicate similar and related dogmas relating to global hood culture and connected to race – particularly to black men and boys – directly interrogating the more complex relationships between class and race appears to have proved more difficult. SPID's artistic director informed me that the company does not deliberately avoid the subject in its work; rather, it has not been addressed because the young people have 'not shown an interest in it' (email exchange, 2013).

Despite being engaged in practice that resists stereotypes, it would appear SPID's young company members are absorbing certain stereotypes of the inner city and using them to understand and articulate their position in relation to the outside world. While forcing the young people to engage with issues they have not expressed an interest in exploring might undermine the emergent, resident-focused way that SPID develops its performance work, its lack of engagement with the issue of race potentially limits the opportunity of the performance work to engage participants and audience members in a useful reflexivity. Although its work often invites audience members to consider their prejudices concerning young estate residents, these interventions work predominately with the spatial relationship between the 'real' and represented. The issues of race, and indeed gender – although predominately male, the performance 'gang' includes both male and female members –

are not called into question in the same way. This limits the opportunity for the performance to engage the audience in a more complex reflexivity, where the intersections between race, class and gender on the estate are highlighted and connections are made between the estate and wider, related inequalities.

Conclusion

Reay and Lucey propose that:

> space needs to be made [in academic discourse] for working-class understandings of locality and place in order to counter the hegemony of middle-class versions. Otherwise we will never move very far from representations of deficit and pathology in relation to the urban poor. (2000: 425)

I would argue that this point extends to dramatic representation, where alternative understandings of council estate space may assist in breaking open enduring stigmas that limit the opportunity structures available to estate residents. The value of SPID's work lies in the ability the company has to create and disseminate alternative depictions of estate space, and to give residents a voice in this process. SPID's practices offer an example of the way that located grass-roots arts practice can highlight the specificity of the council estate struggle, point to the seductive construction of council estate as hood and, at the same time, build upon global traditions of sited resistance in urban environments – which offer residents avenues for survival by giving them the means to share their stories.

However, it is essential that the effects of SPID's work are not exaggerated and that the instrumental nature of the practice is recognized; crucially, it is important to acknowledge that SPID does not operate outside of problematic conceptions of community, which risks reinforcing the discourses they attempt to oppose and isolating individuals who do not identify with the company's vision. Indeed, as I addressed above, the company's existence relies to some extent on the identity of the estate community as marginalized – and its own identity as a radical arts practice which addresses such marginalization. Nonetheless, SPID's long-term engagement with the council estate site, its network of influential partners and techniques for intervening in the habitus of both audience members and participants offer a useful framework for companies seeking to offer marginalized groups strategies for survival. And, indeed, SPID's practice equips individual participants with useful tools for staging further creative resistance beyond the company, both in the immediate location of the estate and via the dissemination of mediatized creative practice on social media platforms where their voices might contribute to an international discourse.

Notes

1. Although the subsidized provision of housing was the initial purpose of council estates, in recent decades they have become more socially diverse. It is now common for owner-occupiers and private renters, as well as social renters, to live on estates, due to the introduction of the 'Right to Buy' policy in the Housing Act 1980, which allowed secure tenants to buy their properties at a discounted price.
2. I have been exposed to SPID's work as part of a larger research project investigating the theatrical representation of council estates in the UK. I have developed a relationship with the company over a number of years, attending performances and interviewing audience and company members in person and via email.
3. Bourdieu's concept of 'habitus' delineates the way that social structures condition a repertoire of behaviours, shared by those who 'practise' similar 'fields'; thus, habitus 'generates meaningful practices and meaning-giving perceptions' (1984: 170).
4. This chapter builds on my earlier article concerned with SPID's practices (Beswick 2011), published in *Research in Drama Education: The Journal of Applied Theatre and Performance*.
5. The term 'chav' may have been derived from the Romany *chavi* meaning 'child' (see Quinon n.d.).
6. See, for example, Reay and Lucey 2000, McKenzie 2009, and Kearns et al. 2013.

Bibliography

Alexander, C., and C. Knowles, 2005. *Making Race Matter: Bodies, Space & Identity*. New York: Palgrave Macmillan.
Ball, J., 2011. 'Who Were the Rioters?' *Guardian*, 5 December, available online at http://www.theguardian.com/uk/2011/dec/05/who-were-the-rioters, accessed 27 May 2014.
Barnett, E., 2009. 'Sixteen'. *The Stage*, 3 August, available online at http://www.thestage.co.uk/reviews/review.php/25167/sixteen, accessed 20 November 2013.
Bauman, Z., 2001. *Community: Seeking Safety in an Insecure World*. Cambridge: Polity Press.
Beswick, K., 2011. 'The Council Estate: Representation, Space and the Potential for Performance'. *Research in Drama Education: The Journal of Applied Theatre and Performance*, 16: 3, pp. 421–35.

Bharucha, R., 2011. 'Problematising Applied Theatre: A Search for Alternative Paradigms'. *Research in Drama Education: The Journal of Applied Theatre and Performance*, 16: 3, pp. 365–84.

Bourdieu, P., 1977. *Outline of a Theory and Practice*. Cambridge: Cambridge University Press.

Bourdieu, P., 1984. *Distinction: A Social Critique on the Judgement of Taste*. London: Routledge.

Couldry, N., 2010. *Why Voice Matters: Culture and Politics After Neo Liberalism*. London: SAGE Publications.

Damer, S., 1974. 'Wine Alley: The Sociology of a Dreadful Enclosure'. *Sociological Review*, 22: 2, pp. 221–48.

hooks, b., 1990. *Yearning: Race, Gender, and Cultural Politics*. Boston: South End Press.

Kearns, A., et al., 2013. 'Notorious Places: Image, Reputation, Stigma. The Role of Newspapers in Area Reputations for Social Housing Estates'. *Housing Studies*, 28: 4, pp. 579–98.

Kelleher, J., 2009. *Theatre & Politics*: Basingstoke: Palgrave Macmillan.

Kitossa, T., 2012. 'Habitus and Rethinking the Discourse of Youth Gangs, Crime, Violence and Ghetto Communities'. In C. Richardson and H. A. Skott-Myhre (eds) *Habitus of the Hood*. Bristol: Intellect, pp. 123–42.

McCann, K., 2011. 'Westminster Vows to Evict Social Tenants Involved in Riots'. *Guardian*, 10 August, available online at http://www.guardian.co.uk/housing-network/2011/aug/10/council-seeks-evictionfor-looters, accessed 23 July 2013.

McKenzie, L. L., 2009. *Finding Value on a Council Estate: Complex Lives, Motherhood and Exclusion*. Unpublished PhD thesis, University of Nottingham.

Pearce, J., and E. J. Milne, 2010. *Participation and Community on Bradford's Traditionally White Estates*. York: Joseph Rowntree Foundation.

Pogatchnik, S., 2011. 'UK Gangs Thrive in August Riots'. *Associated Press*, available online at http://news.yahoo.com/ap-enterprise-uk-gangs-thrive-august-riots-103756755.html, accessed 14 January 2014.

Power, A., 1999. *Estates on the Edge: The Social Consequences of Mass Housing in Northern Europe*. 2nd edition. Basingstoke: Palgrave Macmillan.

Quinon, M., n.d. 'Chav'. *World Wide Words*. Available online at http://www.worldwidewords.org/topicalwords/tw-cha2.htm, accessed 3 June 2013.

Reay, D., and H. Lucey, 2000. 'I Don't Really Like It Here but I Don't Want to Be Anywhere Else: Children and Inner-city Council Estates'. *Antipode*, 32: 4, pp. 410–28.

Richardson, C., and H. A. Skott-Myhre, 2012. 'Introduction'. In C. Richardson and H. A. Skott-Myhre (eds) *Habitus of the Hood*. Bristol: Intellect, pp. 7–25.

Richardson, C., 2012. 'Making "Changes": 2Pac, Nas and the Habitus of the Hood'. I In C. Richardson and H. A. Skott-Myhre (eds) *Habitus of the Hood*. Bristol: Intellect, pp. 123–42.

Rogaly, B., and B. Taylor, 2011. *Moving Histories of Class and Community: Identity, Place and Belonging in Contemporary England*. Basingstoke: Palgrave Macmillan.

Shepherd, S., and M. Wallis, 2004. *Drama/Theatre/Performance*. Abingdon: Routledge.

Skeggs, B., 2005. 'The Making of Class and Gender through Visualising Moral Subject Formation'. *Sociology*, 39: 5, pp. 965–82.

SPID, 2009. *Business Plan 2009–2012*. Unpublished.
Swartz, D., 1997. *Culture and Power: The Sociology of Pierre Bourdieu*. Chicago: University of Chicago Press.
Sweetman, P., 2003. 'Twenty-First Century Dis-ease? Habitual Reflexivity or the Reflexive Habitus'. *Sociological Review*, 51: 4, pp. 528–9.
Takako, D., 2014. 'The Making of Menace II Society'. *Dazed*, available online at http://www.dazeddigital.com/artsandculture/article/16699/1/the-making-of-menace-ii-society, accessed 2 December 2014.
Wacquant, L., 2008. *Urban Outcasts: A Comparative Sociology of Advanced Marginality*. Cambridge: Polity Press.
Watt, P., 2006. 'Respectability, Roughness and "Race": Neighbourhood Place Images and the Making of Working-Class Social Distinctions in London'. *International Journal of Urban and Regional Research*, 30: 4, pp. 776–97.

9
The Art of Survival: Social Circus, Youth Regeneration and Projected Community in the North East of Scotland

Graham Jeffery, Neill Patton, Kerrie Schaefer and Tom Wakeford[1]

Introduction

This chapter examines the creative practice of Theatre Modo in North East Scotland.[2] A self-defined 'social circus' established in 1995, Theatre Modo works throughout Scotland from bases in Glasgow and, since 2012, Peterhead utilizing 'high quality engagement in circus, street theatre and carnival arts as a catalyst for individual and community change' (Theatre Modo). In 2009, Aberdeenshire Community Planning Partnership invited Modo to contribute to a 'Youth Regeneration' project in Peterhead and Fraserburgh, fishing towns located on the north-eastern coastline of the region with small, yet notable, pockets of multiple deprivation. Since 2009 Modo has produced an annual Fireworks Parade, a large celebratory community event coinciding with Bonfire Night, in Peterhead (*Pandemonium* 2009, *Leviathan* 2011) and Fraserburgh (*Fantasmagoria* 2010, *Maelstrom* 2012). Here we focus on the making of *Maelstrom, The Shell Fireworks Parade* in Fraserburgh in 2012, which was the culmination of a four-year programme of community partnership, public engagement and creative practice.

This case study of Modo's programme of work in Aberdeenshire claims to offer an examination of creative and cross-sector community partnership as one possible mode of social organization in situations of extremity. It also claims to broaden the analysis of extremity from the situation of the camp or conflict zone, locating it instead in more mundane and, perhaps, familiar spaces. It is crucial to note that there is nothing exceptional about the Aberdeenshire towns (or the people living in those places) featured in the discussion below. What is under scrutiny in this discussion is the growing gap between wealth and relative poverty or deprivation in the UK, and the fact that social inequality has dramatically increased since the 2008 global financial crisis. Modo's creative practice within a cross-sector community partnership is to be understood in relation to this crisis context, a disturbingly quotidian 'situation of extremity' affecting many communities in the UK today.

Through close analysis of the parade-making process we aim to understand how Modo's long-standing, independent creative practice operates inside a regional community planning and local regeneration partnership. This is key to investigating the role and function of performance within a 'community' (broadly defined to include government, non-government and private/corporate agencies) regeneration process initiated in response to economic and social change. While we readily admit that Modo's work may be situated within practices problematized as 'governing by community' (Rose 1999), we will argue that in creating a 'spatiality of action and performance' (Rose 1997), Modo's creative practice troubles fixed notions of identity and community, particularly in relation to young people and determinations of social exclusion. The researchers assert that it is within the non-representational space of performance created by Modo that alternative possibilities, not necessarily dictated by external intervention, are generated and enacted.

The place of performance and the problem of representing deprivation

Theatre Modo's creative practice is focused on Peterhead (pop. 19,000) and Fraserburgh (pop. 12,500), relatively large settlements located on the coastal fringe of the rural region of Aberdeenshire in Scotland. For the most part, Aberdeenshire is an affluent region. Its economy is buoyed by a significant rate of employment in North Sea/offshore oil and gas and associated service industries, which are based in the city of Aberdeen. While administratively separate from the city, Aberdeenshire's proximity ensures 'low levels of unemployment and crime, high rates of educational attainment and an overall high quality of life' (*Reaching Out Project*: 2). However, the traditional fishing towns of Peterhead and Fraserburgh have been affected, economically and socially, by the imposition of EU quotas to restore falling North Sea fish stocks. While both towns remain commercial fishing ports, parts of Peterhead and Fraserburgh feature prominently in the Scottish

Index for Multiple Deprivation. In order to remediate pockets of multiple deprivation of an order more commonly associated with inner-city neighbourhoods (*Reaching Out Project*: 3), which are perhaps made starker by the relative prosperity within other areas of the local economy, Aberdeenshire Community Planning Partnership (ACPP) initiated the Peterhead (Central-Roanheads) and Fraserburgh (North) Community Regeneration Project, which came to be known as the Reaching Out Project (ROP). Founded in 2005, the ROP is a partnership initiative funded by the Fairer Scotland Fund, awarded locally through the Tackling Poverty and Inequality Group (TPIG) of ACPP. In inviting Modo into the partnership, ACPP identified the ROP as the agency to be lead partner on Modo's work.

Given the themes of this edited volume, it is important to stress here that Peterhead and Fraserburgh are not formally designated as 'sites of crisis'. After a growing literature which problematizes the representation of places as 'poor' or 'deprived', this discussion aims not to exceptionalize the places of Peterhead and Fraserburgh and, by association, the people who live there, who may be similarly 'constructed as exceptional, as characterized by economic deprivation and dependence, social disconnectedness and deviance, political inaction and apathy, and therefore needing the intervention of formal government programmes in order for their human potential to be fulfilled' (Cruikshank 1999: 40). Rather, this discussion identifies growing inequality in the UK as a 'situation of extremity', an exceptional state of permanent (economic) crisis normalized by neoliberal hegemony in order to sustain its ideological attacks on the public sphere.

According to the first report of a major academic study on poverty and social exclusion in the UK, levels of deprivation, based on public determinations of minimum living standards, are returning to the levels of 30 years ago and, while the size of the UK economy has doubled since then, most of the gains have been captured by those on the highest incomes (Gordon et al. 2013: 17). The recent global financial crisis has led to the introduction of 'austerity' measures which have only served to increase levels of deprivation and to exacerbate extremes of wealth and poverty, which leading epidemiologists, influenced by the new public health movement of the 1980s and its recognition of the wider social determinants of health, regard as a serious public heath issue (Marmot and Wilkinson 2003; 2006). Suffice it to say that Aberdeenshire is one amongst many regions in the UK (and globally) confronting this terrifyingly quotidian 'situation of extremity' through growing economic and social inequality. This chapter aims to move beyond debates concerning the impact of the arts on social deficits, wherein the arts are viewed as instrumental to remediating social problems. Drawing instead on work that recognizes a phenomenological connection between participation in arts/cultural activity and survival or human flourishing (White 2009), we will examine how Modo's creative practice figures in the Aberdeenshire community partnership as both respond to the uneven and fluid effects of economic and social change. Again, it is worthwhile being reminded, *pace* White, that while participation in creative activity cannot solve the multidimensional effects of poverty, which 'extend beyond money incomes to education, healthcare, political participation and advancement of one's own culture and social organization', it 'can release visions and voices, and it can tool up some people to break out of the kind of poverty that liberation theology describes as the deprivation of any stimulus to change one's condition' (2009: 35).

Theatre Modo and Creative Community Partnership

Theatre Modo has experienced a slow and gentle journey (see Crehan 2011) into community partnership in Aberdeenshire. Modo's co-founder and artistic director, Martin Danziger, has himself worked creatively with/in remote communities in the Scottish Highlands and North East since the early 1990s. After training in physical and circus performance in Bristol, he returned to establish Modo and develop the company's creative practice in these and other communities. For several months in 2007, Modo were based in Buckie, a town on the Moray Firth coast, to create a performance/parade for the Buckie Festival in the Highland Year of Culture. Katie MacLean, who leads the Community, Learning and Development (CLD) team for the North of Aberdeenshire (Banff and Buchan, and Buchan) was impressed by the level and scale of engagement of young people in a community festival/celebration and invited the company to work on a 'youth engagement' project under the auspices of the CLD in Banff in 2008. MacLean observed that Modo:

> are just really good at enthusing young people, at inspiring them and talking to them and listening to them and believing in them and creating things for them to do themselves without saying 'no that's not the plan, you can't do that'. (2012)

In addition to Modo's ability to engage young people in cultural activity, MacLean noted the scale of engagement of young people in Modo's creative practice:

In terms of working with young people I had never really encountered creative cultural work with young people in the masses before we brought Modo up to do the first project. The cultural involvement of young people tended to be very selective and it was very dependent on young people who were high achieving or high attaining and who were part of a family where there would be cultural experiences. We never succeeded in engaging masses of young people until we found partners like Modo. (2012)

After *Macpherson's Rant* in Banff (2008) MacLean saw the potential for further work with Theatre Modo in Aberdeenshire. Modo's ability to engage young people in huge numbers led MacLean to consider the possibility of scaling up Modo's work to the bigger towns of Peterhead and Fraserburgh. Both towns have large populations of young people: 44 per cent and 49 per cent of the population respectively is between the ages of 0 and 34 years (*Reaching Out Project*: 5–6), and the ROP was attempting to engage this population in the regeneration process. MacLean knew that work of this scale would require, as she stated, 'the freedom and flexibility to work out of the confines of local authority regulatory structures' (2012) and within, instead, a wider community partnership framework. As leader of the CLD with membership of ACPP, she brought Modo into partnership with the ROP. A pilot project in Peterhead, *The Pandemonium Fireworks Parade*, led to a three-year Youth Regeneration project partnership between Theatre Modo, the ROP, Aberdeenshire Community Planning Partners, Shell, Aberdeenshire Council and UZ Arts/Roofless.[3]

Modo in Fraserburgh, 2012

The Modo creative team was led by Danziger as project director. Five practitioners were designated Workshop Leaders, including one each in making costumes and props (Emilie Velluet-Draper), design (Fergus Dunnet), music (Roddy Dickson), and two in performance (Suzie Ferguson and Janine Fearn). The Workshop Leaders in making, design and performance were each joined by an Assistant Workshop Leader (AWL). These Assistants were originally parade participants from previous projects who then volunteered on subsequent parades, and whose development as creative practitioners was mentored by Modo practitioners. A new tranche of funding support from UZ Arts' *Roofless* programme for the 2012 Fireworks Parade meant that Modo could offer the AWLs 'a progressive route through participation' (Danziger 2012) into paid employment. In this way Modo, itself, was able to provide a direct link between skills training, further training and employment, which was a sought after outcome of the community planning/youth regeneration partnership. For Modo, this new development and the formation of workshop teams of two was also significant for increasing the number of young people potentially able to take part in the project, as Danziger explained:

> we concentrate on low-fi, cheap activities like juggling, stilt-walking and fire[4] because 2 of us can work with 30 young people at a time. We don't do aerial, for instance, because it's too expensive. We are always trying to find ways to make sure that our activities are affordable, possible and inclusive so we don't have to make choices about who takes part. (2012)

Modo had two bases in Fraserburgh. One was an empty shop, one of several empty or boarded-up premises located on a street perpendicular to the high street on the edge of the regeneration zone. Modo took over the space, covering the shop front window with images of previous performance parades and information about the company, their work in Scotland, and how to participate in or engage with the work in Fraserburgh. Modo and two ROP workers supporting the project reused this space for project management, administration, planning and meetings. An empty warehouse at the fish market on Fraserburgh harbour was redeployed by Modo as a workshop, rehearsal and drop-in (evenings and school holidays), creative (puppet-making, costume design and making, fire sculpture-making) and storage space. Over the weeks that we visited, the cavernous empty warehouse space, where Modo practitioners and researchers once played football with young men on stilts in an afternoon drop-in session, was progressively filled with all kinds of parade creations. The rest of the process took place in school classrooms and in existing spaces in which youth and community groups already met. Occasionally, workshops spilled out onto the streets as, for instance, when stilt-walkers from Fraserburgh Academy (with a teacher, Modo practitioner and researcher in tow) practised walking the long distance into town or to the beach.

Before workshops got underway parade themes were solicited from the school, youth and community groups that Modo would go on to work with. The final three were determined by polls conducted on various social media. It was decided that the parade would feature the lighthouse at Kinnaird Head, the first built in Scotland by the

Commissioners of Northern Lights (founded 1786) and whose engineers were familial relations of novelist Robert Louis Stevenson; the 'treasure wreck' of the Bonaventura, lost off the north-east coast of Scotland in 1556; and a seal that frequented Fraserburgh harbour. While the parade themes touched on significant local events, stories, legends, personages and/or creatures, these served as frames for the creative activities of different groups, each of which devised a performance to be executed around the large parade puppets – a seal, lighthouse and ship.

The Modo creative team, including Danziger, facilitated approximately 64 weekly workshops in school, youth and community groups in Fraserburgh and the surrounding area over a six-week creative development period. Workshops in puppet-making, lantern-making, stilt-walking, drumming, mural painting, fire juggling/breathing, and circus and street performance were held in schools, youth and community groups. Modo, as Danziger explains, works hard to achieve broad community participation in the project process and event. They work with curriculum (drama, dance, art) classes in schools and with 'mainstream' community groups (dance, drumming, Boy's Brigade, Scouts, Guides, etc.), as well as with students with special education plans in school and with specific issue groups –for example, groups addressing drug and alcohol dependency – in the community. Danziger explains that, while they aim to work with 'lots of people who wouldn't normally take part, lots of challenging, hard-to-reach young people', the parade has to be seen as broadly inclusive because 'if we start describing it as a "parade of the hoodlums" it's going to be clear to those young people why we're doing it and they'll walk away' (2012). According to Danziger, Modo and its partners balance working with excluded young people and maintaining an inclusive creative practice: 'Enough people need to be involved so it's seen as widespread mainstream activity that just happens to involve lots of people who present particular issues or challenges' (2012).

Over six weeks around 1,000 young people from Fraserburgh and the surrounding areas learned circus and performance skills, devised and rehearsed parade routines, designed costume and make-up, and created all the materials (puppets, lanterns, murals, costumes and props) for their performances and the parade. This activity culminated in *Maelstrom, the Shell Fireworks Parade* on the evening of 2 November 2012, which began at the secondary school, Fraserburgh Academy, and wound through the streets of Fraserburgh until it came to a local park where fire performances led by Inferno Fire Troupe, a local cultural group established and nurtured by Modo, and a fireworks display were held. Approximately 7–8,000 people, more than half the population of

Fraserburgh, turned out to watch the parade and fireworks. On a clear, cold November night in North East Scotland many lined the streets, while others watched from windows or from cars parked along the parade route as a mass of young people performed in a parade and community event of their own collective making.

The difference Modo makes

Theatre Modo works in a context where there are significant educational and employability-related challenges affecting the ability of young people to 'flourish' in society. While aware of some of these issues through partnership with social agencies and relationships with young people themselves, Danziger is careful to articulate Modo's creative focus and approach to such knotty social problems:

> Economically and educationally there are limited opportunities and possibilities in the area. Job opportunities are limited, training possibilities are limited and aspirations are limited... we can do something different and provide a different range of opportunities. (Danziger 2012)

While Modo were brought into the regeneration project partnership to address 'major issues around social inclusion' (White and Scott 2012) and to hit 'health and employability targets' (Scott 2012) their process with young people was remarkably free of the discourses of personal responsibility and civic/community renewal (although these themes were raised in reflection prompted by researchers' questions). Modo carved out an active creative space – a 'spatiality of action and performance' (Rose 1997) – in which young people were occupied with the disciplines of physical and circus performance, and the challenge of making a street parade and spectacular community event. As Danziger states:

> We don't do the discourse thing. In an odd way that's one of our strengths. We do the same as lots of people working with young people – try to encourage them to communicate, to have confidence, and self esteem – but we don't ever really mention it. [...] For example, we'll bring out the stilts and people will realize having gone through that journey from terror to exhilaration that actually somewhere along the line they've become proud of what they've achieved. [...] (Danziger 2012)

The focus of interaction between young people and Modo is a practical task, whether devising performance routines, learning a performance skill such as stilt-walking, or stencilling fabric. Recalling her participation in an earlier parade an AWL stated:

> [Modo] made it sound like they really needed us to be in the parade. They made us feel we were wanted for something. [...] In drama classes we came up with movement and choreography to go into the parade [...] They said 'you've got really good ideas'. (2012)

Performance Workshop Leader, Suzie Ferguson, states that the key aim of the process for her – and the same would be true of other Modo practitioners in their respective workshop areas – is to facilitate young people in creating their own performances:

> it's all about the ideas coming from the young people and making sure that they have complete ownership of it...It all comes from them and that's the whole point...the main thing is that they've come up with it, they love it and they want to show people what they've done. (2013)

The same AWL found a similar situation of practical challenge and learning when she advanced to work as a volunteer on the parade the following year. Working with Design Workshop Leader, Fergus Dunnet, the AWL notes that:

> Fergus showed us how to do things and we'd do it. Then he gave us more responsibilities. We got to spray paint all the flags with stencils. If we made a mistake, it wouldn't look as good, but would be used. It made us feel more responsible to make it perfect. (2012)

Young people valued this practical and creative space. They identified a range of experiences (fun, a level of risk/challenge, shared excitement, relaxed informality) that were possible or allowed in the process that weren't in more everyday spaces, such as in school or at home, for instance:

> It was different and I didn't expect it to be that fun. My mum was really over protective...she kept saying that she wouldn't have let me do it [walk on stilts] but she's really proud of me being able to do it. (Participant 1, 2012)

Everyone really likes it, it brings a different feeling...people get excited...my dad is really excited about seeing the Bonaventura. (AWL 1, 2012)

You're not cooped up in a classroom and at Modo you can actually have a laugh with them, it's not all serious like school...[Modo practitioners] are just like teenagers...you can be yourself around them...you don't have to be scared about being a nutter like me because they're all nutters too. (Participant 2, 2012)

I like being in here [the fish market], I don't always feel like speaking to people. I just feel comfortable in here...I feel like I can be and do what I want. (AWL 2, 2012)

While a lot of the Modo activities are presented and perceived as 'fun', rather than formal learning, the discipline required to walk on stilts, juggle-with-fire, choreograph movement routines, make puppets, stencil designs on material, sew costumes, and perform non-stop for hours in a moving street parade presents intrinsic challenges that provide a framework for learning. Dunnet asserts that the young people undergo 'a process and it is creative process...[as well as] a process of learning and creative development' (2013). Community partners such as MacLean and a secondary school teacher viewed the parade as a key learning and development experience for young people. According to MacLean, based on her observation of previous parades, the experience of participating in the parade 'led to a sense of personal achievement and growth for those who took part' (MacLean 2012).

Participants interviewed in the process acknowledged that they were learning new skills and gaining confidence: 'It's given me a heap more confidence, I feel useful. I feel valued as a person' (AWL 1, 2012). Some described enjoying connecting with 'different people', from other young people to theatre technicians, whose skills they admired, to those who came out to watch the parade. Having community members come out to see the parade in large numbers provided a new perspective on the place they lived in: '[I]t makes you realize that Peterhead isn't just full of horrible folk...[Living in Peterhead] was rubbish, I didn't like it and wanted to move away...I'm quite happy where I am at now' (AWL 1, 2012). Others spoke about subtle changes that it had brought about in familial relationships: 'My mum and dad didn't understand me spending all my time on it. They totally disapproved of it for a while...they didn't get it. But when they saw what I had done they were like "I didn't know you could do that" and I was like "aha!"' (AWL 2, 2012). Taking part in the process also presented new possibilities for future directions: 'I always wanted to do something like that [circus/physical performance] but I didn't think you could really... but then when I saw Modo, I thought, "you can do it"' (Participant 1, 2012); 'Before I couldn't think I could do arty things... I've always felt I was too rubbish to do it... [now] I've a little bit [of a plan]... I want to go to college to do art. I want to do the lowest course so I can build up to being good... I just want to learn how to be good at art' (AWL 1, 2012). There is evidence in these accounts from participants of informal learning, of experience of subtle forms of apprenticeship, and the making of new identities and the imagining of possible futures.

Analysis of responses from practitioners, professionals and participants variously engaged in the creative process led the researchers to consider the concept of 'projected community' as best fitting Modo's creative practice. According to Mulligan et al., 'projected community is neither embeddedness in particularistic relations, nor adherence to a particular way of life, but rather the active establishment of a creative space in which individuals engage in an open-ended process of constructing, deconstructing and reconstructing identities and ethics for living' (2006: 18). The notion of projected community underpinning Modo's creative process was also present in the event of the parade, which simultaneously brought people together in the streets of Fraserburgh to witness a celebratory spectacle and, at the same time, shifted preconceptions of identity (particularly that of young people), relationships (with family members and other adult figures of authority) and understandings of place/community, as we will go on to discuss.

Participatory performance process, creative space and projected community

In a study of community arts workers in Edinburgh, cultural geographer Gillian Rose attempts to understand how creative practitioners understand the politics of their practice given criticism of the concept of community (1997: 184). As Rose explains, in its exclusion of difference and in its oppressive uniformity of self-same identity, a politics based on community as collective identity is viewed critically as the antithesis of a radical politics (1997: 185). Analysing the transcripts of numerous interviews with community arts workers, Rose realized that it was what practitioners didn't say, their silences around certain aspects of creative processes and production, that was critically important. She notes that community arts workers were silent or refused to talk about the meaning or significance of what was co-produced in and through the creative process:

> The workers refused to explain the significance of these products for me in any terms other than the processes of their making, or their impact on audiences. The products were never represented, never described as artefacts awaiting interpretation for community arts workers. Instead, they were always placed in the context of performances, both in their making and in their audiencing. These products were understood as moments of 'communication', not as representation, and therefore could not be described... (1997: 193)

At the same time, while community arts workers refuse to describe, interpret or define the products of the creative process, they do celebrate that process in and of itself:

> A product of a particular project is presented in and of itself as an achievement, regardless of what it 'means'. Its importance is not in its meaning but in its facticity; enormous importance is given to the sheer existence of the object itself. [...] the fact that participants got 'to create something that they're proud of' [...] The workers celebrate this making. (Rose 1997: 193)

Drawing on the work of Berlant, Copjec and Bhabha in and through an extended discussion of Nancy's concept of 'inoperative community', Rose asserts that community arts workers engage in a radical politics that works to destabilize power/knowledge by uncovering surplus, excess and lack in relation to 'the dominant culture's discursive myths of identity and community' (Rose 1997: 187). In other words, the resolute focus by community arts workers on process and participation, their creation of a non-representational 'spatiality of action and performance', founds a 'politics of praxis', which is also a 'politics of resistance' (1997). The very existence of a space of creative practice is a threat to the dominant discursive order. Apparently fixed, stable and secure knowledges, meanings and values can, potentially, be un-worked and reworked in and through participatory creative processes.

Theatre Modo's creative practice is to be located in relation to a notion of 'inoperative' or projected (Rose 1997; Mulligan et al. 2006; see also Kwon 2004) community and this is most evident in relation to the event of the parade. According to Danziger it provides an important platform in so far as 'what people seem to want is the liberty to demonstrate that joy of doing stuff' (Danziger 2012). In line with Danziger's assertion, the research team assert that the *Maelstom* parade was less about communicating a narrative story grounded in place-based identity, although if one were looking for representational meaning/significance a link could clearly be drawn between R. L. Stevenson's creative persona and the creative activity of Fraserburgh's young people. Nevertheless, despite the presence of some historical/literary references, the parade was driven by an emphasis on action and performance through participation. Within that experience was the enactment of emergent identities not necessarily simply tied to place, family, school or community, but primarily enacted through the celebratory display of newly learned creative skills in an extravagant performance. As Danziger observes:

> You can remind them as much as you like about what the parade's about and how it's connected into their story but actually... the identity and sense of place that they're interested in is their identity on stilts. It's not about their identity in the story. [It's about] the fact that they're walking down the main street of their hometown on stilts and that place and identity actually always seems stronger than any identity or place that you can create by historical or cultural analogies. (2012)

The carnivalesque sights and sounds and sheer scale of the parade (750 participants, around three quarters of a mile long from start to finish) also provided a moment of social transformation in Fraserburgh where young people were highly visible on the streets and a cold, usually quiet, November evening was illuminated with fireworks, drumming and dancing. The performance spaces thus created allowed for the enactment of 'difference', including new acts of communication and reconnection, which might lead to subtle changes in perception, and future performances, of self and/or others, as Danziger observes:

> Making some of those stilters the centre of attention in a positive way is to change radically how they are normally perceived and what their normal role is in the community context... and there is something about getting criminal justice or drug offenders to come along and steward on the night when they are suddenly in hi-vis vests walking alongside police. There is that sense of 'it can be different'. (2012)

Conclusion

In this chapter we've attempted to explain how Modo's work in a particular part of North East Scotland (Aberdeenshire) has developed, survived, even thrived, and how the work has been shaped by the specific contexts of 'community', both as formally enacted through policy in relation to community development, young people, social inclusion/exclusion and regeneration initiatives, and also informally through engagement and challenge with a complex confluence of values and attitudes towards young people and their creative potential. Rather than discuss the impact or effects of this kind of work in an area of multiple deprivation – the 'arts as a social elastoplast' model (White, n.d.: 21) – we've sought to focus on the process and its connection to a 'politics of praxis and resistance' (Rose 1997) within community planning and regeneration contexts. We have observed and documented the process and explored the perspectives of the creative team, project partners (a mix of government, third sector/charity and corporate), participants *and* researchers, in an attempt to get at the *values underpinning* the work more than the 'effect' it has.

Modo's work has developed in and through these particular contexts, which has influenced the way the company, in the broadest sense, defines the work. There is not a methodologically or theoretically fixed Modo practice; it is dynamic, evolving and dependent on navigating policy and funding opportunities. There is a deep pragmatism and opportunism in the work, which could perhaps be criticized from a more radical political perspective: at a time where sponsorship of major cultural institutions by the oil/gas industry is criticized by campaigners as 'buying legitimacy',[5] there is an expedient local logic for the involvement of Shell, a significant regional employer and 'community stakeholder' in the parade. John Raine, community relations manager, repeatedly emphasized the need for Shell to be seen as a 'good neighbour, as good citizens...as giving something back' (2012). This is an example of the kind of ideologically messy, pragmatic partnership working that characterizes community arts practice, particularly when attempting to achieve large-scale projects at a significant distance away from major centres of cultural power. Modo mediates these narratives and discourses to produce learning situations and encounters which are experienced as meaningful opportunities by the young people that take part, even if they are not explicitly named as 'skills development'.

Thus, energy generation of a different kind is an important part of Modo's practice: they use fire and physical circus skills to generate enthusiasm and fuel creativity. Modo artists spend much time in being encouraging and energizing young people. The Fireworks Parade is the culmination of months of quietly connective and communicative activity which is, in large part, task-focused and produced by the company, but which also allows space for people to *be* – to hang out in social/creative spaces and witness the process. Lots of people, not only those who perform in the parade or participate in workshops, feel like they've taken part, even if only from the sidelines, and they have. By stressing accessible artistic activity Modo create a communicative and performative space which demonstrates spaces of learning and possibility, however small, piecemeal, fragile or compromised. Modo's is a pragmatic politics of praxis rather than a set of sweeping statements or grand gestures or exaggerated claims of 'impact'. However, Modo still manages to enact other possibilities, other modes of value, and other experiences of identity and community beyond dominant social and policy discourses – as a celebratory construction of fragile solidarities through making, performing and learning together.

Notes

1. The authors would like to thank Martin Danziger for comments on a penultimate draft and for gaining necessary permissions to quote participants, and the editors for their insightful comments on earlier drafts.
2. The authors wish to acknowledge the support of the Arts and Humanities Research Council and the cross-council Connected Communities programme. *Remaking Society* (grant number AH/J006882/1) brought an interdisciplinary team of researchers into partnership with community development, community health and participatory arts and media organizations in four contrasting contexts of deprivation in the UK to investigate the pragmatic politics of creative practice in action.
3. UZ Arts Roofless came on board in 2012. For more on the outdoor art programme coordinated by UZ Arts see: http://roofless.org.uk
4. Danziger is referring here to a number of fire-related activities including the making of fire sculptures, fire breathing and juggling fire sticks.
5. See, for example: http://platformlondon.org/2013/08/28/margaret-atwood-talk-at-the-southbank-centre-sponsorship-shell-dystopias/

Bibliography

Assistant Workshop Leader (AWL) 1, 2012. *Interview with N. Patton.* 10 October, Fraserburgh.
Assistant Workshop Leader (AWL) 2, 2012. *Interview with N. Patton.* 10 October, Fraserburgh.
Assistant Workshop Leader (AWL) 3, 2012. *Interview with K. Schaefer and N. Patton.* 9 October, Fraserburgh.
Crehan, K., 2011. *Community Art: An Anthropological Perspective.* London and New York: Berg.
Cruikshank, B., 1999. *The Will to Empower: Democratic Citizens and Other Subjects* Ithaca: Cornell University Press.

Danziger, M., 2012. *Interview with K. Schaefer and N. Patton*. 9 October, Fraserburgh.
Dunnet, F., 2013. *Interview with N. Patton*. 15 January, Glasgow.
Ferguson, S., 2013. *Interview with N. Patton*. 15 January, Glasgow.
Gordon, D., J. Mack, S. Lansley, G. Main, S. Nandy, D. Patsios, and M. Pompati, 2013. *The Impoverishment of the UK. PSE UK First Results: Living Standards*, available online from http://www.poverty.ac.uk/sites/default/files/attachments/The_Impoverishment_of_the_UK_PSE_UK_first_results_summary_report_March_28.pdf, accessed 23 June 2013.
Kwon, M., 2004. *One Place After Another: Site-specific Art and Locational Identity* Massachusetts: MIT Press.
MacLean, K., 2012. *Interview with K. Schaefer*. 2 November, Fraserburgh.
Marmot, M., and R. G. Wilkinson, 2003. *Social Determinants of Health. The Solid Facts*. World Health Organisation, available online from http://www.euro.who.int/__data/assets/pdf_file/0005/98438/e81384.pdf, accessed 10 June 2012.
Marmot, M., and R. G. Wilkinson, 2006. *Social Determinants of Health*. 2nd edition. Oxford: Oxford University Press.
Mulligan, M., K. Humphery, P. James, C. Scanlon, P. Smith, and N. Welch, 2006. *Creating Community: Celebrations, Arts and Wellbeing Within and Across Local Communities*. VicHealth and Globalism Research Centre: Melbourne.
Participant 1, 2012. *Interview with N. Patton*. 10 October, Fraserburgh.
Participant 2, 2012. *Interview with N. Patton*. 10 October, Fraserburgh.
Raine, J., 2012. *Shell Stakeholder Welcome*. 2 November, Fraserburgh Community Centre, Fraserburgh.
Reaching Out Project. Aberdeenshire Community Planning Partnership, available online at http://www.aberdeenshire.gov.uk/communityplanning/AberdeenshireROA.pdf, accessed 18 September 2012.
Rose, G., 1997. 'Performing Inoperative Community. The Space and the Resistance of Some Community Arts Projects. In Pile and Keith (eds) *Geographies of Resistance*. London: Routledge, pp. 184–202.
Rose, N., 1999. *Powers of Freedom: Reframing Political Thought*. Cambridge: Cambridge University Press.
Theatre Modo. *Theatre Modo Website*, available online at http://www.theatremodo.com/startingpage.html, accessed 12 June 2012.
White, C., and L. Scott, 2012. *Interview with N. Patton*. 15 January, Fraserburgh.
White, M., n.d. 'What the Experts Think: Mike White'. In P. Devlin, *Restoring the Balance. The Effect of Arts Participation on Wellbeing and Health*. Voluntary Arts England, pp 19–22, available online at http://www.voluntaryarts.org/wp-content/uploads/2011/10/Restoring-the-Balance.pdf, accessed 12 February 2013.
White, M., 2009. *Arts Development in Community Health: A Social Tonic*. Oxford: Radcliffe.
World Health Organisation. 2006. *Social Determinants of Health*, 2nd edition. Oxford: Oxford University Press.

Part V
Crisis and Extremity as Performance

10
The Paradox of Dis/appearance: Hunger Strike in Athens as a Performance of Survival

Aylwyn Walsh

Introduction[1]

This chapter analyses a large-scale hunger strike act, performed by 300 migrants, staged in a makeshift 'camp' in the Law School building in Athens in January 2011. It began when the 300 men – all asylum seekers and economic migrants – embarked on a hunger strike in order to pressurize the Greek government into paying attention to their demands for legal status. I examine this event as a means of practising resistance and as a spectacle that draws attention to migrants' disappearing bodies in order to create a political space for recognition. The construction of the hunger strike was dramaturgically compelling: the staging and scene can be analysed in relation to their positions on the threshold between public and private. In this chapter, however, I shift the focus from defining the hunger strike as 'performance', which is briefly summarized here, and turn towards considering this performance within the context of crisis and austerity in Greece as a situation of extremity, multiplied by migrants' precarious legal status. Thus, rather than rely on the mapping of performance and hunger strike, my argument seeks to position the social conditions of the crisis contemporary to the hunger strike as a performance that distinctly stages a politics of dispossession. Hunger as a conscious, unravelling performance of resistance displays wider socio-political dispossession.

Most hunger strikes are conducted within the framework of incarceration – in which the bodies of the strikers are considered to be in the care of the state – and to which 'care' the strikers inevitably refer in their attempts to draw attention to its ambivalence. Writings on Irish hunger strikes led by Bobby Sands in the 1980s (Anderson 2009, 2010; Sweeney 1993), and on hunger striking by refugee subjects (Conlon 2013; Grewcock 2013; Hazou 2008), demonstrate that the starving body becomes a point of political contention as wilful self-destruction positions the state as ultimately powerless over the 'survival' of the incarcerated strikers. In the case of political prisoners and refugee detainees, there is heightened awareness of the tensions inherent in carceral spaces as sites of extremity in relation to limitations of freedoms and the curtailment of rights. Hunger strikes provide a potent act of resistance that draws attention to issues of human rights and the responsibility of those in power over the bodies of those subjugated to state authority. For hunger strikers, their resistant acts present the body as the locus of symbolic meaning, as, along with the progress of the strike and its relation to specific political demands, public attention is drawn to the conditions surrounding these demands. Under the universal declaration of human rights, prisons or detention centres can only perform their functions when they are perceived to be housing, feeding and treating inmates with humanity. Incarceration is thus intended to ensure the survival of the inmates.[2] In other words, the limitations of state control are evident in the strikers' deliberate refusal to survive. This is particularly potent in relation to incarcerated strikers. Yet, the chapter uncovers a knotty problem of survival in the conditions of extremity highlighted by such strikes: if the hunger strikers 'succeed' in their intentions, then either their demands are met, or the outcome is death. If they 'fail', or survive the strike, then their continued existence draws attention to the ineffectual strike. However, this fails to take into account the strategic deployment of the strike as a form of resistance in which the threat of non-survival is intended to call the ethical bonds between subject and authority (usually extending to the reach of the state) into question. This chapter proceeds to analyse a hunger strike conducted outside of penal institutions as a performance that is at the same time an act of resistance and a citation of wider tensions that constitute Greece in the first years of austerity (2009–12) as a site of extreme dispossession, suffering and lack of social and political agency.

Yet, while I am interested in teasing out some of the dramaturgical elements of the hunger strikes in Greece, the chapter is underscored by Deirdre Conlon's (2013) recent thinking about the implications of governmentality in the staging of such a strike. She offers the argument that hunger strikes

> enact the right to question how one is governed, which is, at once, to recognize and realize the logic of governmentality while

simultaneously refusing its form or means in a particular situation. In other words, hunger strikes exemplify a process that relies on, yet also calls into question, the rationale and practices that are in place to guide human behaviour or conduct. (2013: 145-6)

The strike is a political performance of resistance against the state, but in its participants' seeking of recognition from the state as human subjects, it legitimized the state's power to determine whose life counts. I will return to this quandary later in the chapter. The migrants' strike gestured towards dissent and destruction of the corpus as metonymically standing in for the wider body politic. Their choice of performative protest was a means of foregrounding their desire for a future within the country as (equal) citizens whose lives count, and therefore whose bodily integrity matters to the wider public as well as the state. In this sense, I am relying on the spectacle and the consequent political pressure experienced by the authorities who were forced to take stock of the human suffering in the centre of the capital. I do not propose that the government actually shifted its sclerotic position on migration, simply that this particular event provided a moment in which they were visibly seen to be paying attention to the related issues. The performative force of the hunger strike relies on the cathartic resolution of recognition by the state. The main focus of this chapter is this paradoxical positioning of performing (for) survival.

The chapter develops a means of framing the Athens hunger strike as an act of political resistance that occurred within a highly symbolic space and not within a prison or detention centre. Indeed, most research on hunger striking correlates with institutional demands and the relationship between detention and human rights. This specific case, however, was a hunger strike conducted in a public space, without the framing of a carceral space in which to set the act of resistance, and therefore with the likelihood that the strike would prove a 'failure', as the state was not directly responsible for the migrants. Rather, these hunger strikers took up position in the Law School building in central Athens. This choice was symbolic since the strikers occupied university spaces (which were, until recently, asylum spaces).[3] In other words, migrants whose legal status did not lend them legitimacy in the eyes of the state staged an 'appearance' in a space of learning loaded with historical capital, the significance of which relates intimately to Greek national identity, as I demonstrate in a subsequent section on asylum spaces.

Their performance was stage-managed by a collective called Migrants' Forum in Crete, along with some voluntary human rights lawyers who acted as gatekeepers. It was constituted to draw attention to the situations of extremity faced by migrants in Greece – precarious workers, some of whom were without documentation (*sans papiers*), and without the right to claim unpaid wages or retrieve unemployment insurance, much less the means to return to their home countries.[4] The migrants' decision to conduct the hunger strike was fuelled by dissatisfaction that many had experienced a change in their working conditions due to the impact of austerity politics. The related social and economic context is explored in more detail in the next section.

I must acknowledge a problem of terminology that arises in the case of the hunger strike in Greece, which relates to the juridico-political distinctions between asylum seekers, refugees, immigrants and migrant workers that run throughout the chapter. This problem is not merely a matter of which 'category' migrants may claim, but is intricately tied up with the bureaucratic state mechanisms that are inherited from the European Union, as implemented by the Greek state. In other words, although persecuted people have the right to claim asylum when they appear at the borders, the corruption and mismanagement of the Greek state has both denied legitimate claims for asylum and prevented such claims from being made (Amnesty 2012). Thus, even though migrants could have legitimate reasons for claiming asylum, they may have been in the country for several years without having made an asylum claim, and therefore their legal status remains in question. In addition, where migrants have managed to lodge legitimate claims, political instability has meant that immigration status has shifted due to the introduction of new laws by successive governments. Previously 'legal' migrants with documentation and the right to work suddenly found themselves unable to pay *ensima*, the equivalent of national insurance contributions, which is matched by employer contributions. This was due to rising unemployment as well as increased reliance on black market labour. In the ontological trap that bureaucrats can implement, the lack of *ensima* means that the right to work is called into question. Thus, migrants who have the right to work are forced to act in the same way as 'illegal' migrants in pursuit of precarious jobs to support themselves and their families.

I have tended to retain the word migrant in this chapter, since this is the term used in their own communication tactics, while drawing on literature that refers to the position of refugees and asylum seekers. However, where it is necessary, I distinguish between migrants who appear to have the choice of returning home and those that do not (for reasons of war, or continued threat of persecution). The issues of migration are centred around definitions, legal status, paperwork and the burden of proof that demands a convincing 'story' of intention and reasons for leaving one's point of origin (also often obscured for a range of complex reasons). I make reference to issues about migration that could equally apply to refugees, asylum seekers or economic migrants because the current state in Greece positions all three 'statuses' as equally marginalized, vulnerable to exploitation and without adequate protection by the law governing persecuted peoples. In other words, very few migrants hold legal rights, and therefore struggle to attain the visibility accorded to those that present themselves as refugees at international borders.[5] The hunger strikers occupied all three positions, and crucially maintained the collective label 'migrants', while refusing to be more specific about their countries of origin, which might otherwise have identified them as economic migrants or asylum seekers. Convivial hospitality towards 'the Other' was put under pressure by Greeks who now had to engage with their own survival. What was more starkly evident, in the state of financial and social 'crisis', was a stark difference between 'us' and 'them'. The distinguishing markers returned to the xenophobic attitudes that are prevalent in times of precarity: firstly, the rigid understanding of nationalistic belonging related to language, culture and religion, and secondly, the increased profiling of racial and ethnic differences. Yet, many of the migrants who constituted the hunger strikers had been living in Greece for many years, had been integrated into the 'host' communities, learnt the language, and worked (often in grey zones as precarious labour, since they were prepared to work without national insurance contributions).

The crisis of austerity related to the global financial crisis beginning 2007/8, and its concomitant increase in xenophobia, state-sanctioned crackdowns, fear of bodily danger, instability in relation to work, and unfair dismissals, served to frame their experience as 'extreme'. Extremity here is understood not as the stark demarcation of loss of liberty represented by incarceration in detention centres, but is dispersed as everyday, insidious violence in the ways 'crisis' resulted in the erosion of human rights. While freedom to move was still permitted, many migrants undoubtedly felt 'stuck' in Greece, unable to report hate crimes against them for fear of victimization (see Golash-Boza 2001). Many wanted to move away from Greece, but were unable to do so due to the Dublin II treaty, and others felt unsafe returning to their home countries. The recent Amnesty International report on the experiences of migrants in Greece cites an asylum seeker who says 'in Syria you die once, here you die many times... we are forced to sleep rough and are scared of racist attacks' (2012: 2).[6] This anecdote was collected before the escalation of the Syrian conflict, but it highlights a number of concerns related to the problems of perceptions of Europe as a space of asylum and hospitality. The report provides further evidence of disillusionment faced by migrants who feel trapped and unable to return home, also highlighting the dual trap of how one of the 'gateways' to Europe is a holding ground with no escape.

Greece as 'gateway to Europe': a body politic in crisis

In Greece, often considered the 'entry point' to Europe, what led to the juridical invisibility of migrants? In 2003, the European Commission passed a regulation (known as Dublin II) relating to the status of asylum claims across the member states. In brief, the regulation sets out a juridical framework for timely asylum claims and seeks to ensure that claims are made to the 'first point of entry'.[7] In practice, that means that all EU member states were obliged to deport all claimants who had crossed EU borders back to the point of initial entry (in a procedure known as *refoulement*).[8] However, in the case of Greece, NGOs and human rights organizations petitioned the EU to demand that EU states did not return 'illegal' immigrants to Greece in particular, since the country's systems and resources would be unable to cope with the volume of returned migrants. Furthermore, EU states believed that there would be little chance that the international standards of human rights in detention would be enforced (Mindova 2013). In short, in the years leading up to what is now called the 'crisis', migration had become a critical social and political concern.

Migrants' rights had been systematically eroded in Greece during the years following the Olympic Games of 2004. There is very little reliable data on immigration figures, as the porous borders meant that entries were undocumented. However, some reports cite figures of up to ten per cent of the population (Kasimis 2012). This, coupled with the lack of transparency in the asylum process, and the routine use of detention and deportation rather than a system of assessment for asylum claims, means that migrants face increased marginalization in relation to their legal status – mainly because the state seems to be unwilling or unable to reform its practices. The international community has noted shortcomings in the Greek system, but there has been very little progress relating to application, assessment and the granting of papers. Against this background of corruption, mismanagement and sheer volumes of migrants, in about 2008 Greece simultaneously entered a deep recession. This meant that, even more than before, the economic squeeze was unevenly felt by the poor and marginalized, including precarious migrant labourers in the agricultural sector. Added to this, as in other eras of austerity, dwindling opportunities correlate with an increase in suspicion of 'others' – in this case, a deep and growing xenophobia that relates to a sense of insecurity in the job market. By early 2011, Greece had already endured three full years of shrinking economy and austerity, and people had become used to referring to 'crisis' in daily life. For non-Greeks, however, the situation was intensified by the increased surveillance by police, racial profiling and criminalization. At the same time, the state mechanisms for processing asylum claims, as well as the resources needed for fair and humane treatment in detention centres, had been eroded by cuts. As a result of poverty, unemployment and instability in public services, commentators noted an increase in crime (Kasimis 2012). Simultaneously, there was a shortage of jobs and farmers and factory owners began to experience delays in payments. This had a knock-on effect, so that the agricultural sector continued to supply goods while, in some cases, refusing to pay workers for more than six months – tantamount to slave labour. In this context, a group of 300 migrant workers (mainly from the Maghreb region) worked closely with human rights lawyers in order to stage a large-scale hunger strike in central Athens, as a means of pressuring the then-socialist government (PASOK, led by George Papandreou) to make significant changes to the ways migrant rights were being handled in Greece. Starting in early January 2011, they initiated their hunger strike. Their chosen site was the Law School in Athens, highly symbolic because of the historical resonance of occupying university spaces in the face of political contestation (particularly in the context of the post-1973 modern Greek state). In this light, the next section details the particular circumstances of the Law School and its significance as constituting the social spectacle of the strike.

Setting the scene: asylum spaces

The setting of the migrants' hunger strike in the Law Building of the University of Athens evoked the ghosts of the early 1970s and of students and radicals locked in conflict with the police since that time.[9] The notion of university as 'sanctuary' was not questioned until immigrants 'appeared' there and demanded to be seen. Writing about refugees, Sophie Nield (2008, 2010) refers to the simultaneous need for them to 'appear' and have 'presence': to be both physically present and to be constituted by the documentation that legitimizes their presence.

'Appearance', then, is being used here to indicate a 'particularly theatrical practice' (2010: 40). Nield says that it is the 'mode by which things, objects, people inhabit that strange dual space – there but not there, here but not here – of the theatre. To appear is to become visible or manifest – to be spectated' (Nield: 40). This means that legitimacy lies with those that can affirm the presence of the subjects as bodies; but what happens when the bodies refuse to be legitimized or 'read' by the system? What does it mean when they call into question the discourses of power and subjection that inscribe them? What questions are thrown up by the desire to be marked as 'legal', while resisting the definition of humans *being* 'illegal'? How, then, does a hunger strike become an ambiguous manifestation of performing (for) survival?

I have already claimed that the choice of the Law School and the second site as the central stage for their performance was a deeply symbolic act that was consciously framed as such in the strikers' communiqués (printed fliers and blogspot; see Assembly of Migrant Workers 2011). Not only did these migrants link their struggle with earlier acts of resistance evoking feelings of empathy and solidarity; they also questioned the essence of a juridical system that refused to recognize them as human beings and visible citizens. I will go on to analyse the means by which visibility and invisibility were central to the strike by considering what such staging calls into question. At the time of the strike, the very public spectacle prefigured an understanding of what it means to be human, and the question of whose lives 'count'. The strike positioned the public as imbricated within the fate of the strikers, though in hindsight I would suggest that the performance of the hunger strike was a spectacle that did not engage in any kind of transformative negotiation with the political status quo. Nevertheless, it served as an important performative protest of resistance that explicitly positioned the migrants' bodies at the centre of public discussion. Initially, however, I attend to the conception of starvation as a paradoxical performance for survival.

Hunger strike: starvation as performance for survival

If we consider Baz Kershaw's notion (2003) of efficacious performance as one which has engaged with an ideological intention in order to effect change, then a reading of the hunger strike of 300 migrants as a performance would only be considered efficacious if they were successful in achieving their intended aim: 'instant legalization for all.' Simultaneously, since the correlative act alongside the intention was starvation, if the strikers 'failed' to complete the strike, then their intention was also called into question. Finally, we must question what efficacy might mean in this instance: to 'succeed' is to be granted their demands; equally, though, the performance must be completed, and thus another way of 'succeeding' is to starve to death. Lucy Nevitt calls this a 'spectacle of harm' (2013: 64), which relies on the durational degeneration of the body. Accordingly, Patrick Anderson says that

> self-starvation conceptually and methodologically obtains its significance as cultural practice not simply in gesturing toward absence, but in viscerally and affectively summoning us to bear witness to the long, slow, wasting away of human flesh. (2010: 2)

Anderson is pointing towards the core spectacular function of hunger strikes. The inherent paradox of the invisible immigrants is their actively willing themselves to 'appear' by diminishing their existence by growing ever thinner, and closer to death – or, as Alan Feldman puts it, the way subject/object are fused in politically material ways through self-starvation (1997). Such attention to witness in the act of martyrdom is key to its success. The critical issue in this rendering of the hunger strike as performance is that the Greek root of the word 'martyr' (*martyria*) refers to witnessing. Thus, a protagonist undertaking an act of martyrdom is at once a witness to the social and political conditions that placed them in the position to become martyrs, as well as a figure that demands witnesses. If self-immolation engages spectators who witness the destruction of self for a wider cause, then spectacle has a function in the political efficacy of the act. If we consider that a particularly important operation in the hunger strike is audience witnessing, we can observe the complex interplay of gaze and subject/object binaries.[10] This shift from material presence to the wasting away of presence is fundamental to thinking of hunger strike as performance.

As with every civil protest that begins at the grass-roots level, in the case of the 300 migrant workers there was an important role for communication and representation. This gatekeeping occurred via the human rights lawyers and supporters who had initially helped ensconce the strikers in the Law School building. These same supporters also helped negotiate the shift from the Law School to another building not in use as a learning space, but nevertheless university property under asylum protection. However, its position was more exposed than the original site, and the decision was made to seal off the building, erecting medical tents that were staffed with volunteers prepared to assist in the event of medical emergencies. The sealing off of the building fulfilled another function: to avert the intrusion of the authorities, and to replicate the conditions of warmth, security and solidarity that would be found in other institutional sites of hunger strikes. One could argue that the banners and plastic wrapping of the fence to protect the strikers from 'the outside' functioned as a challenge to the question of witnessing raised earlier. Yet, it is not precisely the image of the starving body that is fundamental to the communication of the aims of the hunger strike, but the conscious framing and aesthetic marking of the strike as such – in particular, through the very visible constant presence of the Red Cross and other volunteers. This strike, like strikes in prisons or detention conditions, relies less on the image of starvation than on the imagination of the public whose grasp of starvation is mediated through the lists of physical, medical and emotional effects of the strike.[11]

Performance scholars writing about refugeeism engage with this distinction between visibility and invisibility (Balfour 2013; Hazou 2008; Jeffers 2008; Jestrovic 2008; McKinnon 2009; Wake 2013). Performance methodologies help to unpack the ontological precarity of migrants whose identities, personal histories and stories are at the same time integral to their status as well as erased by bureaucratic failures. McKinnon (2009) demonstrates in her analysis of what she calls the performance of credibility in relation to 'audiencing' gender-based asylum claims that there is often vital juridical importance placed on the 'successful' performance of victimhood, suffering, persecution and perceived danger.[12] It might thus be expedient for migrants claiming asylum to predicate their everyday performance on victimhood, since the more credible their claim of persecution, the more likely (in theory) they would be to gain asylum status (Jeffers 2008). These categories are not merely discursive, but embodied. For example, asylum claims that refer to torture in countries of origin would need to provide bodily 'evidence' of the claim to harm, such as scars, images of bruising, medical reports indicating broken bones, etc. A believable 'victim' would be able to present his or her embodied evidence for scrutiny. This suggests that it is via both the embodied and the written archive that claims would be considered. Thus, 'presenting' oneself as an asylum seeker demands a performance of 'hyper-authenticity' (see Jestrovic 2008) that is predicated upon both victimhood and survival, as well as the conscious framing and staging of suffering that sediments the migrant body into these categories. The implication: it becomes nearly impossible to escape from these limited dramaturgies of written records and stories told on skin. This is what Dwight Conquergood refers to in his consideration of the legibility of claims for asylum.

His characterization of the interface between the law and the dispossessed is worth citing at length:

> More often than not, subordinate people experience texts and the bureaucracy of literacy as instruments of control and displacement, e.g., green cards, passports, arrest warrants, deportation orders – what de Certeau calls 'intextuation' [...] [Undocumented immigrants/*sans papiers*] are illegal because they are not legible, they trouble 'the writing machine of the law'. The hegemony of textualism needs to be exposed and undermined. (de Certeau 1984, cited in Conquergood 2002: 147)

Conquergood's reflection on *sans papiers* provides a productive point of return to the hunger strikers, who attempted to construct a further, embodied discourse around what 'bare life' may mean in the context of Greece. Their hunger strike demanded political responses that engaged with the bodies of migrants, and not merely as a largely invisible problem. Thus, hunger striking became a performative reaction to their own position as a 'problem'. Starvation became a tactic to engage critically with the framework of human rights, and the discourse of 'hospitality' in Europe. The strikers positioned themselves within the Law School precisely to render themselves legible in the core of the domain of juridical power and oppression. For Butler and Athanasiou (2013), such a performance of the dispossessed renders a valuable function in the political sphere: that of demanding a response. By attending to the ways in which the hunger strike was both a performance of resistance enacted on the bodies of the migrants and a staged spectacle of political agency within the state of exception that constitutes Greek asylum practices, I have demonstrated that self-starvation was an attempt to render political struggle visible.

The rather bleak description of conditions for migrants in Greece has already positioned them as victims of the state's inability to deal with asylum claims and regular migration in a timely and humane manner. Many migrants narrate desperate circumstances in their home countries and terrifying journeys to reach Greece. Without wishing to essentialize their suffering, such journeys position migrants as already victims – not necessarily of political violence or oppression, but of the implications of capitalist, neoliberal systems that perpetuate myths of ever-increasing wealth that relies on cheap labour. Furthermore, the pressure on migrants (whether regular or irregular) is related to a set of regulations governing mobility, and how refugees 'present' themselves to the authorities. Alison Jeffers' important work on the problem of refugee performance positions the migrants' story within a wider systemic performance.

In the course of arguing their case as 'Convention refugees' they become enmeshed in bureaucratic performance, which often casts them as conventional refugees, those who conform to cultural expectations of suffering, passivity and silence (2011: i).[13]

Based on some of the communiqués, the 300 hunger-striking migrants in Greece had survived perilous journeys – either entering the country across the river Evros, at the borders of Turkey, or having arrived on boats or rafts across the Libyan Sea.[14] Furthermore, they had survived in their host country by adapting in various ways, such as learning the language, forming communities, finding work and paying taxes. In the instance of the hunger strike, these migrants deliberately drew attention to the difficulties and precariousness of bodily survival. They used their own capacity for protest in order to make visible these struggles. However, the strike does not exactly distantiate the migrants from the 'conventional' representations Jeffers is talking about. The migrants remain passive, silent and suffering – still subject to the recognition of the state.

Towards an understanding of resistant acts in political crisis

The attention to specific local struggles by migrants to Greece provides an argument for reimagining the ethical position of nations in relation to human rights and welfare. The case of the 300 migrants interrelates the argument about migration deeply with austerity, precarity and crisis. The events (and their stage-management) were an attempt to re-evaluate and recompose the fixed polarities that have been central to the narratives playing out about economic and social crisis in Greece: self/other; inside/outside; order/chaos. These 300 migrants did not seek to seize state power. Rather, they were calling for a democratic transformation directed by civil society, or to use their own words: 'a civil society [where] people are actors rather than subjects' (Walsh and Tsilimpounidi 2012: 96).

Herein lies the central paradox that I wish to highlight: the slippage between recognition and action. Hunger strikes provide a particular kind of problem of recognition for the authorities since they are compelled to acknowledge the value of human life and ensure the survival of peoples (even if they are detained). At the same time, such strikes are conducted in order to force wider public awareness of the conditions faced by the strikers, in order to pressure the relevant authorities to change. As such, this wider recognition directly reinforces the authority of the state over the welfare and survival of the bodies of the strikers. Yet, what is necessary is a much deeper ethical engagement with what lies beyond mere survival. The strikes are at the same time resistant as well as compliant to the gaze of the law. Conlon, for example, draws attention to the need to transcend the conception of bare life (2013):

> [T]o posit that hunger strikes and lip sewing by asylum seekers are political acts that embrace bare life is to lay claim to mere physical life as a kind of human right. [...] What is significant and political about asylum seekers' lip sewing protests in particular is that these desperate acts call forth reaction, and, by doing so, they generate the space for dialogue and exchange that form the basis of political action. (2013: 140)

Conlon hones in on lip sewing specifically because it is usually a strategic public spectacle that draws attention to the political requests of the protesters, as opposed to hunger strikes. In light of the ambiguous siting of the Athens hunger strike as non-transparent, yet a public spectacle, we can conceive of its value as political performance. By considering the strike as a performance, I have approached the spectacle in a particular way in order to unpack some of the roles performance played in the specific context. Namely, I have argued that the setting of the strike was significant; that hunger strike itself has a specific resonance in terms of performance as it straddles the divide between political agency, 'visibility' and 'invisibility'. I have also framed this shifting ocular relationship between migrants' bodies and the wider public as particularly important in the case of refugees and asylum seekers. In particular, the ways in which visible 'difference' (in other words, racial and ethnic markers of non-Europeanness) renders migrants visible in public spaces, and therefore vulnerable to xenophobic and racist attacks.[15] Rather than positioning dissent against particular authorities, the hunger strike as performance positions the act of resistance as a moral and ethical call to account for all those in the civic sphere to witness, contemplate and respond to wilful destruction of human life in relation to the political and social context that circumscribes the act.

Performance, then, was necessary for placing the bodies (and lives) of the migrants in public space, and thus at the centre of the daily lives of inhabitants of that space (albeit in the sealed-off building and thus ostensibly invisible). Yet, the sudden occupation of a public space and its invisibility draws attention to it. In this case, and in the case of large-scale protest movements, staging resistant protest by conducting the hunger strike was about mass mobilization in relation to the ethical concerns at stake. Large numbers of starving people calling attention to the political issues of migration could not be fobbed off as irrelevant or an isolated incident. The strike was simultaneously invisible and a spectacle, and its force thus relied on the power of the public as witness. This argument rests on the relationship between a wider local, national and international public (mediated through online platforms) and the notion of the suffering of others.[16] I have already accounted for the blogspot and fliers that were distributed across the city. The strike was documented with (anonymized) photographs, texts by the strikers and interviews with spokespeople. There were audio recordings of the texts played on street corners, designed to make the public aware of the demands of the strikers. There was also a large protest march that coincided with the strike, and the gatekeepers (mentioned previously as human rights lawyers) made statements and gathered signatures for petitions to government.

The example of the migrant hunger strike explicitly rendered the precarious lives of migrants in Greece visible. The statements, testimonies and public debates that surrounded the strike itself provided further contextual information on living conditions: extreme vulnerability relating to poverty, unemployment and lack of access to social welfare. These particular migrants were not all amongst the most marginalized in Greece (such as those considered 'illegal'/*sans papiers*, and therefore without any visibility before the law). The particular hunger-striking bodies pointed towards bodies of others while at the same time remaining distinctive in their own demands through resistance. But the performance was also important for a wider understanding of the ontological 'problem' of refugees in relation to 'host' communities. Hunger, staged as a macabre durational performance, became a means of seeking the connections between political agency, civic responsibilities, public visibility and moral standards. In particular, following Sophie Nield (2008), questions are raised about whether rights adhere to the natural body, the political body, the human or to the representations of those bodies.[17]

In conclusion, I have examined the ways in which the hunger strike by 300 migrant workers was conducted at a particular point in what is being called the contemporary Greek 'crisis'. The chapter considers the hunger strike as a performance explicitly designed to mobilize the political sphere in active rethinking about migrants' precarity as imbricated within the wider social, economic and political 'crisis'. The value of mass protest and resistant action is particularly important in times of political 'crisis', with their function of making visible the embodied experiences of others. In relation to the example I have offered of 300 hunger strikers, there is the distinction between personal sovereignty – the right to starve oneself to death (if necessary) to achieve a political purpose – and the sovereignty of the state. In the case of Greece, despite the strike holding valuable bargaining power at the time it was conducted, the rapid decline in social and economic conditions led to the political gains made by the strikers being overruled. In particular, the critical decision to legalize the 300 migrants – or accede to their demands – was revoked. The symbolic achievement of the strikers was quickly rendered empty of significance.

Ultimately, the value of this particular hunger strike as performance in rendering the struggle for survival visible has been undermined by 'crisis', change in government and social unrest. Yet, despite the lack of recognition for these migrants, the example provides a means of understanding how hunger strikes simultaneously call into question the government's right to grant recognition and yet demand such recognition. In other words, they question binaries like insider/outsider while demanding to be made insiders. However, following Conlon, the very opening of discussion and awareness of the culpability of the state and the conditions faced by the migrants constitutes an effective resistance to governmentality. There is thus the potential for the wider public to add to these resistant protests by developing aesthetic, durational, and if necessary risky performances of and for survival that insist on attending to the limits of whose lives count, as well as the role of the witness to the suffering of others.

Notes

1. This chapter is an extension of an article co-authored with Myrto Tsilimpounidi, 'Disappearing Immigrants: Hunger Strike and Invisible Struggles' (2012), in *Journal of Theory in Action*, 5: 2: pp. 82–97. I am also grateful to colleagues at the Royal Holloway Conference 'Asylum and Displacement in the Twenty-First Century: Performing Community, Crisis and Belonging' (April 2012) for their questions, which deepened my engagement with questions of political subjectivity.
2. This is, of course, only true in countries without the death penalty. However, there are strict international laws governing the human rights of those people in prisons and detention centres that relate to their humane treatment (See CPT 2011).
3. Asylum spaces were historically significant in Greece as the Church was the only asylum space under Ottoman rule. Later, the 1973 military junta fell

218 *The Paradox of Dis/appearance*

after significant human casualties, symbolized by army tanks bulldozing the gates to the university buildings. The post-junta constitution declared all university spaces asylum spaces to protect freedom of thought and expression in pursuit of knowledge. This asylum status was revoked under George Papandreou's leadership in 2011.
4. The Migrants' Forum had no prior history and was specifically brought together for the purposes of the hunger strike. It still exists, however, as a collective with hubs in Crete, Athens and Thessaloniki.
5. The notion of being constituted a refugee at the borders is integral to the understanding of migration. That is, the system proposes that migrants are accorded specific rights when they lodge an official claim to asylum. In other words, they present themselves as subject to the care and protection of another state. The existence of 'illegal' migrants does not mean that they would not have had the right to such categories of protection, but rather that the system is so overburdened and inadequate that it does not adequately address the issues of asylum status.
6. Amnesty International (2012).
7. 'The Dublin Regulation, which is part of EU asylum policy, aims to determine which member state is responsible for an asylum application lodged within the EU (and in some other European countries to which the Regulation also applies). It usually requires asylum seekers be returned to the first country they entered upon arrival in the EU. The Regulation is based on the assumption that all member states have equivalent standards of protection, which in practice is not the case' (Amnesty 2012: 6).
8. Council Regulation (EC) No. 343/2003 of 18 February 2003 establishes the criteria and mechanisms for determining the member state responsible for examining an asylum application lodged in one of the member states by a third-country national. See EC (2003).
9. In the period since the junta, university spaces have been asylum spaces in which values relating to democracy and freedom of speech are prized. In short, asylum status was deeply intertwined with narratives of the nation.
10. Jakovljevik refers to Kafka's short story *A Hunger Artist* and the tension between starvation and spectacle, suggesting that 'the central paradox of Kafka's tale is that, if the monastic practice of fasting is put on public display, the longer the performance lasts, the less of the performer there is' (2005: 169).
11. In the Athens example, since the hunger strike was conducted privately, in a sealed-off building, there needed to be a platform to communicate their struggles and demands. This protest did so on a wide scale, through blogspots, social networking and via mobile telephones. For more on the constructed gatekeeping and public awareness of the hunger strike, see Walsh and Tsilimpounidi (2012).
12. The 1951 United Nations High Commissioner for Refugees' definition of a refugee is 'a person outside of his or her own country with a well-founded fear of future persecution on the basis of race, religion, nationality, political opinion or membership in a social group' (United Nations High Commissioner for Refugees, cited in McKinnon 2009: 206).
13. 'Convention refugees' refers to the 1951 Refugee Convention that resulted in a key legal document that defines who is considered a refugee, and outlined

rights and the legal obligation of states. This was amended by the 1967 protocol.
14. See Amnesty International (2012).
15. These have grown more common since the hunger strike, particularly under the watch of far-right (Golden Dawn) factions whose nationalist ideologies proclaim supremacy in their own 'performance for survival'. For further information on these violent attacks, see Amnesty (2012), Human Rights Watch (2012) and Human Rights Watch (2013). It would be reductionist to claim that violent racist attacks are a deliberate public performance (although there is a sense of 'reassuring' local communities that this is a 'clean-up' operation). What might be most appropriate is the use of the term 'spectacle' in both cases. I am not making a causal argument here, but drawing attention to the ambiguous space that is created when an issue of human rights violations and subsequent resistance makes a minority vulnerable by rendering them visible.
16. I draw here on the work of Lilie Chouliaraki (2006) whose work on the spectatorship of suffering demonstrates the interplay between (moving) images of suffering disseminated in order to inspire responses in the viewer or audience. In particular, she provides the framework for thinking about how concepts such as 'us'/'them', 'belonging' and 'nation' are replicated within the screening (or indeed staging) of performances of survival.
17. The theatre's spaces of representation have staged these questions in relation to hunger strikes in Australia by immigrant detainees in *Refugitive* by Shahin Shafaei (cited in Hazou 2008). The aesthetic possibilities of theatrical representations allow for the solo performer (an Iranian asylum seeker) to locate and specify the conditions of hunger as intricately connected to the suffering and humiliation of detention – as Hazou argues, as manifesting the disembodied 'dys-appearance' of the human subject (2008: 182).

Bibliography

Amnesty International, 2012. 'Greece: The End of the Road for Refugees, Asylum-Seekers and Migrants', available online at http://files.amnesty.org/archives/eur250112012eng.pdf, accessed 19 August 2013.
Anderson, P., 2004. ' "To Lie Down to Death for Days": The Turkish Hunger Strike, 2000–2003'. *Cultural Studies*, 18: 6, pp. 816–46.
Anderson, P., 2009. 'There Will Be No Bobby Sands in Guantanamo Bay'. *PMLA*, 124: 5, pp. 1729–36.
Anderson, P., 2010. *So Much Wasted: Hunger, Performance, and the Morbidity of Resistance*. Durham: Duke University Press.
Anderson, P., and J. Menon (eds), 2008. *Violence Performed: Local Roots and Global Routes of Conflict*. Basingstoke: Palgrave.
Assembly of Migrant Workers, 2011. *Hunger Strike 300 Website*, available online at http://hungerstrike300.espivblogs.net/2011/, accessed 30 January 2011.
Balfour, M. (ed.), 2013. *Refugee Performance: Practical Encounters*. Bristol: Intellect.
Butler, J., and A. Athanasiou, 2013. *Dispossession: The Performative in the Political*. Cambridge: Polity Press.
Chouliaraki, L., 2006. *The Spectatorship of Suffering*. London: Sage.

Conlon, D., 2013. 'Hungering for Freedom: Asylum Seekers' Hunger Strikes – Rethinking Resistance as Counter Conduct'. In D. Moran, N. Gill, and D. Conlon (eds) *Carceral Spaces: Mobility and Agency in Imprisonment and Migrant Detention.* Farnham: Ashgate, pp. 133–48.

Conquergood, D., 2002. 'Performance Studies: Interventions and Radical Research'. *TDR: The Drama Review,* 46: 2, pp. 145–56.

CPT, 2011. 'European Committee for the Prevention of Torture and Inhuman or Degrading Treatment or Punishment (CPT): Public Statement Concerning Greece'. *CPT,* available online at http://www.cpt.coe.int/documents/grc/2011-10-inf-eng.pdf, accessed 20 August 2013.

Ellmann, M., 1993. *The Hunger Artists: Starving, Writing, and Imprisonment.* Cambridge: Harvard University Press.

European Commission, 2003. 'Council Regulation No. 343/2003 of 18 February 2003, to establish the criteria and mechanisms for determining the Member State responsible for examining an asylum application lodged in one of the Member States by a third-country national'. Available online at http://eur-lex.europa.eu/LexUriServ/LexUriServ.do?uri=OJ:L:2003:050:0001:0010:EN:PDF, accessed 5 March 2014.

Feldman, A., 1997. *Formations of Violence: The Narrative of the Body and Political Terror In Northern Ireland,* 3rd edition. Chicago: University of Chicago Press.

Golash-Boza, T., 2001. 'Notes from the Field: The Criminalization of Undocumented Migrants: Legalities and Realities'. *Societies Without Borders,* 5: 1, pp. 81–90.

Grewcock, M., 2013. 'The Great Escape: Refugees, Detention and Resistance'. In E. Stanley and J. McCulloch (eds) *State Crime and Resistance.* London: Routledge, pp. 54–67.

Hazou, R., 2008. 'Refugitive and the Theatre of Dys-appearance'. *Research in Drama Education: The Journal of Applied Theatre and Performance,* 13: 2, pp. 181–6.

Human Rights Watch, 2012. 'Hate on the Streets: Xenophobic Violence in Greece'. Available online at http://www.hrw.org/sites/default/files/reports/greece0712ForUpload_0.pdf, accessed 20 August 2013.

Human Rights Watch, 2013. 'Unwelcome Guests: Greek Police Abuses of Migrants in Athens'. Available online at http://www.hrw.org/sites/default/files/reports/greece0613_ForUpload.pdf, accessed 20 August 2013.

Jakovljevic, B., 2005. 'Daniil Kharms, the Hunger Artist: Toward Eden, and the Other Way Around'. *Theatre Journal,* 57: 2, pp. 167–89.

Jeffers, A., 2008. 'Dirty Truth: Personal Narrative, Victimhood and Participatory Theatre Work with People Seeking Asylum'. *Research in Drama Education,* 13: 2, pp. 217–21.

Jeffers, A., 2011. *Refugees, Theatre and Crisis: Performing Global Identities.* Basingstoke: Palgrave Macmillan.

Jestrovic, S., 2008. 'Performing Like an Asylum Seeker: Paradoxes of Hyper-authenticity'. *Research in Drama Education: The Journal of Applied Theatre and Performance,* 13: 2, pp. 159–70.

Kasimis, C., 2012. 'Greece: Illegal Immigration in the Midst of Crisis'. *Migration Information Source,* available online at http://www.migrationinformation.org/Profiles/display.cfm?ID=884, accessed 31 July 2013.

Kershaw, B., 2003. 'Curiosity or Contempt: On Spectacle, the Human, and Activism'. *Theatre Journal*, 55: 4, pp. 591–611.
McKinnon, S. L., 2009. 'Citizenship and the Performance of Credibility: Audiencing Gender-based Asylum Seekers in U.S. Immigration Courts'. *Text and Performance Quarterly*, 29: 3, pp. 205–21.
Mindova, V., 2013. 'The Dublin Regulation Has Turned Greece into a "Parking Lot" for Illegal Immigrants'. *GRReporter*, available online at http://www.grreporter.info/en/dublin_regulation_has_turned_greece_"parking_lot"_illegal_immigrants/9462, accessed 31 July 2013.
Nevitt, L., 2013. *Theatre & Violence*. Basingstoke: Palgrave Macmillan.
Nield, S., 2008. 'The Proteus Cabinet, or "we are Here but not Here"'. *Research in Drama Education: The Journal of Applied Theatre and Performance*, 13: 2, pp. 137–45.
Nield, S., 2010. 'Galileo's Finger and the Perspiring Waxwork: On Death, Appearance and the Promise of Flesh'. *Performance Research*, 15: 2, pp. 39–43.
Sweeney, G., 1993. 'Self-immolation in Ireland: Hunger Strikes and Political Confrontation'. *Anthropology Today*, 9: 5, pp. 10–14.
Thompson, J., 2006. 'Performance of Pain, Performance of Beauty'. *Research in Drama Education*, 11: 1, pp. 47–58.
Wake, C., 2013. 'Testimonial Theatre in *Through the Wire*'. *Modern Drama*, 56: 1, pp. 102–25.
Walsh, A., and M. Tsilimpounidi, 2012. 'Disappearing Immigrants: Hunger Strike and Invisible Struggles'. *Journal of Theory in Action*, 5: 2, pp. 82–97.

11
'Dis-ease' and the Performance of Radical Resistance in the Maze Prison[1]

Patrick Duggan

In his study of Northern Ireland, *Formations of Violence: The Narrative of the Body and Political Terror in Northern Ireland* (1991), anthropologist Allen Feldman proposes that the H-Blocks of the Maze prison were full of 'myths, local histories, performance spaces, carnivals of violence, symbolic kinship, death rituals, and animal totems' (Feldman 1991: 166).[2] Throughout *Formations of Violence* – and indeed elsewhere in the extant literature on the Maze prison – the events that took place in the Maze are described as 'theatre', 'theatrical' and/or as 'performance'. To a certain degree these terms are deployed poetically to highlight the spectacular, internally spectated and performance-like nature of many of the events within that carcerial space. Even so, the use of such terminology in studies that are not from performance or theatre studies calls to mind the fact that, to some degree, all theatre and performance is concerned to explore presence and absence, visibility and invisibility, representation and 'reality'. This concern with visibility or presence is precisely at the heart of the different protests performed in the Maze prison between 1976 and 1981. My contention in this chapter is that the learning of Gaelic (the Irish language), the so-called 'dirty protests' (1979–81) and the 1981 hunger strikes were performative attempts to rewrite the narrative of the prison space and to make radically visible the body and body politic. The first two were explicit attempts to intervene in the politics of the institution (to literally change the space and write the protest on the walls) and secondarily to support and increase the visibility of the wider politics of the Republican cause. The hunger striking, particularly as manifested in the 1981 strikes, was an attempt to become present to the wider public, to highlight the politics of incarceration and republicanism through death. The death of ten of the hunger strikers functioned philosophically and ideo-politically as an appearance through disappearance; death was deployed as a mechanism for political and ideological 'survival'. The residues of both the hunger striking and dirty protests function (or perform) as political and cultural capital, historically and in the contemporary moment of their remembering.

This chapter looks at protest as performance and while the protests discussed here are not aesthetic performances in Schechner's sense (2003: 214–15) they call upon the spectacular, the theatrical and the dramaturgical in order to function with affective impact. Each mode of protest explored is participating in what Umberto Eco defined as a 'performative situation': 'a human body, along with its conventionally recognizable properties, surrounded by or supplied with a set of objects, inserted within a physical space, *stands for something else to a reacting audience*' (Eco 1977: 117; my emphasis). In the context of this chapter, then, suggesting that these protests might be read as performances is more than merely poetic or convenient in so far as they accord to what Adrian Heathfield has, in a different context, termed performances' 'temporal paradox': '[performance] exists both now and then, it leaves and lasts; its tendencies towards disappearance and dematerialization are countered by its capacities to adhere, mark, and trace itself otherwise' (2012: 27). While the conditions of the protest events of the Maze self-evidently map onto this definition of performance they are also what we might think of as radical examples of it as they are staged longitudinally (extreme duration), in a complex and violent social-real context.

The durational nature of the protests suggests a further performative link (as does the correlation of dates) in so far as durational performances of the 1970s and 1980s have been seen as 'vital form[s] of cultural resistance to orders of temporal regulation and acceleration' (Heathfield 2012: 29). While the contextual dissonance between the events Heathfield is discussing and those that form the centre of this chapter is vast, the political, cultural and aesthetic similarities are quite readily navigable: physicality, endurance, limits of the body, disruption and elongation of time and narrative, 'extremity' and a blurring of reality and representation are fundamental to both the history of live/performance art and to the events focused on here.

The Maze, and particularly the 1981 hunger strikes, have been the subject of numerous artistic endeavours since their happening, particularly literature, film, theatre and installation art. While many of these works, such as Peter Sheridan's 1982 play *Diary of a Hunger-Strike*, Steve McQueen's 2008 film *Hunger* and Martin Lynch's 2009 play *Chronicles of Long Kesh*, are rigorously researched and, as Emilie Pine argues, determinedly concerned to create an 'aura of authenticity' (2011: 106), they are of course responses to the crisis, retroactive engagements with the history of the 'Troubles' and the particular context of the hunger strikes especially. As Pine suggests, the interweaving 'of fictional and factual performances of the history of the hunger strikes...blur[s] the edges of the context of dramatic and imagined representations by using real cultural artefacts to underscore the veracity of what is being depicted' (2011: 107). Nevertheless, while such performances are useful to the concerns of this chapter, insofar as they provide a clear sense of the cultural importance of the original performance of the protests and strikes, they remain outside its central investigation. Instead I am focusing on three interrelated, social performances from within the prison between 1976 and 1981: call and response learning of Gaelic through closed doors; 'dirty protests' and the disruption of normative penal narratives this caused; and the performance of death as political survival in hunger striking. Each of these is a determinedly performative act both insofar as they are 'performance-like' or theatrical in some way *and* in the sense of J. L. Austin's original use of that term as acts that are world making (cf. Austin 1962).³ For Austin, in certain circumstances signs can produce reality. In Austinian terms, the events I explore in this chapter are not just constative in the sense of responding to and commenting on the context of the prison, but are precisely performative, radically reality-producing acts and means of regaining individual and political agency over the body, space and, perhaps most importantly, ideology.

A brief history

In 1976 the British government removed 'special category status' (SCS) from all paramilitary prisoners, thus refusing to recognize them as political prisoners. Anyone convicted after March of that year was classified an 'ordinary decent criminal'. The term was designed to position the paramilitary prisoners at the same level as 'normal' criminals such as rapists, drug dealers and car thieves. Thus the 1976 decision was intended to position all terrorist acts as ordinary crimes rather than as politically motivated offences. This was part of a larger move to position the violence as an apolitical question of law and order in an attempt to delegitimate the IRA and other paramilitary groups and to deny the colonial roots of the conflict. The move was read as an attempt by the British government to 'criminalize' those involved in the conflict. No longer were the prisoners granted free association, the right to wear their own clothes and exemption from prison work. This quickly reinforced a collective solidarity among those arrested and those already in prison and instigated a policy of non-conformity among the Republican prisoners that was to have radical consequences for the way in which prison life and political discourse progressed thereafter. Thus, when the first prisoner sentenced after this, Kieran Nugent, was sent to Long Kesh/the Maze in September 1976 he refused to recognize his status as an 'ordinary criminal', demanded political status and would not conform to prison regulations such as wearing the uniform and instead wrapped himself in a blanket. Thus, partly of necessity, the 'blanket protest' was born (cf. McKeown 2001: 17–18) and the men on it became known by the aptly theatrical moniker of 'Blanketmen'. In March 1980 all prisoners with paramilitary connections were denied SCS irrespective of sentencing date or date of crime. The importance of being recognized as political prisoners is commonly highlighted in historical analyses of the time as well as in published prisoner memoirs and it is unsurprising that the removal of political status was seen as a (symbolically) violent attack by the British. It became a central preoccupation of the Troubles both inside and beyond the walls of the prison.

The blanket protest that began in 1976 lasted until the beginning of the 1981 hunger strikes (in March, exactly five years after the removal of SCS), when this new mode of protest took precedence. During this time, the deliberate non-conformity by the prisoners was met with disdain by the prison authorities and by the government; there was a sustained attempt to break the resolve of the prisoners, which resulted in an escalation of the tactics deployed by both sides. In an effort to force conformity and break the blanket protest the prison authorities enacted a series of changes to the daily routine of the prisoners' life. They enforced 24-hour lock-up and strip and cavity searches. Prisoners had to request toilet visits, which were frequently denied or delayed, or else the right to 'slop out' (empty buckets containing bodily waste) was refused; visitation rights were severely limited; routine violence was meted out; visits to washing facilities were restricted and when they did happen the prisoners' bodies were forced into naked display through the removal of towels (cf. Feldman 1991: 165–74; McKeown 2001: 17). The response by the Blanketmen was to escalate the situation by refusing to shave or wash, pouring their urine under the doors into the corridor, and throwing faecal matter out of the windows, until these were blocked up, at which point they resorted to smearing it on the walls.

> ... keep fucking us about and we'll not use the toilets; so we stopped using the toilets, just used a slop bowl in the cell. At that time we were throwing the shit out the window and pouring the urine under the door. So the screws had to mop it up. The cells were still basically clean. So then the screws blocked off the windows. So you couldn't throw it out the window. They started squeeging the urine back under the door into the cells. So the guys said all right, we'll just put the shit in the corner.
>
> ... The screws would [then] come in and all the shit and urine was in the corner. They lifted your blankets and fucked it into that corner and walked the shite all over your blankets or fucked the mattress into a wad of it. So the only effective way of combating that was to spread it on the walls. (INLA prisoner, cited in Feldman 1991: 167–8)

This brief description of the blanket protest and its escalation into the no-wash or dirty protest is of course not intended as an exhaustive account of the complexities of the political and physical context of the Maze, but should give some sense of the extremity of the physical resistance the prisoners were engaged in from 1976 onwards. Four years later, ten prisoners (seven in the Maze and three women in Armagh prison) went on hunger strike as a means of furthering the protest over political status through different tactics. All ten started at the same time and then, after 53 days, the strike was called off because the then prisoner leader, Brendan Hughes, was under the impression that the British government were about to accede to the prisoners' demands. However, this proved not to be the case and the dirty protest began afresh.

Despite the failure of the 1980 hunger strikes, in 1981 Bobby Sands, by then the commanding officer in the H-Blocks, determined to try hunger striking again, but this time took a more strategic approach. He designed a process of rolling start points rather than a single mass strike. This was to be a key dramaturgical strategy, as I will explicate below. The 1981 hunger strikes began with Sands on 1 March and lasted until 3.15 pm on 3 October, during which time ten hunger strikers died.

Performative acts of identity

> The first time I heard Irish spoken in the H-Blocks, it was like magic. (PIRA prisoner, cited in Feldman 1991: 211)

Aside from a perceived attempt to criminalize the paramilitaries by removing their political status, the move to brand them as ordinary criminals and thus integrate them into the normal penal narratives of the Maze began also to remove their individual identity (or expression of identity) by ensuring their symbolic disappearance into one indistinguishable homogeneous group of 'prisoners'. As such, part of the prisoners' resistance to wearing prison uniform and to participating in normal prison chores and rituals was an attempt to retain both individual identity, expressed, for example, in choice of clothes, and collective political, Republican identity through free association, dormitory sleeping arrangements and increased visitation and communication rights.

While the dirty and violent modes of resistance came to characterize this time in Long Kesh (which I will attend to below), one tactic that became crucial to the inmates maintaining some level of ownership over their bodies, communications and collective politics was the teaching and learning of, and communicating in, Gaelic. Participation in this pedagogy was a deeply performative act. Firstly, in the sense of being performance-like: particular inmates would perform the role of teacher through a 'call and response' system of learning. Secondarily, this performance-based learning was productively world or reality making. It worked as a mechanism of resistance on multiple levels. At its most fundamental, Gaelic was a language little understood by the prison guards and even less by the British government, and as such the aural environment caused by its oral teaching (being called out of windows, along pipes and under doors) worked as a means of secretive (and 'illegal') communication that might be deployed alongside the more invasive 'bangling' (slang used to define the smuggling of things within the folds and orifices of the body). Beyond this, it also worked to create a sense of collective identity. In the context of the prison, Gaelic was something owned by the Republican prisoners; it was beyond capture, so to speak. Alongside other liminoid oral performances, storytelling and singing, it bound them together ideologically.

Echoing the idea of the reality-producing capacity of the performative act, Homi Bhabha has argued that a nation creates itself, projects itself in the world and is thus perceived through the cultural narratives it tells itself and creates for itself both in content and form (1990: 3). The singing of songs, storytelling and learning of Gaelic might be read as functioning as a sort of two-fold sonic nation building: creating a proto-nation state within the confines of the prison while representing and reinforcing the national identity of Republican Ireland. This functioned to erode the abstract violence of penal liminality and identity erasure that can be seen as part of incarceration, and it brought the men together to develop a sense of communitas through performance:

> At the end of the week you would set aside a day of storytelling... [and] Irish history all done in Gaelic from the head... Bobby [Sands] was the main advocate of cultural separatism. That was the message that came from inside the jails out to the whole community now. Bobby told us that the proof of the pudding was in the eating. The jails proved that when you became culturally separate it breaks the enemy, that it builds walls they can't cross... (PIRA prisoner, cited in Feldman 1991: 213)

The performance-like call and response learning of Gaelic became an important means by which the prisoners created a collective identity and thus a mechanism for surviving the violence of the prison and later for coping with the self-enacted violence of the hunger strikes (cf. Pine 2011: 100–26).

The power of this performative work went beyond creating a sense of collective identity, however; it was a fundamental part of rewriting the penal narratives of the Maze and materializing a space that was alien to the prison authorities and one in which the prisoners gained a level of agency despite the removal of SCS. As one ex-prisoner put it, 'We changed the prison. When I first went to jail you couldn't talk out the door. You would get done for "disturbing the peace of the prison". Less than a year later we were having singsongs out the door, giving the Gaelic lessons and the political lectures. *We just broke down the whole prison discipline*' (INLA prisoner, cited in Feldman 1991: 214; my emphasis). The incomprehensibility and alterity of Gaelic provided a means by which to subvert the rules of the prison. This was a performance of power that was necessitated by, emerged out of, and was aimed at the conditions of the prison. As well as gaining the skill of a new language and the development of a collective national political identity, this oral/aural performance was a sort of symbolic freedom and protection from the daily rhythms of the prison, the violence inflicted on the prisoners' bodies and the enveloping, polluting confines of the dirty cells. It was not merely a desire to be subversive for the sake of it, but rather a deliberate strategy because learning Gaelic became 'a matter of survival' (PIRA prisoner, cited in Feldman 1991: 214). As Feldman posits:

> Gaelic speaking, its grammar, its lexicon, its phonics, its 'beat', once enunciated in the prison, enabled migration to alterity... The

prison leadership identified the intensive Gaelic enculturation as the required cognitive preparation for the collective commitment to hunger striking [and to coping with the dirty protests. It was seen as] the necessary precipitant of the political solidarity that would enable chosen prisoners to act materially on their own bodies as the central structure of their captivity. (Feldman 1991: 217)

From exclamation to excrement

The learning of storytelling and singing in Gaelic is only one of the ways in which the prisoners engaged in modes of protest that called on the theatrical and performative. Sophie Nield has made the case that very often protests are read as theatrical simply 'because they share attributes with conventional theatrical practice' (2006: 53); that they are very often 'theatre-like' in so far as they are 'organised around the symbolic production of meaning, they refer to concepts, things and ideas that are not otherwise materially present, and they are "stage-managed" in order to be read' (Nield 2006). The problem inherent in this mapping, for Nield, is that it can present the protest event as being 'only a symbolic action referring to some "real" activity or set of relations elsewhere'. As such, the moniker of 'theatrical' can highlight the temporality of the event to detrimental effect as 'the symbolic exchange between power and opposition [is seen to take] place and then both sides depart and all continues as before' (2006: 54). We might add to this the long history of anti-theatrical prejudice, with all that that signifies, as attending to protest once it is named as theatre. While this argument is important, the events in the Maze are undeniably spectacular and quite evidently theatrical in their organization. They are, moreover, longitudinal, with neither side able to 'depart' and 'continue as before' because of the unique conditions of prison (the inability to leave, power imbalances, and so on), and the clarity of the power dynamics is put into flux as a result of the protest and, it is my contention, precisely *because of* their theatrical and performative composition.

The dirty protest and the 1981 hunger strikes (that I will return to below) were carefully stage-managed and employed costuming, scenography, dramaturgy, ensemble performance and individual characterization to create an environment that was incomprehensible, alienating and disgusting to those who encountered it from the outside (prison guards, governmental authorities, press and public). Alongside the enveloping orality of the learning of Gaelic, the all-pervasive stink of faecal matter doubly enfolded the bodies of the guards, and symbolically the prison administration, in a space of alterity and incomprehensibility.

These protests are not 'theatre', but rather employ theatrical techniques as strategy for the disruption of space and negotiation of power dynamics. One of the fundamentals of performance is its engagement with and in space, the way in which performance gives space meaning through a deliberate and explicit redesigning of it, as with a representational set, or through social dramas such as protests or riots. At a basic level, then, we might contend that the Maze prison, even before the performative protests of dirt and starvation, was a theatricalized space. At the level of institutional organization (and demonstrations of authority) the prison is cut up into sections with specific narratives and meaning attached to each: punishment blocks, isolation cells, interrogation centres. While all institutional spaces – schools, universities, office buildings, and so on – have such arrangements of space, within a carcerial context the prominence of spatial design is writ large at an explicit embodied level. The configuration of space is intended to control bodies, and encounters between them, as routes are blocked by locked doors, and exercise, meal times and visits are all strictly controlled. Although not unique to the Maze, these architectural elements might be thought of as a dramaturgical control of power in so far as they very precisely shape the movement of bodies, provide stages for interactions and place those bodies and interactions under panoptic spectatorship (cf. Kershaw 1999: 126–56).[4] This theatricalization of space is made more apparent when we consider the ways in which the dirty protest rewrote the normative penal narratives of Long Kesh (as outlined above). Moreover, their faecal interventions were not solely a means of disruption, but became also a means of communication with the next prisoners to be put in the cell; smearing shit on the walls became a medium of artistic expression and ultimately a means to 'own' the space (cf. McKeown 2001: 53–8; Feldman 1991: 147–217; O'Malley 1990).

While the protests of the Republican prisoners were absolutely a response to the conditions of incarceration they were also fundamentally engaged in a symbolic representation of that space on the prisoners' terms. The dirty protest was part of a process of transforming the prison into a site of cultural otherness as a form of political resistance and, fundamentally, as a means of performing for everyday 'survival':

> Their condition of faecal disorder was to be an escape from the suspensions of juridical time [such as being denied access to a toilet on demand] – a fundamental structure of their oppression – and an entry

into the resolving finitude of biological time [answering their own bodies' call when they felt like it]... As they transgressed customary biological boundaries and adapted to the scatological ecology of their cells, the Blanketmen began to extract political lessons from their relative biological immunity and survival. The scatological began to cohere into a system of positive meaning that defined their relationship to the prison and to the outside world. The faecal body and cell began to function as an encoding mechanism from which a variety of political texts could be mined. (Feldman 1991: 182)

The tactics (and even aesthetics) of the dirty protest were strategically employed to make the greatest impact on the normal rhythms and narratives of the penal space. In so doing there was an explicit attempt to change what Henri Lefebvre might term the 'social space' that the prisoners found themselves in.

In *The Production of Space* (1991), Henri Lefebvre suggests, in an argument that is similar to Bhabha's on nationhood, that social actions produce space and inscribe themselves into space as they produce it: actions in space produce new meaning for that space. These theatrically made protests might be seen, in Sophie Nield's terms, to 'temporarily materialise' (2006: 53) a space in which the power of the institution is usurped and turned back on itself, but here over a prolonged period of time: refusing to allow the prisoner to freely associate necessitates the learning of and speaking in a 'foreign' language; restricting access to toilet and washing facilities is ratcheted up to smearing shit on the walls; denying visits, access to news sources and open communications ensures clandestine 'bangling', the body as hiding-place for anything from handwritten communiques to short-wave radios. These performatives materialize a resistant space physically within the walls and, crucially, imaginatively outside of it (in galvanizing Republican support for the prisoners).

Nield usefully argues that while space is 'produced and shaped by human actions', space by return is able to 'shape and direct human activity and experience'. As such, even 'temporary appropriation of a space can have a longer and more profound impact on how people feel about themselves and their environments than the temporary nature of the intervention may at first suggest' (2006: 54). While the interventions of the blanket and dirty protests into the prison space are physically *apparent* (visually and in terms of smell) their impact and thus subsequent continued deployment is in the capacity of the acts to materialize a space of alterity that the prisoners have ownership over and then, crucially, to rematerialize that space beyond the prison walls. The events in the prison are very materially present to all who experience them, but, as Feldman has pointed out, this physical impact was not merely confined to within the compound as the stench remained on the skin and in the clothes of the prison workers for hours after shifts finished (1991: 193). This ensured that the space of the protest was extended into the personal real of daily existence for those workers.

> For a prison officer who was in for a twelve-hour shift and who then went home, he would usually have to spend about four hours trying to get the smell off of his uniform and his body and then go back into that situation twelve hours later. That became a daily barrier that he had to overcome, both returning home and entering back into the prison. The inmates didn't have that adjustment. You could actually see, as I saw and the inmates must have seen, the revulsion of the prison officers as they were coming onto their shifts. The smell would stick to his uniform and to his body and was hard to get off... The prison offers [felt] defiled because it extended into their private lives, their bodies, their sense of cleanliness, their marital relations, and their relations to their children... Physical contact with the prisoner and the cell was abhorrent. (Welfare Officer, cited in Feldman 1991: 193–4)

So while the institution of the prison is designed to control and make subservient the prisoners, their protests were able to penetrate the screws' everyday existence and so relentlessly make imaginatively present the prisons' now abject spaces and the prisoners themselves.

The dirty protests thus come to represent a spatial disruption that reinscribes the meaning of the physical space; the protests make manifest both a new interaction with and atmosphere in the physical space and a representational space that impacts upon the bodies and lives of the prison workers and in the social real via news media and community representations.[5] These spaces (prison space, domestic spaces of the workers and media space) exist in a looped relationship with each other – the material space and actions in it influence the representational spaces and vice versa. As Lefebvre proposes, social actions produce the meaning of a particular space; thus, while the dominant discourse of the prison might be about control and domination, the dirty protest began a process of subverting the dominant and inscribing a different political meaning to the space (cf. Lefebvre 1991: 390–93). Thus, if, as Foucault contends, 'space is fundamental in any exercise of power' (in

Rainbow 1984: 252), the (successful) disruption of that space, physically and in representation, must in turn be the fundamental exercise of the disruption of that power.

However, Nield raises an interesting complication here as she contends that 'authority actively encourages both legible resistance and the interpretation of resistance as legible' as a means of ensuring such resistance is read and encountered on the terms of that authority (2006: 59). In such instances, resistance can be reduced to 'mere' representation. What is interesting in relation to my current context is that, while the dirty protests are readable (perhaps more readily retroactively), they are in the same moment illegible in so far as the actions of the men participating are what we might think of as abhorrent or disgusting. In almost all instances of the protest, from smearing faecal matter on the walls, to sloshing urine under doors, to 'bangling', to simply not washing, the modalities of protest and the representations they raise are incomprehensible in 'normal' or everyday society. While many accounts from the men on the protest contend an enculturation or acclimatization to the environment, however feted, the workers 'never really got accustomed to the stench and atmosphere of the place... The psychology of the Dirty Protest was so alien' (Welfare Officer, cited in Feldman 1991: 193–4).

Nield contends that while 'authority produces space precisely by cutting it up, marking it with borders and controlling and regulating movement', resistance, to be effective, must 'intervene in the illusory homogeneity of abstract space, expose its weaknesses and contradictions, and materialise an alternative space' (2006: 61), which is precisely the function of the dirty protests and the learning of Gaelic (and then latterly the hunger strikes). The protests disrupted normative readings of the penal space and of the political narrative of Northern Ireland at the time. This disruption is implemented through a performance of a particular sort of strategic disgust where bodily functions are deployed to create an abject space, physically and mimetically, that refuses the power dynamic of the prison, even in the face of continued physical violence.[6] The fundamental schema of disgust, Winfried Menninghaus argues, is 'the experience of a nearness that is not wanted' (Menninghaus 2003: 1). An encounter with disgust affects the whole nervous system; it is an overloading experience in which 'everything seems at risk' to create a 'state of alarm and emergency, an acute crisis of self-preservation in the face of an unassimilable otherness, a convulsive struggle, in which what is in question is, quite literally, whether "to be or not to be"' (Menninghaus 2003: 1). The dirty protest, then, becomes a prime candidate for what we might think of as an abject space, one in which aesthetic, moral and olfactory disgust envelop the bodies of the prison guards in pervasive proximity. The protest not only refuses the normal narrative of the prison space and thus of the State, but tactically rematerializes it to become a space of political identification (for the inmates) and resistance (as symbol in the wider world). In the same way that Adrian Heathfield describes performance as 'leaving *and* lasting', as having a trace (2012: 27; my emphasis), this particular protest leaves a physical residue on the bodies of the guards that materializes an echo of the protest space beyond the physical parameters of the event itself.

The dirty protest is a dramaturgy of bodily functions that creates an environment that surrounds and envelops, but which at the same time is disgusting and violently distancing; it is inescapably near, yet violently distancing.[7] This disruption is theatrically made and lays the ground for the efficacy of the hunger strikes in terms of bodily discipline, collective identity and united action. It also works as a strikingly different form of action at an aesthetic level: while one is dirty, smelly and violently visible, the other is quiet, clean, medical, slow, inevitable and perturbing in the extreme.[8] This precisely accords with Lefebvre's note that resistance has to make its own space, and not adhere to the rules and limits of representation imposed by the penal authority (cf. Lefebvre 1991: 393).

However, elsewhere Lefebvre contends that a revolution that does not produce a new space has not realized its full potential; indeed it has failed in that it has not changed life itself, but has merely changed ideological superstructures, institutions or political apparatuses. A social transformation, to be truly revolutionary in character, must manifest a creative capacity in its effects on daily life, on language and on space – though its impact need not occur at the same rate, or with equal force, in each of these areas (1991: 54).

While arguably the dirty protests were successful in changing the daily life of the prisoners and prison guards, they were less successful in achieving their ideological political goals: political status was not reinstated, institutional violence increased and the situation became untenable. A new tactic was needed and, for Bobby Sands, that was a return to the ancient practice of hunger striking.

'I pledge myself to abstain from food to the death' (Sheridan 1982: 106)

Ex-hunger striker Laurence McKeown notes the atmospheric shift that the announcement of the 1981 hunger strikes had: 'The mood in the

Blocks began to change. The screws were unsure of just what was going to happen and appeared more friendly, or at least less aggressive. Our hopes were high' (2001: 75). McKeown tells us that the decision to end the blanket/dirty protest was because it had 'outlived its usefulness' and because clarity of representation was needed on 'the outside' (the functional incomprehensibility of the dirty protest, however internally productively, was clouding the representation of the struggle outside, i.e. people were disgusted and unsympathetic). Furthermore it was also a 'tactical move' to demonstrate flexibility on the part of the prisoners and at the same time manoeuvring to a position (physical and metaphorical) from which 'it would be much easier to move on if the hunger strike did not produce the desired results' (77). As McKeown narrates it, the 1981 hunger strikes were composed with a deliberate attention to dramaturgical strategy. The key element of this is the way the strikes were structured around rolling start points rather than being a mass event, thus ensuring maximum impact through media exposure. This is perhaps most apparent in Sands' election to Westminster while on hunger strike. Sands' nomination and election pushed the protest into the wider political and social domain and gave 'worldwide publicity to our protest and struggle but he still died' (McKeown 2001: 78).[9]

Beyond this, the act of hunger striking is in itself performative. Dwight Conquergood has eloquently argued that '[e]xecutions are awesome rituals of human sacrifice through which the state dramatizes its absolute power and monopoly on violence' (Conquergood 2002: 342). If this is the case, then the act of hunger striking in contexts of incarceration seems to suggest a similarly 'awesome ritual of human sacrifice' in which the individual – or individuals – dramatize their *lack* of institutional (or state) agency and power through the spectacle of violent disappearance. This is a precisely theatrical/performative formulation: these events are politically charged, dynamically embodied instances of protest performance, which, to borrow from Peggy Phelan, create a 'maniacally charged' present (Phelan 1993: 148) and in their passing leave visceral, lasting traces. During the hunger strikes the bodies of the prisoners became surveilled as never before and ultimately became most present, most visible (ideologically, politically and in the media) at the moment of disappearance (cf. Feldman 1991: 251; Anderson 2009). This is the performance of death in so far as it is deliberately and publically staged: the hunger strikers were seeking an audience, seeking exposure and seeking to be read.

In aligning the hunger strike with performance there is an implicit framing of it as an embodied cultural practice engaged in a rewriting or resymbolization of the individual strikers' identities (Sands became an icon of the Republican movement and all ten who died were hailed as heroes and martyrs, for example), their 'cause', those who encounter the hunger strike and the hunger strike's representation in news (and other) media. The hunger striking created to a very powerful presentness in so far as the ontological presence of the bodies in the space is writ large by the (possible) immanence of death. The strikes are more than theatre-like, however. The radical presence of the bodies of the strikers might be seen to be created through what Barba and Savarese (1991) term 'pre-expressivity': the way in which a character's energy is brought alive scenically rather than psychologically. Their proposition is that it is the quality of the scenic elements of the production, such as the set, lighting, costume and (especially) the actor's actions that creates presence and meaning. They contend that 'the totality of a performer's performance... [is] made up of distinct levels of organisation' and that there is a basic level of organization which is common to all performers, the pre-expressive (Barba and Savarese 1991: 187). Pre-expressivity does not take into account the usual elements of a performer's presence on stage; no heed is paid to intentions, emotions or identification, and so on: '[i]t is the *doing* and *how the doing is done* which determine what one expresses' (187; emphasis is original). In short, the 'psycho-techniques', as Barba and Savarese term them, are ignored in favour of a focus on the performer's physical presence and actions. Through this, the bodies of the hunger strikers might be seen to come to occupy a sort of fictive zone in which they perform disappearance. The hunger strikers become what Moriaki Watanabe might call 'fictive bodies'. That is, bodies that (in theatre) are 'in an intermediate state' where they are 'performing [their] own absence. But this absence is performance and is therefore a present absence [...] which stimulates a kind of transformation of the daily body at the pre-expressive level' (Watanabe, cited in Barba and Savarese 1991: 187; emphasis is original). The hunger strikers are at once present and absent. While of course the seriousness of this performance is extreme compared to the Noh actor Watanabe is discussing, the hunger strikes, it seems to me, occupy what might be termed a dis-easing fictive zone (I will return to this shortly).

Read in light of Peggy Phelan's argument that the political efficacy of performance is in the fact of its disappearance, and indeed that disappearance is the *sine qua non* of performance, the hunger strikes are a sort of absolute performance in so far as the political impact of the event can only become itself through the disappearance of the body.

Two things arise here. Firstly, although, as Patrick Anderson contends, 'self-starvation becomes itself most fully, and becomes meaningful in the logic of its own image most vividly, at the moment of death' (2010: 12), I argue that, in the context of the Maze prison, the efficacy of the event is tied more complexly to the earlier creation of an oral-aural environment of alterity in the learning of Gaelic and to the hunger strikes' aesthetic juxtaposition to the aesthetics previously employed. This is because the aesthetic shift mediates the space once more and thus makes complex the readability of that space for the institution and its representatives. From making the body and bodily functions violently, materially present in the move to hunger striking, the prisoners withdraw from the space instead of radically occupying it. Secondly, and arising out of the first, the hunger strikes move from an aesthetic strategy of disgust to one of 'dis-ease'. By which I mean that the shift from the noisy spectacle of dirty protests to the relative quiet of dying and disappearing places the bodies of the prisoners into an in-between space, one that no longer gains agency through disgusting, but which creates anxiety, uncertainty and insecurity. Here, my suggestion is that the world is not rendered meaningless, as Critchley (2009) contends is the case with Heidegger's 'anxiety', but becomes othered, distanced and shimmers in and out of readability in an experience that makes one feel slightly other *in* it and perturbed by the experience *of* it. Unlike Heidegger's anxiety, dis-ease is not a sudden experience of being *unheimlich*, but exposure to a constant threat of being ripped from a state of normalcy, and as such it pervades or persists in the everyday. In the context of the Maze this most clearly applies to the prison workers who come in and out of the environments materialized by the protests, but it might also apply to the British government as they wrestle with what the event 'is' and how to 'deal' with it.[10] Within the context of the Maze the different modes of protest produce a dis-ease that is not only 'productive' in the prison itself – each facilitated gaining some level of ownership of the space and the prisoners retaking control of their bodies – but also beyond its walls in the political realm. The 'liveness' of the performance of hunger striking is ratcheted up in seriousness when one considers that this performance really will disappear, never to be repeated. What is interesting in the case of the Maze protests (though given the preponderance of hunger strikes by political prisoners, the argument can be applicable elsewhere) is that death is deployed as symbolic of and perhaps even vital to the survival of the local body politic as represented by the Republican prisoners. At least at an ideo-political level, (the performance of) death *is* survival.

Conclusion

The triumvirate of protests discussed here call upon the spectacular, the theatrical and the dramaturgical in order to function with impact. The ultimate goal of such resistance is of course to function as a countervailing force that may be able to disassemble the monolithic power structures of the prison and ultimately, here, the British government's removal of SCS (and more broadly British rule in Northern Ireland). While the success or failure of the protests is debatable, and most historical accounts tend towards the latter, they were performatively and theatrically made. They functioned through the prisoners' bodies against the fabric and body of the prison in an attempt, after Foucault, to disrupt the capacity of the prison to act 'as an instrument and vector of power' (cited in Rainbow 1984: 178). The performative acts of the call and response learning of Gaelic, the spectacular disgust of the dirty protests and dis-easing fictive bodies of the hunger strikers are organized around what Cathy Turner might term a 'porous dramaturgy' in which the protests gain meaning through their co-relation, interaction and via their violently immersive nature (cf. Turner 2013). Thus they operated as a *strategy of tactics* (after de Certeau) that reinscribed the meaning of, and to a certain degree took ownership over, the carceral space. These social performances for ever altered the reading of the prison space – the Maze is still and especially read in light of this history – through organized use of bodies and bodily functions, reorganization of space, disruption of time and narrative progression and certain 'aesthetic' decisions. In so doing the protests and the institutional response to them created a sort of diegetic world that operated through a theatricalized deployment of disgust and dis-ease, the natural result of which was a deeply politicized and violently charged longitudinal public action *as* performance.

Notes

1. 'The Maze' refers to Her Majesty's Prison Maze in Co. Antrim, Northern Ireland. The prison was used primarily to house paramilitary prisoners during the Troubles from mid-1971 to mid-2000. Prisoners were segregated along sectarian lines; thus Unionists and Republicans were housed in separate wings and did not mix.
2. I have drawn heavily on the extensive primary source interview material collected in Feldman's work, but this essay is not an explicit attempt to reframe or renegotiate Feldman's broader arguments.
3. With 'theatrical' I am suggesting that the protests in some way make use of the conventions of theatre – scenography, costume, dramaturgy, characterization, audience, and so on.

4. Indeed, theatricality might be seen to be at the heart of the development of the prison at the height of the Enlightenment given that the Bentham brothers' idea of a Panopticon was to 'induce in the prisoner an awareness of an omniscient and permanent state of visibility'; there was then a constant audience (cf. Branco 2010: 279).
5. For a detailed discussion of the protests in the press and in popular discourse see Coogan 2002.
6. I am here drawing on philosopher Carolyn Korsmeyer's idea of 'aesthetic disgust', which she develops as a means for discussing art that deliberately arouses disgust in its viewer in order to shape a particular narrative or to intensify the impact of that artwork (cf. 2012: 758–61).
7. Valerie Curtis (Reader in Hygiene, LSHTM) contends that 'people feel shame when disgust is turned on them' (cf. http://www.nytimes.com/2012/01/24/science/disgusts-evolutionary-role-is-irresistible-to-researchers.html?page wanted=all&_r=0).
8. This is an aesthetic difference that is foregrounded in Steve McQueen's 2008 film *Hunger* and is central to the dramaturgical coherence of the film.
9. The dramatic potential of this structuring principle is also evidenced in Peter Sheridan's decision to use it as the dramaturgical structure for, or dramatic centre of, *Diary of a Hunger Strike* (1982).
10. State papers recently released by the National Archives in Kew, London, from the period give interesting accounts of how the British government were discussing the events in the Maze. For a useful summary, see http://www.bbc.co.uk/news/uk-northern-ireland-16355142, accessed 14 November 2014.

Bibliography

Anderson, P., 2009. 'There Will Be No Bobby Sands in Guantánamo Bay'. In *PMLA*, 124: 5, pp. 1729–36

Anderson, P., 2010. *So Much Wasted: Hunger, Performance and the Morbidity of Resistance*. Durham, NC: Duke University Press.

Austin, J. L., 1962. *How to Do Things with Words: The William James Lectures Delivered at Harvard University in 1955*, ed. J. O. Urmson. Oxford: Clarendon.

Barba, E., and N. Savarese, 1991. *The Secret Art of the Performer: A Dictionary of Theatre Anthropology*. London: Routledge.

Bhabha, H. K., 1990. *Nation and Narration*. London: Routledge.

Branco, P., 2010. 'On Prisons and Theatres: Santo Stefano and San Carlo'. In *Law Text Culture*, 14: 1, pp. 277–85.

Conquergood, D., 2002. 'Lethal Theatre: Performance, Punishment, and the Death Penalty'. *Theatre Journal*, 54: 3, pp. 339–67.

Coogan, T. P., 2002. *On the Blanket: The Inside Story of the IRA Prisoners' 'Dirty' Protest*. Basingstoke: Palgrave Macmillan, pp. 169–93

Critchley, S., 2009. 'Being and Time, Part 5: Anxiety'. *Guardian Online*, available online at http://www.theguardian.com/commentisfree/belief/2009/jul/06/heidegger-philosophy-being, accessed 14 July 2014.

Eco, U., 1977. 'Semiotics of Theatrical Performance'. *Drama Review*, 30: 1, pp. 107–17.

Feldman, A., 1991. *Formations of Violence: The Narrative of the Body and Political Terror in Northern Ireland*. Chicago: University of Chicago Press.

Heathfield, A., 2012. 'Then Again'. In A. Jones and A. Heathfield (eds) *Perform, Repeat, Record: Live Art in History.* Bristol: Intellect, pp. 11–35.

Kershaw, B., 1999. *The Radical in Performance: Between Brecht and Baudrillard.* London: Routledge.

Korsmeyer, C., 2011. *Savouring Disgust: The Foul and the Fair in Aesthetics.* Oxford: Oxford University Press.

Korsmeyer, C., 2012. 'Disgust and Aesthetics'. In *Philosophy Compass*, 7: 11, pp. 753–61.

Lefebvre, H., 1991. *The Production of Space*, trans. Donald Nicholson-Smith. Oxford: Blackwell.

Lynch, M., 2011. *Chronicles of Long Kesh.* London: Oberon Books.

McKeown, L., 2001. *Out of Time: Irish Republican Prisoners Long Kesh 1972–2000.* Belfast: Beyond the Pale.

Menninghaus, W., 2003. *Disgust: Theory and History of a Strong Sensation.* Albany: State University of New York Press.

Nield, S., 2006. 'There Is Another World: Space, Theatre and Global Anti-Capitalism'. *Contemporary Theatre Review*, 16: 1, pp. 51–61.

O'Malley, P., 1990. *Biting at the Grave: The Irish Hunger Strikes and the Politics of Despair.* Boston, MA: Beacon Press.

Phelan, P., 1993. *Unmarked: The Politics of Performance.* London: Routledge.

Pine, E., 2011. *The Politics of Irish Memory: Performing Remembrance in Contemporary Irish Culture.* Basingstoke: Palgrave Macmillan.

Rainbow, P., 1984. *The Foucault Reader.* London: Penguin Books.

Schechner, R., 2003. *Performance Theory.* London: Routledge Classics.

Sheridan, P., 1982. *Diary of a Hunger Strike.* Unpublished manuscript.

Turner, C., 2013. *Porous Dramaturgies Project.* Available online at http://expandeddramaturgies.com/category/porousdramaturgy/, accessed 10 July 2014.

Coda: Picturing *Charlie Hebdo*

Sophie Nield

This volume is predicated upon a particular kind of doubling, captured in its title: *Performing (for) Survival: Theatre, Crisis, Extremity*. For the theatre and performance makers who created the performances under discussion are not only making a claim for a particular mode of survival: articulating an alternative, shaping a future, staging a different kind of life. They are also staging those alternatives: materializing and performing them, for however temporary or provisional a moment. They are performing survival and performing *for* survival, working in registers of both presence and representation simultaneously.

Having drawn productively for several decades on critical models drawn from adjacent (and even not so adjacent) disciplines, performance analysis is increasingly exporting perspectives, arguments, frameworks of interpretation and critique into the fields of philosophy, critical geography, law, historiography and politics, and impacting both disciplinary formations and the scope and focus of critical interrogation. The chapters in this volume offer a new and important set of insights to these interdisciplinary exchanges, focusing as they do on performance work generated out of/against/in spite of its material political contexts. They address multifarious ways in which performance constitutes things; objects, ideas, identities. The focus of the book – on those works arising materially out of their immediate context of crisis, rather than those being developed later in retrospect – puts increasing and welcome pressure on the binary division of the world and the world of its 'imitation' (so often the category assignation of performance work). It opens up questions of what can actually count as performance, and further, explores what sets of definitions and determinations drawn from the performance field can do to help us shape wider frameworks for the interpretation of culture, of politics and of social life.

There is much we can learn as political actors from the examples and instances explored by the contributors here. What is it to put one's own body on the line in a representational gambit – to stage the possibility of one's own non-survival? What is it to gather the materials of mimesis in the conditions of the gravest danger – to insist on an elsewhere and an elsewhen? What is it to forge community in the face of the most horrific attacks on humanity itself? What is it to challenge power and its instrumentalities by materializing the limits of its jurisdictions in performance?

When I was invited to write a coda to this volume, I wondered what I could usefully do that would not simply describe again to the reader everything which they have just read. It occurred to me, given the theme of the collection is survival and what survives, that it might be interesting to begin to think about the potential afterlife of the inspirations offered here: what insights, perspectives, models and questions might we take forward, and what sorts of problems might they help us solve. I want therefore to briefly examine some of the circumstances of a crisis current at the time of writing, in order to open up some of this potential space – the shootings at French satirical magazine *Charlie Hebdo*, and the outpouring of demonstrative and symbolic commemoration which followed. I choose this example not simply for its currency: it is one in which the intertwining of material and symbolic gestures is a fundamental part of how it has evolved.

On 7 January 2015, brothers Saïd and Chérif Kouachi entered the offices of the French satirical weekly *Charlie Hebdo* and opened fire on the people they found inside, They killed a number of the magazine's staff and the protection service officer assigned to guard the editor, Stephane Charbonnier ('Charb'), and wounded a further 11 people. As they left the building, they shot and killed a wounded police officer as he lay helpless in the street. The two men fled in a stolen vehicle which was later found abandoned. On 9 January, having been tracked to a signage company building in Dammartin-en-Goële, not far from Paris, the pair were killed in an exchange of gunfire with police and security forces. A second attack took place on 9 January in a kosher supermarket in Porte de Vincennes on the east side of Paris. Amedy Coulibady shot and killed four Jewish shoppers in the store, before police entered the building and killed him. It emerged that he had also been responsible for the killing of a policewoman the previous day. The two sets of gunmen had been in contact, though the Kouachi brothers claimed to be acting on behalf of al-Qaeda in Yemen, and Coulibady had pledged allegiance to the so-called Islamic State of Iraq and the Levant.

It goes without saying that these events were deeply shocking: the murder of 17 people in broad daylight in a major European city, followed by a massive police and security operation, was profoundly disturbing and the resonances extended globally. Of interest here in particular, however, is what happened next, as people began to respond to the events, and to organize their responses in performative and symbolic vocabularies. First, of course, there was the symbolic act of standing together in public space. Even on the day of the killings, spontaneous demonstrations of support and solidarity began to occur in Paris, across France, and also internationally. The French president, François Hollande, declared 8 January would be a national day of mourning for France, and there were also upwards of 100 demonstrations internationally in cities such as Sydney, Amsterdam and Chicago. On 11 January (the Sunday following the attacks) an estimated two million people participated in a rally of national unity on the streets of Paris.

In a way, the *Charlie Hebdo* events stand as an example of the ways in which traumatic events, and the subsequent performative responses to them, are being configured in public space. They illustrate the ways in which people reach for symbolic vocabularies within which to express their views. More broadly, they can be understood as the ways in which events begin to enter history as representation. Forty world leaders attended the rally in Paris, and walked (or pretended to walk) in front of the march for the first half hour. In actual fact, of course, their presence was very carefully stage-managed, as they meandered short distances for the press cameras, before stopping arm-in-arm for photo opportunities. There was little attempt to disguise the fact that this was what was happening: live camera coverage on the day showed clearly the ranks of security men and soldiers from various nations who were keeping a vigilant and secure eye on their principals. Nevertheless, gestural politics was very much in play. Despite what was evidently intended to look as casual as possible (as though the leaders had simply gathered in the street), the final placement was diplomatic in the extreme. Adjacent to Hollande (who of course was centre front row) was Malian president Ibrahim Boubacar Keïta, to whose nation France has provided troops to help fight Islamist insurgents. On Hollande's other arm was Germany's Angela Merkel. Benjamin Netanyahu of Israel and Mahmoud Abbas, the Palestinian President, were both in attendance, and were positioned equidistantly from Hollande, both prominently in the front row. David Cameron, the British prime minister, was positioned some distance from the centre, and was clearly less than pleased.

Hundreds of marches also took place worldwide, but it was not simply a matter of the physical presence of bodies staging horror and affront which was to become the most prominent symbolic gesture. What began as a hashtag on Twitter on 7 January, #jesuischarlie, had gathered extraordinary momentum, and become effectively the motto of solidarity with the victims, adopted by both the public, and, increasingly, by state institutions and politicians. By the time of the Sunday demonstration, the black and white poster 'Je suis Charlie' was everywhere – on hand-held banners, badges, in windows and of course, on social media – and had been joined by the corresponding identifications for the other victims: 'Je suis flic (cop)' and 'Je suis Juif'. Interestingly, cartoons had also begun to appear in many newspapers, both print and online, featuring pens and pencils. In particular, images which counterpointed a pen with a gun, or showed a pencil regenerating, redoubling or being resharpened, illustrated that while the *Charlie* artists may have been killed, freedom of speech could not be destroyed.

The use of symbols and images in political demonstration and expression is of course nothing new. The speed and spread of these symbolic expressions was, perhaps, exceptional, but it is probably as much to do with the widespread use and immediacy of social media as anything particular to this event. In this context, though, there are some potential questions and complexities which arise, as both the crisis, and the reaction to it, were in part already fundamentally implicated in the politics of symbols. Not least, it was the publication of satirical images of the Prophet Muhammad by *Charlie Hebdo* which was cited as provocation by the attackers: as they fled they are alleged to have shouted 'We have avenged the Prophet Muhammad; we have killed *Charlie Hebdo*'.

Famously, the 'survivors' issue' of *Charlie*, which came out a week after the attacks, carried Renald Luzier's ('Luz') cartoon of the Prophet (carrying a 'Je suis Charlie' banner and weeping) on its front cover. 'We are sorry to draw him again,' he said at a televised press conference held to introduce the issue. In 2006, *Charlie Hebdo* had reprinted the *Jyllands-Posten* cartoons (the so-called 'Danish' cartoons), and in 2011 the magazine's previous offices had been subject to an arson attack after they ran a special issue entitled 'Charia (Sharia) Hebdo', again featuring images of the Prophet. Luz, who survived the attack through the accident of 7 January being his birthday, gave an interview on 10 January in which he spoke frankly about some of the difficulties he was having with the reconfiguring of *Charlie* itself as symbol. Noting the way that *Charlie* was being commandeered by everyone from President François Hollande to far right leader Marine le Pen, he explained that the problem with a symbol is that it is too malleable.

'Symbolism in every sense can be used by everyone to do whatever they like.' Furthermore, the role of *Charlie Hebdo* as a satirical magazine had always been to work against the pomposity of symbols, to break down taboos and burst bubbles of gloss and surface. 'Right now,' he commented, 'we're covered in gloss and I'm going to find that difficult... How can you destroy a symbol when it is yourself?' Even to publish the survivors' issue, in response to the 'symbolism of the attack' was, he suggested, perhaps to 'reply to symbolism with symbolism'. Our friends, he concluded, did not fall for France (Les Inrocks.com 2015).

In fact, this anxiety around what was happening in the realm of the image was not restricted to Luz. A lot of the criticism, from all sides of the debate, pivoted around the use of symbols, and whether or not they were working in the ways they were intended to work. For those angry or anxious about the cartoons of the Prophet (considering any such image unacceptable and disrespectful in the extreme), there was further difficulty in the way that they came to be deployed as an – even *the* – emblem of freedom of speech. This happened to such a degree that several newspapers found themselves pressed to publish the *Charlie* front page or find themselves declared as being 'against free speech' – as though a single possible example of the principle of free speech had come to function as its only literal means of being exercised. The foregrounding of pens and pencils as emblems of Western enlightenment standing against the guns and weapons of barbarism managed, of course, to occlude the guns and weapons which have been deployed in recent years by Western states in the Middle East on Muslim populations. For, of course, symbols deployed in these kinds of ways tend to oversimplify things. There is an assumption that they somehow 'speak for themselves', when in fact they speak *of*, and *for*, extremely complex political and ideological positions. They materialize something vague and intangible, something (such as the idea of a nation) which may have no physical form elsewhere. As Hanna Fenichel Pitkin notes in *The Concept of Representation*, 'When we speak of something symbolizing, we are... emphasizing the symbol's power to evoke feelings or attitudes... a symbol is not a substitute for what it symbolizes' (Fenichel Pitkin 1967: 98–9). What seemed to be happening in some of the *Charlie Hebdo* fall-out was that symbols were beginning to circulate independently of their referents, causing the debate to refigure as a sequence of gestures, able therefore to express gestural positions (support for the victims; support for freedom of speech; hostility to violence), but not to hold any complexity, or address the contradictions inherent in the political realities cycling within the situation of crisis.

How, then, might we find a way to understand symbolic and material gestures (even, as in this case, criminal acts which are also operating as symbolic gestures) as part of the same exchange and the same meaning-making articulation, without diminishing or trivializing the significant impacts which they make on real people in real circumstances? What if it were possible to open a critical space within which the vocabulary of expression itself could be discussed? Could we access the ways in which it is being deployed and mobilized as a grammar; not just in terms of its units of meaning (Je suis Charlie! Je ne suis pas Charlie!), but as a structure of meaning within which we might begin to approach the wider issues, difficulties and deep divisions at work in the world? If we were to look at the events of the *Charlie Hebdo* aftermath through such a lens – not as a matter of nuance, interpretation, or reflection, but as acts *in the same register* and *in the same historical moment*; not as mirrors to each other but interdependent and mutually constitutive strands of meaning – might we be able to iron out some of the circularities and inconsistencies which have emerged?

What the approaches taken by the contributors to this volume show are a series of ways in which the political and performative can be seen to be constituted by, and constitutive of, the same present. We are enabled to read performances, acts of theatre and acts of dramaturgy not simply as that which follows, explains and interprets 'actual' events, but as a set of real, material, political, (even violent) practices which intervene in, impact and affect the process of the histories in which they take place. In the case of what happened after the *Charlie Hebdo* shootings, it becomes possible, through such a lens, to see the organization of appearances, the manipulation of symbolic vocabularies, and the ways in which claim-making took place around agents and ideologies as *part of the very crisis itself*. Rather than continue to argue about the meaning and counter-meaning of symbols, the work of representation itself is promoted to a constitutive element. It is not a matter of providing different answers; the questions are able to be reframed.

More than this: I think there is a further lesson. What these essays teach us is that performance has the capacity to disrupt the ability of power to speak itself uninterrupted, to create and preserve the fiction that it is whole and entire and permanent. It is, perhaps, merely a form of permanent tactic, disguising its provisionality, its gloss and its illusion as the authentic, the immovable and the transhistorical. Of course reality is manufactured – invented, made and then sustained through faith and belief and violence. We shouldn't have to make the case, any more, that performance is constitutive of material experience, that it forms spaces and consciousnesses, forges imaginaries, and makes worlds in which people are able (even if only temporarily) to live. It is a serious business. Important questions are asked by performance analysis, which is able to see narrative, time, space, and identity as stagings: strategic, impermanent and malleable. It is able to show not only what performance is built of, but by extension what power, its 'other', is built of too. The forms of survival enacted and enabled by the performances discussed in this volume are significant. They are not simply responses, or counter-claims, or reactions, though they are all those things as well. They are re-makings, re-manufacturings, re-phrasings, re-translations and re-presentations of the worlds which give them birth. And it is through the schisms and fissures in those worlds, which are produced by conditions of crisis, that they have been able to find expression.

Bibliography

Fenichel Pitkin, H., 1967. *The Concept of Representation*. Berkeley, London, Los Angeles: University of California Press.
Les Inrocks, 2015. 'Luz: "All eyes are on us, we've become a symbol"'. Interview: Anne Laffeter. Translation: Nick Haughton. Available online at: www.lesinrocks.com/2015/01/10/actualite/luz-eyes-us-weve-become-symbol-11545347/, accessed 15 January 2015.

Index

Aberdeenshire Community Planning Partnership, 185, 187
absurdism/absurdist, 9–10, 123– 5, 129, 131, 134, 136–7, 138n11
Abu Salem, François, 146, 150 –1
Adler, H. G., 61, 63
Agamben, Giorgio, 95–6
agency, 1, 4, 6, 9, 12, 43, 71, 176, 204, 213, 215–16, 224, 228, 235–7
Anderson, Patrick, 204, 211, 235, 237
asylum, 12, 203, 205–9, 211–15, 217n1, 3, 218nn3,5,7,8,9, 218n17
audience(s), 5, 8, 10, 21–2, 24, 29–30, 39, 42–4, 50, 66, 70, 74, 89, 96, 108, 111, 116, 127, 128, 135–6, 137n8, 138n16, 144, 145, 147, 148, 149, 152, 155, 174, 175–6, 180–1, 196, 211, 223, 235, 238
Auschwitz, 79, 80, 83, 87–8, 91–3, 109
austerity, 187, 203, 204, 206, 207, 209, 214
Austin, J. L., 3, 224
authenticity, 86, 94, 96, 212, 224

Bartered Bride, The, 73
Ben Akiba Lied, 74
Bhabha, Homi K., 1, 7, 196, 227
Blanketmen, 225, 231
Brundibár, 63
Burian, E. F., 65–9, 74, 75

call and response, 224, 227–8, 238
Caruth, Cathy, 61
censorship, 8, 10, 103, 107, 113, 123, 126, 137n7, 141–2, 147, 148–50, 152, 154, 155, 156nn1,2,8, 157n13
Charbonnier ('Charb'), Stephane, 242
Charlie Hebdo, 242, 243–6
Chekhov, Anton, 72

Chile, 10, 104, 112–18
colonial, 10, 17, 22, 45, 48, 53n1, 54nn15,16, 113, 121, 129, 130, 131, 132, 134, 135, 145, 153, 167, 225
Communist, 28, 60, 65, 73, 75, 78, 79, 98n11, 148
communitas, 1, 9, 79, 81, 91, 93–7, 228
community, 2, 5, 11, 21, 23, 29, 31, 45, 47, 71, 72, 81, 95, 103, 119n10, 135, 136, 153, 164–5, 171–2, 175, 178, 179, 185, 186, 188, 189, 190–1, 192, 194, 195–6, 197, 198, 199, 208, 228, 232, 242
community arts, 195–6, 198
concentrationary literature (see littérature concentrationnaire)
Conquergood, Dwight, 212, 213, 235
costume(s), 29, 75, 147, 189, 190, 191, 194, 236, 238n3
Coulibady, Amedy, 242, 243
council estate, 11, 163–7, 168–71, 173–8, 181
cultural politics, 164, 166, 171–2
Czechoslovakia, 9, 10, 59, 66, 74, 76, 105–6, 108, 110, 117

dance, 21, 23, 24, 29, 44, 46, 48, 50, 51–2
Delbo, Charlotte, 9, 78–97
democracy, 31, 111–14, 131, 148, 154
deprivation, 6, 163, 168, 171, 174, 185–8, 198
Dergi Zergi, 22
diaspora, 18, 23, 37, 38, 46, 51, 179
dictatorship, 4, 10, 103–4, 106, 109–18, 121–3, 125, 133, 135
'dirty protest', 12, 222, 223, 224, 226, 229–35, 237–8
dis–ease, 236–7

disgust, 229, 233–4, 237, 238, 239nn6,7
dissent, 1, 6, 10, 27, 106–7, 123, 129, 133, 134, 205, 215
Dyk, Viktor, 74

El-Hakawati (theatre troupe), 142–3, 145, 146, 148–55, 156n3
Emperor, 19–20
Erben, Karel Jaromír, 75
Eritrea, 7–8, 17–31
Eritrean Liberation Front (ELF), 8, 17, 18–23
Eritrean People's Liberation Front (EPLF), 8, 17, 18–19, 21, 23–30, 31
Esther, 60–1, 65, 66–8, 75
ethnicity, 26, 45–6, 169, 180
European Union, 206
exilic conditions, 38, 39, 42

fictive body, 236, 238
Fischer, Jan, 60, 65, 67, 68, 74
Foucault, Michel, 2, 126, 232, 238
Fraserburgh, 11, 185, 186, 187, 189–92, 195, 197
Freizeitgestaltung, 62, 63
Frýd, Norbert, 60, 61, 63, 65, 66–8, 70, 72, 73

gacaca courts, 50
Gaelic, 12, 222, 224, 227–9, 233, 237, 238
Gebre, Ramadan, 19, 20
Gellner, Ernest, 22, 23
genocide, 37, 46–52, 54n16
Gogol, Nicolai, 60, 65, 68–9
grass-roots, 28, 164, 167, 172, 174, 179, 181, 211

habitus, 11, 164, 170, 174–6, 177, 181, 182n3
Habtemariam, Asmerom, 25
Haile, Negusse 'Mensa'ai', 17, 20, 22
Halas, František, 74
Heidegger, Martin, 86, 93, 237
Herman, Judith, 9, 59, 61–2, 64, 70, 71–2
Hollande, François, 243–4, 245
Honzl, Jindřich, 74, 75

hood, the, 165–8, 170–1, 174, 180
hunger strike, 3, 12, 203–7, 209–17, 218n11, 219n17, 222–4, 226, 228, 234–7, 238
Hutu, 7, 45, 46–7, 49, 53n1

identity, 7–8, 12, 24, 26, 38–9, 42, 44, 45–6, 52, 71, 73, 74, 107–8, 109, 115, 117–18, 119n10, 144, 145–7, 154, 164, 168, 170, 172, 178–9, 181, 186, 195–7, 205, 226–8, 234, 247
immigrants, 206, 208, 209, 211
inequality, 186–7
inoperative community, 196
Iryo Nabonye, viii, 46–51
Israel, 76, 141–2, 144–5, 147–53, 155, 156nn1,2,11, 243

'je suis Charlie', 12, 244, 246
Jerusalem, 10, 144–5, 147, 153, 155
Ježek, Jaroslav, 74
Jouvet, Louis, 78, 82–5
Jyllands-Posten, 244

Kanafani, Ghassan, 150, 157n17
Kavanová, Eva, 61, 69–70
Kayishema, Jean-Marie Vianney, 38–40, 53n3
Khruschev, Nikita, 73
Kongo religious practices, 10, 123–4, 133, 136, 138n17
Kouachi, Cherif, 242
Kouachi, Said, 242

Langer, Lawrence, 80, 90–1
Last Cyclist, The, 65–6
Laub, Dori, 70
Lefebvre, Henri, 3–4, 8, 231–2, 234
Liberated Theatre, The, 74–5
littérature concentrationnaire, 80, 97n2
Long Kesh, see Maze prison
Lubeck, Jackie, 147, 150, 156nn3,4, 23
Lustig, Josef, 74
Luzier ('Luz'), Renald, 244

Index

Mahber Teyatre Asmera (Ma.Te.A., Asmara Theatre Association), 20, 25
Marriage, The, 65, 68–9
martyr(s), martyrdom, 24–5, 423, 126–7, 211, 236
Marxist, 8, 17, 20, 121–2
Maze prison, 12, 222–30, 237
Mengisteab, Bereket, 20, 22, 25, 27, 32n11
migrant(s), viii, 12, 203, 205–19
Miška, František, 60, 67–9, 72
Modo, 11, 185–99
Molière, 83, 87, 89, 96

Nancy, Jean–Luc, 9, 79, 93, 98n10, 196
national identity, ix, 7–8, 12, 26, 39, 45, 74, 108, 205, 227
nationalism, 22–3, 45, 51–2, 73
Nazi(s), nazism, 9–10, 59, 61–3, 65–6, 71–3, 78, 80, 90, 92, 96, 104–9, 117
Neruda, Jan, 74, 76n7
Nield, Sophie, 12, 209–10, 216, 229, 231, 233
Northern Ireland, 222, 233, 238

occupation, 9, 17, 24, 28, 30, 67, 104–8, 117, 143–50, 152–3, 155, 156n1, 215
Oliver, Kelly, 70–1
oral history, 39, 44, 53n3
Orientalism, 154

Palestine, 141, 145, 150, 152–5
performative, 3, 6, 9, 12, 199, 205, 210, 213, 222–5, 226–31, 235, 238, 243, 246
Peterhead, 11, 185–7, 189, 194
political education, 21
Popperová, Truda (see Šedová, Jana)
postcolonial, ix, x, 123, 125, 130
poverty, 11, 40, 164, 170, 174, 186–8, 209, 216
Prince Bettliegend, 74
projected community, 185, 195
propaganda, 17, 19, 21, 25–6, 32n7, 48, 130, 142

puppet(s), puppetry, ix, 9–11, 103–19, 191, 194

race, ix, 109, 135, 168–9, 173, 178–80
realism, 28
reconciliation, 19, 46, 49–52, 114, 116, 119n11
reflexivity, 174–6, 178, 180–1
regeneration, 172, 185–7, 189–90, 192, 198
Reinerová, Hana, 61, 65, 75
Republican, Ireland, 12, 222–3, 225, 227, 230–31, 236–7, 238n1
Resistance, 1, 9, 20, 59, 80, 90, 92–3, 95–6, 109, 117, 121, 123–30, 136, 143, 146–51, 153, 155, 165, 166–8, 170, 174, 177–8, 181–2, 196, 198, 203–5, 210, 213, 215–17, 222–4, 226–8, 230, 233–4, 236–8
revolution(s), revolutionary, 18–9, 24, 26, 28, 30, 39, 52, 53n1, 74, 122–3, 125, 127, 147, 157n18, 166, 170–1, 234
riots, UK, 2011 163–4, 173
Rocado Zulu Theatre, 132
Rugano, Kalisa, viii, 38, 41, 53n3
Ruganzu, 38–44, 53nn4,6
Rugari rwa Gasabo, 38–44
Růžička, Ota, 72
Rwandan Patriotic Front (RPF), 38, 40, 42–3, 48–52, 53n2
Rwandanicity, 7–8, 37, 45–6, 51–2

Said, Edward, 10, 141–2
Sands, Bobby, 204, 226, 228, 234–6
sans papiers, 206, 213, 216
Schönová, Vlasta, 72
Schorsch, Gustav, 61, 65, 68–70, 72–4
Šedová, Jana, 60–1, 63, 65–8, 71–2, 74, 76n4
Smetana, Bedřich, 73
social circus, 185
socialism, 73
solidarity, 9, 67, 71–4, 78–80, 87, 91, 93–4, 96–7, 201, 212, 225, 229, 243–4
Šormová, Eva, 60, 66, 76
Soyinka, Wole, 133

Spain, 104, 111
spectatorship, vii, 73, 219n16, 230
Spitz, Jiří, 74
strategy of tactics, 6, 8, 238
subjectivity, 38, 70–1, 128–9, 217n1
Suleiman, Fatuma, 29
Švenk, Karel, 61, 63, 65–6, 69

Tam'si, Tchicaya U, 137n1
Tesfahunei, Tebereh, 25, 27, 32n16, 18
Tesfai, Alemseged, 29
Testimony, vii, 9, 59–65, 67, 71, 75, 79–81, 83, 117
Trauma, vii–viii, 9–10, 59–62, 64–5, 70–2, 75, 92, 97n8, 9, 104, 112–14, 117–18, 128, 243

Tutsi, 7–8, 37–9, 41, 43–50, 52
Twa, 7, 45, 53n1
Twahirwa, Aimable, 46–7

Ubu Roi, 134

Verfremdungseffekt, 5
voiceband, 75
Voskovec, Jiří, 74

Werich, Jan, 74
witness(ing), vii, viii, 50, 69–71, 79, 81, 83, 91–2, 97, 108, 114, 121, 195, 199, 211–12, 215–17